KU-412-961

C0063 09348

How Trump Thinks

PETER OBORNE is a columnist for the *Daily Mail* and former chief political commentator of the *Daily Telegraph*. One of Britain's most distinguished and independent political writers, his books include *The Triumph of the Political Class* and *Wounded Tiger*.

TOM ROBERTS, PhD, is a media historian and author of *Before Rupert: Keith Murdoch and the Birth of a Dynasty*.

How Trump Thinks
His Tweets and the Birth
of a New Political Language

Peter Oborne
and Tom Roberts

HEAD
of ZEUS

First published in the UK in 2017 by Head of Zeus Ltd

Copyright © Peter Oborne and Tom Roberts, 2017

The n   ntified
as th   with

reproc   y form
or by   rding,
or otl   right

Glasgow Life Glasgow Libraries	
CD	
C 006309348	
Askews & Holts	17-May-2017
973.933092 H	£10.00

A catalogue record for this book is available
from the British Library.

ISBN (HB) 9781786696656
ISBN (ANZTPB): 9781786697073
ISBN (PB): 9781786698018
ISBN (E): 9781786696649

Typeset by Adrian McLaughlin

Printed and bound in Great Britain by
CPI Group (UK) Ltd, Croydon CR0 4YY

Head of Zeus Ltd
First Floor East
5–8 Hardwick Street
London EC1R 4RG

WWW.HEADOFZEUS.COM

Contents

"I think that maybe I wouldn't be here if it wasn't for Twitter."

"Twitter is a wonderful thing for me, because I get the word out… I might not be here talking to you right now as President if I didn't have an honest way of getting the word out."

DONALD TRUMP *to Fox News, 15 March 2017*

Introduction

Before Donald Trump, politics had been captured by experts. They manipulated and policed public discourse. They set the rules. They believed that they alone understood the secrets and had mastered the techniques that won elections: focus groups; opinion polls; voter targeting.

Trump humiliated then destroyed these experts.

Raymond Chandler said that the thriller writer Dashiell Hammett "gave murder back to the people who commit it".

Trump gave politics back to the people who vote.

He was by no means the first to achieve this. Indeed, the United States from its early history has been ready to respond to leaders and movements that turned angry and disappointed people against its ruling establishment.

But Trump achieved this in a number of new ways. The most significant of these was the reinvention of political communication through Twitter.

His Tweets brought politics back to life, playing a huge role in enabling the earthquake that took place in November 2016. He exploited Twitter's ability to express raw sentiment instantly, without nuance or subtext, and its ability to blur, even extinguish, the boundary between sentiment and fact.

Donald Trump's Tweets are therefore a serious matter, worthy of study because they changed America and thus the world.

Donald Trump joined Twitter in 2009, only three years after the medium was invented. He wanted to promote his personal brand, to sell his books and to generate publicity for his TV programme, *The Apprentice*.

At this point he was not yet a politician, but a political groupie who flaunted his personality and boasted about his achievements. He was positive and upbeat, and sought out celebrities. He was friendly with Bill and Hillary Clinton (later to be eviscerated as "Crooked Hilary").

They were more famous than he was. Trump basked in their celebrity.

He was also generous about President Obama, later to become the subject of prolonged, vicious attack. At this point Trump's Tweets display intellectual and moral horizons defined by TV ratings, ostentatious wealth, celebrity endorsements and brand management. Politics for him was a variety of show business.

Peter Costanzo, a marketing expert, introduced Trump to Twitter. Trump had produced a book: *Think Like a Champion: An Informal Education in Business and Life*. Costanzo, an online marketing director, argued that a Twitter account would boost sales.

Costanzo told the future US President: "Let's call you @RealDonald Trump."

Trump said: "I like it. Let's do it."

Costanzo later recalled: "He seemed very excited about the idea of being able to reach people so directly. I think he immediately got it."[1]

Only 216 people followed Trump when he began tweeting in May 2009, and for a long time the number increased slowly.[2] His early Tweets were dull and with good reason: public relations advisers seem to have taken care of his first utterances in the medium.

The tone changed in the summer of 2011 when he toyed with running in the following year's Presidential election. Donald Trump was still fascinated by celebrities, TV ratings and brand endorsements. But the mood was no longer so benign. He brutally parted company from the code of mutual congratulation that defines celebrity relationships.

Now he wrote his own Tweets on his personal Samsung mobile phone.[3] Trump started to use the exclamation marks, the capital letters and the staccato insults that have defined his Twitter discourse ever since.

He made enemies, pursued feuds and communicated a sense of apocalyptic doom.

He was very funny and often acute: "Wake up America… China is eating our lunch," wrote Trump in early August 2011. Here at last was Donald Trump's unique voice. All creative artists are familiar with the thrilling moment when they discover a voice capable of talking to the world. So too are politicians.

The 140-character Twitter message was perfect for Trump. It was ideal for painting pictures of a black-and-white world. In the hands of Trump it became a lethal political weapon.

Trump told lies, smeared and fabricated in order to destroy opponents. If the facts proved what he was saying to be untrue, Trump didn't care. He constructed a personal epistemology. His truth claims were purely instrumental. He made assertions about his own honesty – and the lies of his enemies – in order to gain power and win arguments.

According to the rules of conventional politics, this resort to deceit should have been the end of Trump. The media would duly have exposed him as a liar, and as a result he should have remained a fringe figure.

Most informed people were certain he would be discredited. But his failure and disgrace never transpired, and he became President. What happened?

Trump – the heir of tradition

Trump won as the heir to two great American traditions. One is contempt for the elite, real or imaginary, in charge of Washington politics, expressed in periodic fits of "populism". The second is that of fake news – the successful conversion of propaganda into fact.

Both of these traditions were very powerful in the nineteenth century.

The first great anti-Establishment Presidential candidate was Andrew Jackson. He gatecrashed national politics with a (generally deserved) reputation as a military hero and a white nationalist, who on his own initiative had launched wars against Indians and Spaniards.

He also gave the vote in conquered Florida to all free (white) men without property qualifications. His programme mobilized mass democracy to overcome vested interests and perceived corruption in Washington, especially in the operations of the banks.

As Trump would later do, Jackson used exaggerated rhetoric against his collective enemy, "The Great Whore of Babylon".

Jackson's astute chief of staff, Major (later Senator) Eaton codified his thoughts into a programme for delivering the country from the "Hands of Mammon". With the aid of Democratic newspapers, Jackson and Eaton fashioned the first real nationwide Presidential campaign in 1824. He was balked of victory by a private deal between two rivals, John Quincy Adams and Henry Clay, which he described in very Trumpian terms as a "corrupt bargain".

When Jackson ran against Adams in 1828 it produced one of the bitterest election campaigns in American history, with a barrage of fake news stories against both candidates and indeed their families.

Adams was depicted as an alcoholic, who had lived in sin before his marriage. Jackson was described as the son of a prostitute and a mulatto (i.e. he had Negro blood), a murderer and an adulterer.

The smears against his wife Rachel induced her severe depression and death before his inauguration.

Jackson, however, hit back with positive propaganda, exploiting his image as Old Hickory, "the toughest wood in creation". Although he continued to run as an outsider, he benefited hugely from America's first political machine, the Albany Regency, which was created by his dandyish lieutenant, Martin Van Buren, a consummate wheeler-dealer.[4]

Jackson's inauguration in 1829 produced a mass descent on Washington of 10,000 poor supporters and their families – outsiders who horrified local property owners by camping all over the city and drinking it dry of alcoholic beverages. (One of Donald Trump's first acts as President was to pay a reverential visit to Andrew Jackson's home in Tennessee. Jackson is the favourite President of Trump's Chief Strategist Steve Bannon and his populism, white nationalism, hostility to federal power and abolitionism commends him to the alt-right).

This period saw a spectacular example of truly "fake news": the publication in 1836 of Maria Monk's *Awful Disclosures* of her alleged abuse in a Roman Catholic nunnery. Contemporary inquiries exposed many errors and inconsistencies in her story, which was almost certainly concocted by her ghostwriters, but by the standards of the time the book was a runaway bestseller, and helped to sustain the popular backlash against Roman Catholic immigrants from Ireland and Germany.[5]

In the mid-nineteenth century, after Jackson's death, the US saw the brief but phenomenal rise of an "outsider" uprising, an anti-immigrant, anti-Catholic party that sprang from a secret society and rejoiced defiantly in the name "Know-Nothing", although officially it was the American Party.

This was the first political movement to make systematic use of conspiracy theories, peddling theories of Catholic plots to subvert the American working man through Irish whiskey, German lager and cheap migrant labour.

It also exploited a fake martyr – a political bruiser called William Poole, also known as Bill the Butcher, who was killed in a Bowery tavern brawl. At their peak in the 1850s the Know-Nothings had elected over 100 Congressmen and eight state governors. In 1856 they secured a former President, Millard Fillmore, as their own Presidential candidate.

Although he was undone by the party's support for slavery, detested by many of the Northern working class, Fillmore secured 873,000 votes, about a fifth of the total poll. The party then disappeared, but its anti-immigrant, anti-Catholic message endured.[6]

Another "outsider" eruption occurred in 1892 when a powerful third party actually called the Populists emerged, as a splinter from the Democratic Party.

The Populists' main supporters were struggling indebted farmers and some low-paid industrial workers. Its platform proposed a characteristic mix of redistributive measures (federal income tax – then an innovation – low interest rates, the break-up of banks, a boost to veterans' pensions), monetary and fiscal expansion, and a clampdown on immigration.

Its candidate was an Iowa Congressman, James B. Weaver. He won a million votes (from a total of 12 million, all male and nearly all white) and carried four rural states with a combined 22 electoral votes – the best third-party Presidential performance until the white supremacist Strom Thurmond ran against Harry Truman in 1948.[7]

The Populist programme was taken over by the Democratic firebrand William Jennings Bryan – three times a Presidential candidate. Although he was a mesmerizing orator who kept a lasting hold on the Populist coalition of struggling farmers and workers, his message never had enough appeal to voters basking in general prosperity, particularly when he had to oppose Theodore Roosevelt, an activist, reforming President and a master communicator, who also presented himself as an outsider battling vested interests.[8]

It is also worth recalling the career and methods of William Randolph Hearst. It is no surprise that *Citizen Kane*, the masterpiece by Orson Welles based on Hearst's life, is Trump's favourite film.[9]

Politically, the two men have much in common although they represented different parties. Hearst was a serious contender for the Democratic Presidential nomination in 1904.

Like Trump, Hearst was anti-immigrant (in his time the main fear was Chinese immigration, the so-called Yellow Peril). Like Trump, he used the slogan "America First". Like Trump, he positioned himself as a champion of forgotten working-class Americans, and as an outsider who would fight the corruption of the ruling elite. Like Trump, he courted veterans.[10]

Hearst also foreshadowed Trump in his use of language. At one point he appeared to call for the assassination of President McKinley (which was held against him when McKinley was indeed assassinated by an anarchist, although not for any reason suggested by Hearst.)[11] Hearst's Yellow Press was also a lavish provider of "fake news" – and foreshadowing the Murdoch press, it blurred the boundary between news and entertainment, even if Hearst's papers preferred to concentrate on lurid crime rather than lurid sex.

Proto Trumps of the twentieth century

Some twentieth-century forerunners of Donald Trump shared one or more of his objectives: bypassing hostile conventional media, securing the acceptance of their perceptions as fact, or defining themselves with the forgotten masses against a powerful elite.

One of our examples is fictional, but the others achieved their political objectives. It is sobering to think how much more they could have done with the aid of Twitter and the circulation of rumour on the internet.

Franklin Delano Roosevelt

Franklin Roosevelt was the first President to use radio regularly to communicate directly to the American people. This was rightly considered revolutionary. He had pioneered this approach as Democratic governor of New York from 1929 to 1932, in order to circumvent the largely hostile Republican press.

The first "fireside chat" was delivered on 12 March 1933, just eight days after his inauguration (in those days this did not happen until March, a very long "lame-duck" period for a defeated or retiring President). The purpose was to combat panic over the emergency bank holiday that Roosevelt had announced to give breathing space to America's failing banks.

Roosevelt had a clear objective: to combat fear of renewed bank failures and prevent a new run on banks when they reopened after the holiday. By talking directly to the American people, he ensured that his message was not lost or suppressed by hostile newspapers, or political opponents, or by simple word of mouth.

He was successful: listeners actually returned money to the banks after the holiday rather than withdrawing their deposits.

The President spoke for 13 minutes 42 seconds. He used 1,798 words and 10,001 characters including spacing and punctuation. His average word length was 4.56 letters. His broadcast reached an estimated 60 million listeners – almost half the American population at the time.

The term "fireside chat" seems to have been invented by a CBS radio executive. It struck a chord with Roosevelt's press secretary, Steven Early, and the President himself, by capturing the intimate atmosphere he wanted to create: he and his listeners actually sharing the same hearth.[12]

The fireside chats were so successful that it is commonly assumed that FDR delivered them every week. In fact he rationed them carefully, delivering just thirty over all four terms of his Presidency from 1933 to 1945 and only when he had something important to say. It was Ronald Reagan, the Great Communicator, who began the practice of delivering weekly addresses in 1982.

The Radio Priest

Indeed, Roosevelt in the 1930s had a smaller following on radio than a lowly Roman Catholic priest, Father Charles Coughlin. In the mid-1920s his powerful preaching in churches inspired his diocese in Detroit to try him out on radio to combat the anti-Catholic Ku Klux Klan, which enjoyed a revival after the Great War and expanded its political base well beyond the American South. In 1930 as the Depression took hold, Coughlin's message grew increasingly political and his language more strident. His weekly broadcasts won a national following.

Coughlin combined militant anti-Communism with equally fierce attacks on the greed of capitalism. They were both emanations of Satan, from whom the American working man needed deliverance. At first a militant supporter of Franklin Roosevelt ("The New Deal is Christ's Deal") he broke with Roosevelt to support the populist Huey Long, who had himself won a nationwide following with his slogans "Share Our Wealth" and "Every Man a King." When Long was assassinated, Coughlin formed his own Social Justice Movement. It proposed income guarantees for workers, high public spending and redistributive taxation and extensive nationalization (measures generally far to the Left of the New Deal). At his peak, Coughlin's weekly broadcasts were getting an audience of tens of millions and he claimed to receive 80,000 letters in response to each address.[13]

In 1936, Coughlin took a sharp turn to the Right, and his broadcasts became increasingly anti-Semitic and isolationist, and even sympathetic to Nazism and Fascism. But he continued to claim that he was a champion of the (white) working class.

Huey Long is often bracketed with Coughlin and depicted as the nearest American incarnation of a Fascist leader. Fear of his supposed dictatorial ambitions prompted his assassination in 1935. But there were significant differences with the demagogic priest, in policy and style.

Long had actually governed his state, Louisiana, and achieved real results for his poor supporters, particularly in education and public works. Unlike his fellow Southern politicians, he was not a rabid racist or an anti-Semite. His radio broadcasts, almost as popular as Coughlin's, were far less vituperative and laced with folksy humour. He was happy to be nicknamed Kingfish after the tricky black conman in the popular radio comedy *Amos 'n' Andy*.[14]

The prophecy of Sinclair Lewis

Both Coughlin (disguised as Bishop Prang) and Long, under his own name, figure in Sinclair Lewis's 1935 novel *It Can't Happen Here*. This is currently enjoying a revival for its supposed prophecy of Trump's Presidency. In the novel Roosevelt is defeated in the 1936 election (which he in fact won by a landslide). The winner is a charismatic populist Senator "Buzz" Windrip, who exploits and eventually takes over a mass movement of Forgotten Men.

It is significant that Trump used Twitter to make this phrase his own. Just before dawn on the morning after his election victory he tweeted: "Such a beautiful and important evening! The forgotten man and woman will never be forgotten again. We will all come together as never before."

Immediately after the inauguration he returned to the theme: "The forgotten men and women of our country will be forgotten no longer. From this moment on it's going to be America First."

The fictional Senator Windrip promises the restoration of American greatness, a universal annual income of $5,000 and complete protection of American industry and agriculture from all foreign imports. He picks a quarrel with Mexico. He is a sexist and racist. In office, Windrip establishes an imitation Nazi state, with concentration camps and a version of the SS.

Windrip is much nastier than Trump, although he is essentially a weak and dependent figure with no mind of his own. However, one passage is a striking anticipation of Trump's handling of facts. It is taken from "Zero Hour", Windrip's only book (in fact written for him, like Trump's books, by an amanuensis):

"Any honest propagandist for any Cause, that is, one who honestly studies and figures out the most effective way of putting over his Message, will learn fairly early that it is not fair to ordinary folks – it just confuses them – to make them try to swallow all the true facts that would be suitable to a higher class of people."[15]

Irving Kristol, founder of *The Public Interest* magazine and sometimes called the godfather of neo-Conservatism, later made the identical point: "There are different kinds of truths for different kinds of people. There are truths appropriate for children; truths that are appropriate for students; truths that are appropriate for educated adults; and truths that are appropriate for highly educated adults; and the notion that there should be one set of truths available to everyone is a modern democratic fallacy. It doesn't work."[16]

Joe McCarthy's Silly Numbers

For a short period in the 1950s Senator Joseph McCarthy became the most powerful politician in the United States by exploiting and promoting the anti-Communist hysteria of the time. Even President Eisenhower, an ex-soldier, victor of the war in Europe and winner of a landslide mandate in the election of 1952, was afraid to confront him.[17]

McCarthy is one of the rare politicians to become an eponym, although one used as a term of abuse to refer to any unjustified accusation against any political cause, particularly to shut down accusations against liberals.

Such is the power of McCarthy's personality and the melodrama of his methods, that he is often identified as the instigator of all the anti-Communist and anti-progressive campaigns in postwar America. In fact, McCarthy was by no means the first and by no means the most successful of these campaigners. Despite all his scattergun charges he never uncovered a single actual Communist.[18]

He initially made little impact after being elected to the Senate in 1946, but his fortunes were transformed when he was booked on a national Republican speaking tour. He was considered no great attraction as an orator, as was revealed by the first venue on his itinerary, the Republican Ladies Club in the provincial backwater of Wheeling, West Virginia.

McCarthy was undecided whether to talk about Communism or the postwar housing crisis. He eventually chose Communism. His researchers and speechwriters supplied him with this history-making passage: "While I cannot take the time to name all the men in the State Department who have been named as active members of the Communist party and members of a spy ring, I have here in my hand a list of 205 – a list of names that were made known to the Secretary of State as being members of the Communist Party and who nevertheless are still working and shaping policy in the State Department."[19]

The eye-catching number of 205 was almost total invention. It was derived (by faulty subtraction) from a document that was more than three years old and had not in fact mentioned Communists at all. It caused a sensation, but McCarthy was quite unable to produce the list of 205 at his next speaking stop in Denver.

He told reporters he had left this vital evidence in his other suit on the aeroplane. Instead McCarthy switched to another list altogether, of "57 card-carrying Communists" in the State Department. He volunteered four names in his next speech, but then in a drunken tirade in his hotel bar accused two hostile reporters of stealing his new list.

However, he made national headlines and he had discovered a crucial law in the modern science of manufacturing news:

numbers are metaphors. They do not have to be true. They simply bolster a basic message and give it colour.

McCarthy proved this when he took the issue to the Senate for the first time. No longer a failure, established overnight as a national saviour, he had no trouble browbeating his critics. He oscillated confidently between 205 and 57 Communist sympathizers or agents and then came up with a new list of 81 State Department employees with a Communist agenda.

This was also based on old information, and McCarthy could reach a figure of 81 only by conflating liberals and supporters of Roosevelt's New Deal with Communists. McCarthy also began to identify people as homosexuals (and thus automatically subversive).[20]

When challenged on his conflicting totals by the then Senate Majority Leader, Scott Lucas, McCarthy actually said, "Let's stop this silly numbers game."[21] Only a few days after the Wheeling speech, McCarthy knew that most of the American people were not interested in the actual number of Communists in the State Department. They had assumed that there were some Communists in the Department and that they were being protected. No one asked if there were any actual Communists there at all.

McCarthy was eventually destroyed by two factors. First, he chose the wrong target, the Army, a revered institution where charges of Communist influence had little traction. If McCarthy had stuck to the State Department or branched out into the entertainment industry and the media, like the House Un-American Activities Committee, he would have found less resistance.

More important, McCarthy was fatally exposed by his performances on television, particularly under inquisition. Unlike later politicians, he was never taught to perform on what was then a new medium and exposed himself, particularly to conservative, respectable voters, as crass, unkempt, strident and bullying. He lapsed into depression and alcoholism, ignored in the Senate (which finally nerved itself to censure him) and in the media.

Trump has also been rude and bullying on television, especially during the campaign debates, but benefits from a celebrity culture that has come to admire certain kinds of boorishness and sneering as honest self-expression, and revels in the spectacle of public humiliation – as on *Big Brother* and Trump's own programme *The Apprentice*.

Even so, McCarthy still has a substantial following in the United States, particularly in his home state of Wisconsin. Supporters still believe that he was murdered by Communists.[22]

Now let's imagine that Joe McCarthy could tweet. Imagine that he can change numbers and invent new facts and select new targets at will without any hostile scrutiny at all. "205 Commies in State Dpt. All protected by POTUS." If that fails to take hold of the public he could try "Queers in Army promote each other" the same day. Or "23 White House staff paid by Commies."

Imagine that he substitutes Tweets for television as his prime means of communication. McCarthy could have forced the American people and media to respond to all his "stories" on his own terms.

Has Trump learned anything from Joe McCarthy? He was only ten when McCarthy died. But his lawyer and mentor for much of the 1970s was McCarthy's fearsome chief counsel, Roy Cohn.[23]

Cohn was one of the most obnoxious men in American history, with no admirers even among ultra-conservatives. He was a racist, a Jew who spoke viciously of "kikes" and a predatory gay man who spoke viciously of "faggots". He was, however, a brilliant lawyer and a master of political networking. He collected a portfolio of Mob-related clients and defended them successfully by aggressive courtroom tactics and the use of political patronage and media management. He not only represented Trump for over ten years but initiated him into his world of unrestricted sex, corruption and favouritism, while feeding copy to privileged journalists from his tables in New York's leading nightclubs.[24]

Trump revives Nixon's "silent majority"

In November 1969 President Richard Nixon was beset by vocal and at times violent political enemies. He had an enduring hatred of the liberal media and the fashionable elite who in his view had consistently looked down on him throughout his political career. Nixon turned on all his foes by calling into being an imaginary coalition against them: the "silent majority".

Nixon's able speechwriter, Pat Buchanan, recalled later that the "silent majority" speech was Nixon's own work, handwritten on the yellow legal pads he favoured. Buchanan had offered him a number of phrases in a memo, including "forgotten Americans" and "quiet Americans" but Nixon spotted "silent majority", double-underlined it, and built his televised speech on it.[25]

The immediate impact of the speech was to give Nixon a huge lift in opinion polls: his national approval ratings rose from around 50 per cent to 81 per cent.[26] The longer-term effect was to create a political coalition by negation. Nixon's short phrase gave a home to *everyone* who did *not* protest against the Vietnam War (or anything else), who did *not* criticize the police, who did *not* reject authority, religion and conventional mores and family life. Nixon knew from his Presidential campaign that many of his supporters felt threatened, ignored and despised and were ready to identify his foes as theirs.

Only two months after the speech, *Time* magazine named "Middle America" as its "Man of the Year" (although they added a representative Middle American woman to the cover illustration). The magazine's publisher, Roy E. Larsen, explained that "the events of 1969 transcended specific individuals. In a time of dissent and 'confrontation', the most striking new factor was the emergence of the so-called 'Silent Majority' as a powerfully assertive force in US society."[27]

It is small wonder that Trump reinvoked the "silent majority". As far back as July 2015, he announced in Phoenix, Arizona, that "the silent majority is back, and we're going to take our country back".[28]

Two weeks later he affirmed through Twitter: "I truly LOVE all of the millions of people who are sticking with me despite so many media lies. There is a great SILENT MAJORITY looming." He followed this up with: "The polls have been consistently great. The silent majority is speaking. Politicians are failing." The phrase then appeared regularly in Trump banners and rallies throughout his campaign.[29]

There is some irony in that Trump's voters are not a majority – by some 2.9 million – a fact which greatly pained him. But he found enough "silent" supporters in states where it mattered to win handily in the Electoral College.

Why Hillary Clinton could not hit back

These precedents for Trump are far from exhaustive but they show that he is not a new phenomenon. There are many before him who relied on the rage of forgotten voters against the ruling elite and who manipulated their emotions by propaganda and "fake news".

But American voters are now more diverse and more sophisticated than those of the last two centuries and have access to vastly more sources of information. They should not have fallen for a campaign based on rage and lies.

Trump's opponent, Hillary Clinton, was the co-creator and legatee of the most successful political machine in American history. Over their forty-odd years together in politics, Bill and Hillary Clinton raised an estimated four billion dollars.[30]

With the backing of so much money, with a huge staff of supposed political experts, with the support of the majority of the nation's journalists and opinion-formers, why did Hillary Clinton not nail Trump as an empty-headed fantasist?

In our view, it was because she, and the progressive elite which supported her, were themselves hopelessly compromised by their own methods of controlling political discourse. Put less grandly – they had lied every bit as often and deeply as Donald Trump. In doing so, they forfeited the basic trust of millions of voters.

Even before Trump emerged, much of the political class in the US (and Britain) had turned its back on truth. Hillary Clinton could not call him out because she was also a liar and a cheat.

So was Mrs Clinton's husband. So was Tony Blair, Clinton's disciple on the other side of the Atlantic. Indeed, Blair told more serious lies than any that Donald Trump has yet uttered. These concerned Saddam Hussein's imaginary weapons of mass destruction, the justification for the calamitous invasion of Iraq.

There is, however, a significant difference between the lies told by the Clintons (and the liberal establishment) and the lies now being told by Donald Trump.

The Clintons and their followers convinced themselves that their lies were virtuous. They saw truth telling, due process, and respect for the law as minor points, compared to the greater good they could achieve once in power.

This point is nicely made in Joe Klein's comic masterpiece, *Primary Colors*. Governor Stanton (a thinly veiled portrait of Bill Clinton) justified his mendacity as follows:

"We live in an eternity of false smiles – and why? Because it's the price you pay to lead. You don't think Abraham Lincoln was a whore before he was a president? He had to tell his little stories and smile his shit-eating, back-country grin. He did it all just so he'd get the opportunity, one day, to stand in front of the nation and appeal to 'the better angels of our nature'. That's when the bullshit stops. And that's what this is all about."

This is the message of the *West Wing* TV series, much admired by the political class on both sides of the Atlantic. It was the story the liberal establishment told to itself, helped by the media and with the blessing of a progressive United States academic establishment entranced by the doctrine of postmodernism.

Postmodernists played with the idea of truth and falsehood.

Michel Foucault described truth as an effect of the rules of discourse, and for Foucault, all discourses were equally valid. He declared: "I have not written anything but fictions."

The American philosopher, Richard Rorty, helped bring postmodernism to the United States. He too dismissed the idea of independent truth, and argued that the best we could do was to "construct" what he liked to call "a narrative".

These distinguished philosophers were fashionable in liberal universities at the start of the twenty-first century, with their claim that truth was nothing more than a manifestation of power.

This helps to explain how liberals didn't mind at all about lying – so long as they were the ones that lied or "controlled the discourse", as the academics liked to put it. But this meant that they had no defence when Trump turned up.

The 45th United States President, even more than Tony Blair or Bill Clinton, is the perfect politician for the postmodern age where all truths are equal, there is no such thing as an independent reality and all truths are really competing narratives.

When Donald Trump's campaign manager Kellyanne Conway leapt to the defence of White House press spokesman Sean Spicer following his false claims about the size of the crowd on Inauguration Day, she used language that would have made sense to Michel Foucault: "Our press secretary, Sean Spicer, gave alternative facts to that."

This was postmodernism turned into practical politics. Trump's facts were alternative and equally valid.

Donald Trump, however, possessed another advantage that his Democratic opponent lacked. He used Twitter to create a narrative that reached far beyond the normal audience of politics. His language about disenfranchisement of the United States working class spoke directly to the experience of tens of millions of Americans.

However many lies Trump told, he spoke to voters in a way that nobody else could and Twitter enabled him to do it.

He viscerally understood the power of this new medium to simplify complex ideas, to remove nuance and subtext and, above all, to remove any boundary between assertion and fact. Donald Trump was the first modern politician to have grasped social media's full potential to define issues in his own terms and even to create a world of belief impervious to reality.

He understood that politics was entertainment. Hence the name-calling, the bullying, the public humiliation, the relish in combat.

The power of Twitter

Twitter is an ideal medium for appealing to any supposed "silent majority". It is completely democratic. Anyone can join, at no cost. There are no restrictions and no filtering (except in rare extreme cases). Twitter allows a candidate to appeal at a personal level to anyone who is *against* anything and make him or her feel like part of a vast shared community without having to meet or even acknowledge any of its other members.

Donald Trump quickly recognized that Twitter gives the silent majority a voice. A very high proportion of Trump's Twitter output during his Presidential run were Retweets from ordinary accounts. He never vetted these accounts, even though some were run by white supremacists and even worse. One was from an account with the macabre Twitter handle "White Genocide" whose author on inspection turned out to be an apologist for Nazi Germany.

Trump made the revolutionary discovery that Twitter enabled instantaneous connection with voters. Hence his enthusiasm for "live tweeting" of TV events or public occasions. He tried out this technique first with televised awards ceremonies before moving on to political debates and speeches.

TV channels – above all Fox – soon started to flash up his Twitter reactions to televised debates. This meant that Trump in his dressing gown in front of the television at home was brilliantly able to shape the interpretation of live public events, both as critic and entertainer.

Hillary Clinton also did Twitter – at the time of writing she still has 13.7 million followers – but her Tweets were decided by committee. There was no spontaneity. Allegedly one Tweet took nine hours to be agreed. By then the moment had passed and the sentiment was stale.

Trump just plunged with his thumbs. This gave his campaign danger and raw excitement. His Retweets played a crucial role in linking him with voters and creating the "Trump Train" – the term embraced by Trump supporters for the movement that took him to the White House.

In selecting the Tweets for this book from the nearly thirty-five thousand Trump has issued over the last eight years, we have included a significant number of Retweets to demonstrate the direct, unfiltered, personal engagement between Donald Trump and the voters of middle America.

This in turn brings us to an unavoidable question. No populist movement has yet posed a threat to the US political system itself. Will Trump's be the first to do so?

Sir Richard Evans, distinguished historian of Nazi Germany, has noted similarities between Donald Trump and twentieth-century authoritarian rulers:[31] "When you look at President Trump's statements, I'm afraid you do see echoes, and they are very alarming. For example, the stigmatization of minorities. First of all, the Trump White House failed to mention the Jews in its statement on Holocaust Remembrance Day. And that is very worrying because the Nazi Holocaust of the Jews was not just a genocide; it had a special quality, because Hitler and the Nazis regarded the Jews as an existential threat to Germany. They used hyperbolic and exaggerated language about Jews. If the Jews were not killed, the Nazis said, they would destroy Germany completely, whereas other groups that the Nazis stigmatized, discriminated against, and indeed murdered, like the handicapped, were only to be gotten out of the way."

Richard Evans noted that while Trump's White House is contaminated with anti-Semitism, the Muslims have yet more reason to be afraid: "If you look at the language the Trump team has been using about Islamic extremists, it is exactly the same: They are an existential threat to America. They will defeat, dominate, and destroy America. That is a very extreme kind of language and a very disturbing echo."

Sir Richard noted further similarities between Trump and the Nazis, including hostility to the press, and contempt for the courts and the rule of law. He noted that in his early days Hitler was not taken any more seriously than Trump is now, and many people assumed he was a buffoon who "could calm down when he assumed the responsibilities of office".

However, Evans takes comfort from the fact that the rise of Fascism in the 1930s was accompanied by the rise of political violence on the streets. This is so far a relatively minor feature of Donald Trump's America, though (as we show in this book) Trump encouraged violence in his rallies, and (in subsequently deleted Tweets) came close to advocating insurrection in the hours after Barack Obama's victory in 2012.

We were inclined to dismiss Donald Trump as a buffoon when we embarked on this study. This was perhaps a reasonable conclusion at the time Trump started to tweet in 2009, and there is no doubt that the US President remains a notorious loudmouth.

But his identity evolved as he pondered running for the White House. The first serious change, as we have noted, came during the summer of 2011 when Trump discovered his unique Twitter voice and converted it into a political weapon.

An even more pivotal moment came five years later when Ted Cruz pulled out of the race for the Republican nomination.

The machine behind Cruz needed a new vehicle, and discovered one in the shape of Trump. Cruz's most important supporter had been a financier called Robert Mercer, a mathematical genius who has made a fortune as a hedge fund manager.

Though brilliant with numbers, Mercer is close to inarticulate and finds it hard to communicate with human beings. Yet he shares almost all of Trump's instincts. He is contemptuous of the Washington Establishment, believes that politicians (including the Republican high command) are crooks, and wants a drastic reduction in the size of the state.

According to an agenda-setting profile in the *New Yorker*,[32] Mercer believes that the civil rights legislation of the 1960s was a mistake, that the problem of racism in the United States is exaggerated, and that too much has been made of climate change.

Robert Mercer (according to one former colleague, Nick Patterson)[33] considers that the United States should have seized Iraqi oil after the 2003 invasion. This is one of many views that he shares with Donald Trump.

Mercer is reportedly fascinated by conspiracy theories, some of the most lurid and improbable of which involve the Clintons (he apparently thinks, for example, that they ordered the murder of opponents). He is also said to downplay the dangers posed by nuclear weapons, maintaining that the explosions at Hiroshima and Nagasaki which brought World War Two to an end in 1945 made Japanese people (except those caught up in the immediate blast) healthier.

He holds a stake in a firm called Centre Firearms, which claims to possess the largest private collection of machine guns in the United States. It is hard to avoid the conclusion that Mercer's superb mathematical mind is allied to a deranged social and political outlook which, if turned into a programme for government, would prove a profound threat to the stability of the United States and to world peace.

It is an unfortunate feature of American politics that very rich men can and do purchase political power. Mercer arguably proved decisive in getting Trump to the White House. He brought money, organization – and up-to-date techniques of voter targeting. Mercer, having made his fortune by revolutionizing data management techniques on Wall Street, performed the same trick in politics. His hugely sophisticated analysis of voting patterns and social media has reportedly also been used by the NO campaign during the Brexit referendum.

More important still Mercer delivered personnel. He and his politically involved daughter Rebekah Mercer successfully pressed for the appointment of Kellyanne Conway, campaign manager for Cruz, as Trump's campaign chief in the final months. He also helped to deliver Steve Bannon, today Trump's main strategist in the White House and one of the most powerful men on the planet.

Many political leaders depend on a subordinate individual who provides them with a world view and intellectual muscle of which they are otherwise bereft. In Britain Downing Street chief of staff Nick Timothy performs this function for Theresa May.

Just as there would be no Theresa May without Nick Timothy, there could be no Trump without Bannon. Bannon is mentioned only three times in Trump's tweets. However, his Breitbart news organization gets multiple references. This is because, by smashing political convention and rewriting the rules of modern political discourse, Breitbart has shaped Trump's strategy and validated his often barbaric interpretation of public events.

The Mercers met Andrew Breitbart, founder of the eponymous news organization, in 2011. Breitbart died shortly afterwards, aged just forty-three, of a heart attack. Steve Bannon, backed by the Mercers, then became executive chairman. He shaped an outlet which has domesticated far-right extremists, amplified white nationalist voices, and torn down the mainstream Republican Establishment.

Study of Donald Trump's Tweets shows that Breitbart was an essential source of news and ideological reassurance as he made his run for the Presidency in the face of entrenched Establishment hostility. Again and again Trump retweeted Breitbart, which promoted Trump's campaign in a way that few other outlets were prepared to do. It gave credibility to many of Trump's most outlandish themes, for instance to his repeated assertion that President Obama had not been born an American citizen and was therefore ineligible to be President.

A great deal has been written about Steve Bannon, and there is no need to reiterate here the biography of this former naval officer, Wall Street banker, film-maker, propagandist, moral warrior and political alchemist. Steve Bannon is an especially interesting figure because he repudiates modernity, progess and the enlightenment values which have lain at the heart of the American project ever since the time of the founding fathers.

His film *Generation Zero*, made in the aftermath of the financial crash, is especially revealing. It is framed explicitly around a book called *The Fourth Turning: An American Prophecy*, written in 1997 by Neil Howe and William Strauss.

In the words of one of the co-authors, their analysis "rejects the deep premise of modern Western historians that social time is either linear (continuous progress or decline) or chaotic (too complex to reveal any direction). Instead we adopt the insight of nearly all traditional societies: that social time is a recurring cycle…"

Bannon follows Howe and Strauss in the belief that the United States has reached a turning point, and is destined for an immensely painful period of collapse and reconstruction after a long period of profligacy and decadence. There is evidence Trump shares at least some of this apocalyptic vision. The future President wrote in *The America We Deserve*: "I hope I am wrong, but I think we may be facing an economic crash like we've never seen before."[34]

One of the reasons that Trump's Tweets are powerful is that they repeatedly articulate the apprehension that the United States is under mortal threat from multiple enemies, and that only decisive action can avert it.

A large part of this threat is economic, and Bannon's *Generation Zero* is mainly about impending financial collapse. Islam is another element. Trump and Bannon are both convinced that the United States faces an existential challenge from what they call radical Islam.

Bannon believes that what he calls the "Judaeo-Christian West" is engaged in a grand conflict against what he calls an "expansionist Islamic ideology". Trump agrees, and his Tweets dispatch messages of alarm and despondency to his twenty-seven million followers. There is a paradox in this analysis because the notion that Islam and Christianity are irreconcilable exactly mirrors the way Islamic State and Al Qaeda view the world.

Both sides believe in the clash of civilizations, and both believe that they are engaged in an existential war. Both turn rhetoric into action, in Trump's case with his call for a "total and complete shutdown of Muslims entering the United States". This proposition that Islam is a mortal enemy helps explain Trump and Bannon's admiration for Vladimir Putin's Russia. They see him less as a competitor for global power and influence than as a fellow Christian warrior against the Islamic menace.

Donald Trump embodies limitless contradictions. Here is a billionaire who speaks for America's "forgotten men"; a Christian without compassion; a budget hawk who wants to tax less and spend more; a Republican President who shares a great deal of the same geopolitical analysis as Julian Assange, an anarchist fugitive from justice; an isolationist determined to go to war against Islam.

Many populists have tried to reach the White House, but very few have made it. Steve Bannon likes to compare Trump to Andrew Jackson. This comparison, with its implication that Bannon himself is a wheeler-dealing Martin Van Buren, is not without merit. But the White House in 2017 is an infinitely more complex place than it was in the 1830s. In due course – most likely sooner than later – Donald Trump will collapse under the weight of his own contradictions.

The options are narrowing. He is at war on all sides, with the CIA, with the judges, with Congress, with the Republican Party, and the press. America's forgotten men and women are still on his side. The United States somehow needs to discover a leader who can speak for the liberal elites and the working classes, the cities and the small towns, the government and the people. That leader needs wisdom, goodwill, a great deal of luck, and a new political language. The United States is a great nation. Eventually he or she will emerge.

2009

★ ★ ★ ★ ★

Pushing Product:
Trump's early Tweets

Editorial note: All spelling and punctuation in the Tweets have been left as originally broadcast.

Be sure to tune in and watch Donald Trump on Late Night with David Letterman as he presents the Top Ten List tonight!
1:54 PM – 4 May 2009

> Donald Trump's first Tweet was an act of self-promotion. He appeared on the popular NBC show to advise viewers on how to deal with the aftermath of the financial collapse. His top ten tips included "Only buy things that are essential, like golf courses and beauty pageants." Golf courses and beauty pageants obsessed Donald Trump. There would be countless references to both in his future Tweets.

Donald Trump will be appearing on The View tomorrow morning to discuss Celebrity Apprentice and his new book Think Like A Champion!
8:00 PM – 4 May 2009

> Trump remained an executive producer of NBC's *The Apprentice* even after he entered the White House, a sign of the show's importance in his career. When it started in 2004, Trump was emerging from a period of desperate financial trouble. In that year Trump Hotels and Casinos had filed for bankruptcy. The show enabled him to present himself to a national audience as a successful international businessman once more, even though some banks had pulled the plug on him. At the end of each episode of *The Apprentice*, Trump would point his finger at whoever he deemed that week's loser before delivering his trademark "You're fired!" Trump's Tweet refers to the celebrity version of *The Apprentice*, launched in 2008.

"My persona will never be that of a wallflower - I'd rather build walls than cling to them" --Donald J. Trump
9:07 AM – 12 May 2009

> Four years later, in October 2013, Trump was to tweet a quotation from Isaac Newton that stated the opposite – "We

3

build too many walls and not enough bridges." But this early Tweet would turn out to be more prescient.

Did you know Donald Trump is on Facebook?
http://www.facebook.com/DonaldTrump -
Become a fan today!
11:11 AM – 23 May 2009

Trump was building a following across all social media platforms.

Thanks to all for your thoughtful birthday wishes –
Donald Trump
6:13 PM – 15 Jun 2009

Donald John Trump was born on 14 June 1946 in Queens, across the East River from the conspicuous success and wealth of Manhattan. He was the fourth of the five children of Frederick C. and Mary MacLeod Trump. Frederick was a builder-developer specializing in apartment buildings for middle-earners. Donald, a wilful child, was sent aged thirteen to New York Military Academy. After two years at Fordham University he transferred to the Wharton School of Finance at the University of Pennsylvania, graduating in 1968 with a degree in economics. He joined his father's business. In 1973 the Trumps were subject to a complaint filed by the federal government accusing them of racial discrimination against tenants and prospective tenants, a violation of civil rights legislation. The case was settled only after a protracted legal fight during which the Trumps tried to countersue the Justice Department for $100 million for making false statements, allegations that were dismissed by the court. Donald expanded into commercial real estate, benefiting from his father's contacts and willingness to stand as guarantor for loans, sowing the seeds of the Trump Organization. Casinos, hotels, luxury apartment buildings and golf courses would all follow.

RE: Michael Jackson: "He was a great friend and a spectacular entertainer. It's a devastating loss!" -Donald J. Trump
11:51 AM – 26 Jun 2009

> This Tweet can be read alongside a later one, on 24 February 2012: "Clive Davis gave a great eulogy at my friend Whitney Houston's funeral – absolutely amazing!" These Tweets are characteristic of Trump's view of celebrity: these famous people have died; I met them, once or twice, and exchanged pleasantries with them; therefore they were my friends; therefore I am bereaved.

Donald Trump backs 'Apprentice' Randal Pinkett for N.J. Lieutenant Governor
8:40 AM – 15 Jul 2009

> Trump's first political campaign message, in support of a former contestant from his television show, was retweeted just once. Pinkett, an African-American Democrat, failed to become Jon Corzine's running mate.

Ivanka is now on Twitter - You can follow her @IvankaTrump - Have a terrific weekend!
9:33 AM – 14 Aug 2009

> This Tweet welcomed Ivanka, Trump's eldest daughter, to Twitter. She now has 3.4 million followers. Born in 1981 to Trump's first wife, Czech-born Ivana, Ivanka modelled in her teens before following her father to the Wharton School of Finance. After working in real estate development she joined the Trump Organization in 2005. From 2006 to 2015, she worked alongside her father and younger brother Eric (born 1984) and older brother Donald Jr (born 1977) as a judge on *The Apprentice*. She also founded her own fashion brand, the Ivanka Trump Collection. Hers is the only phonecall Trump will "*always* take". She is said to be the heir apparent to the Trump business empire, although she resigned as an executive vice

president of the Trump Organization when her father entered the White House. In late March 2017 it was announced Ivanka was going to work in the White House as a special assistant to the President.

--From Donald Trump: "Ivanka and Jared's wedding was spectacular, and they make a beautiful couple. I'm a very proud father."
10:31 AM – 27 Oct 2009

The first reference to Jared Kushner who would play a dominant role in Trump's Presidential campaign and later in the White House. Kushner was born in 1981, son of Seryl (née Stadtmauer) and Charles, New York real estate developer, landlord and founder of Kushner Companies. The family fortune is estimated at nearly $2 billion, making the Kushners almost as rich as Trump himself. Jared's paternal grandparents were Holocaust survivors who came to America from Poland after World War Two. Jared studied at Harvard and New York universities. While still in his mid-twenties, he was already striking deals of his own, for instance arranging the purchase of a Fifth Avenue office building for a record $1.8bn. In 2005 the Kushners met with a severe setback. Jared's father Charles was sentenced to two years in prison on eighteen counts of tax evasion, witness tampering and making illegal campaign donations. Trump's ally Chris Christie, then a US attorney for the New Jersey district, was part of the prosecution team. It is speculated that Christie's role was one of the reasons for the power struggle inside the Trump camp in mid-2016, won decisively by Jared. Ivanka converted to Judaism on their wedding and they are raising their children as Modern Orthodox Jews.

--Work has begun, ahead of schedule, to build the greatest golf course in history: Trump International – Scotland.
9:57 AM – 2 Nov 2009

The project on the Aberdeenshire coast provided a perfect meeting of Trump's passions for golf (a topic he has mentioned in over 600 Tweets) and Scotland (300 Tweets). But plans by the Scottish government for an offshore wind farm near the development would also stir Trump's hatred of renewable energy and stimulate his cynicism about climate change.

From Donald Trump: Wishing everyone a wonderful holiday & a happy, healthy, prosperous New Year. Let's think like champions in 2010!

12:38 PM – 23 Dec 2009

2010

★ ★ ★ ★ ★

"I saw Lady Gaga last night
and she was fantastic"

Trump Tycoon App for iPhone & iPod Touch - It's $2.99
but the advice is priceless!
11:28 AM – 15 Jan 2010

> Described in promotional literature as "a unique speculation
> game in which players find themselves in a dream job – working
> for Donald Trump".

from Donald Trump: "I saw Lady Gaga last night and she
was fantastic!"
11:58 AM – 21 Jan 2010

> In early 2017 Lady Gaga had 65.3m. followers, making her
> the eighth most followed person in the world. Trump ranked
> forty-eighth.

From Donald Trump: "I'm so proud of my wife Melania
and the launch of her new jewelry line, to debut on QVC
on April 30th at 9 p.m."
4:18 PM – 26 Feb 2010

> Melania, Trump's third wife, was born in 1970 in then
> Communist Yugoslavia. She is today a hero in her native land.
> Her father was the manager of a state-owned car dealership.
> The future First Lady began her modelling career as a child,
> signing with an international agency in Milan when she was
> eighteen. She speaks Slovene, English, French, German and
> Serbian. In the mid-1990s she moved to New York and became
> friendly with Trump. Melania and Donald married in 2005 in
> a lavish ceremony attended by Hillary and Bill Clinton. A year
> later Melania gave birth to a son, Barron, whom the family
> refers to as "Little Donald" on account of his liking for suits
> and ties.
>
> After Donald Trump entered the White House, it was soon
> announced that Melania would remain living in Trump Tower
> at least until Barron finishes the school year. The cost to the
> New York Police Department of providing security for this

arrangement has been estimated by its Commissioner to be between $127,000 and $146,000 a day.

From Donald Trump: Andrea Bocelli @ Mar-a-Lago - Many say best night of entertainment in long history of Palm Beach
9:51 AM – 5 Mar 2010

Trump's pride and joy, Mar-a-Lago is his Florida home and a members-only club. Marjorie Merrieweather Post, owner of General Foods Inc., built the property in the 1920s before bequeathing it to the nation as a winter retreat for the President, intending it as the US equivalent of Chequers. Successive Presidents ignored it and the ungrateful nation, tired of paying taxes on an unused property, gave it back to the Post estate in 1980. The Posts put it on the market at $20m. Trump offered $15m., but his offer was refused. He then told the Post family that he had bought the land between Mar-a-Lago and the ocean, and that he intended to build on it. As a result, in 1985 the shaken Posts finally accepted less than $8m. from Trump. Following his election victory the membership fee was doubled to $200,000. He now terms the property the Southern White House and often spends the weekends there.

Trump is fond of the very popular Italian tenor Andrea Bocelli. Critically he is less esteemed. *The New York Times* wrote in 2006: "Mr. Bocelli is not a very good singer. The tone is rasping, thin and, in general, poorly supported."

The new season of the Celebrity Apprentice is off to a great start-- last night it swept the 10 p.m. hour in every key demographic.
1:21 PM – 15 Mar 2010

I am happy to announce that the original Apprentice --which will offer job opportunities to those in need--is coming back.
1:17 PM – 18 Mar 2010

Job opportunities, at least, for those in need of television exposure and attention. It is less clear how useful the show is in starting business careers.

Last night Melania and I attended the Skating with the Stars Gala at Wollman Rink in Central Park, it was fantastic. Stay tuned for Part 2..
8:33 AM – 6 Apr 2010

Then we attended the Scottish fashion show that benefits veterans, Dressed to Kilt 2010, which I co-hosted with Sir Sean and Lady Connery.
9:34 AM – 6 Apr 2010

My bestselling book from last April, Think Like a Champion, is now available in paperback. It's inspiring, entertaining, and a great read.
1:08 PM – 6 Apr 2010

Trump reviews his own book, ghostwritten like all the volumes he has published.

This is a terrific day for downtown New York. Trump SoHo is unlike anything else. Be sure to visit this fantastic hotel soon!
11:36 AM – 9 Apr 2010

The *Financial Times* later revealed that Trump SoHo had embarrassing links to a Kazakhstan-based money-laundering network. In 2008 Donald Trump Jnr stated: "Russians make up a pretty disproportionate cross-section of a lot of our assets; say in Dubai, and certainly our project in SoHo and anywhere in New York. We see a lot of money pouring in from Russia."

The premiere of "Donald J. Trump's Fabulous World of Golf" is tomorrow night at 9 p.m. ET on Golf Channel. Tune in for a great adventure!
12:37 PM – 12 Apr 2010

> Golf: where business and pleasure meet in Trumpworld. Trump revels in playing against politicians and celebrities. The boxer Oscar De La Hoya and the actor Samuel L. Jackson are among those who have claimed he has a tendency to cheat. Responding to De La Hoya's detailed account of multiple balls and missed strokes, Trump issued a statement insisting "he respects the game too much to cheat and is good enough to have won a number of club championships."

"Before Kids Can Go Places, They Need a Place To Go" -- the motto of The Police Athletic League, an organization I'm very proud to support
3:49 PM – 14 Apr 2010

> A rare example of a regular charitable donation that can be verified. Despite claims of philanthropic largesse, according to *Forbes* magazine this was the only charity to receive a donation from the Trump Foundation each year from 2001–2014. An investigation by the *Washington Post* raised serious questions about the Trump Foundation, both about its income and the destination of its donations. In October 2016 the New York authorities issued a "notice of violation" ordering the Foundation to stop soliciting charitable donations with immediate effect.

Melania and I will be appearing on Larry King Live tonight, 9 p.m. on CNN. Be sure to tune in for some great conversation!
9:13 AM – 28 Apr 2010

Congratulations to our new Miss USA, the beautiful Rima
Fakih. Rima will represent us well at Miss Universe and be
a wonderful Miss USA

11:48 AM – 17 May 2010

> Miss Fakih was a Lebanese American Muslim. She converted to
> Christianity in May 2016. Trump owned the rights to the Miss
> USA and Miss Universe competitions, and it is apparent that
> their glossy version of attractiveness in women conforms to
> his. Trump's verbal abuse of female opponents – Carly Fiorina,
> Hillary Clinton, the various women who accused him of groping
> them – was often based on the fact that they do not resemble
> beauty-pageant contestants and are therefore unworthy of
> serious attention. On 23 March 2016 he retweeted contrasting
> pictures of his wife Melania, a former model, and Ted Cruz's
> spouse Heidi, who is an investment manager at Goldman Sachs,
> with the caption: "A picture is worth a thousand words".

The ratings for the Celebrity Apprentice were fantastic and
everyone had a great time. It was a terrific season -- congrats
to everyone!

10:31 AM – 25 May 2010

Scotland is beautiful. I spent several years looking for the right
place, visiting over 200 sites, and this is absolutely the right
place!

8:51 AM – 26 May 2010

The Dunes here are amazing, and they're how I learned about
geomorphology, which is the study of movement landforms.
We've had a great trip

12:24 PM – 27 May 2010

> The long search for the right place to build a golf resort in his
> mother's homeland was over. But a battle with the Scottish
> authorities over a proposed wind farm nearby loomed.

I'll be turning the table on Larry King this Saturday night. I'll be interviewing him in honor of the 25th Anniversary of his show.
3:37 PM – 2 Jun 2010

Rima Fakih, our beautiful Miss USA, rode with me on the Gray Line Ride of Fame yesterday …
8:46 AM – 9 Jun 2010

> This Tweet prompted three likes and seven Retweets.

Tonight be sure to watch Melania and Ivanka on Larry King Live for a Celebrity Relief Telethon http://larrykinglive.blogs.cnn.com/
8:18 AM – 21 Jun 2010

> The Trumps doing their bit to help in the wake of the Gulf of Mexico oil spill, alongside teen pop star Justin Bieber, Robert Redford and Sting.

The Eric Trump Foundation has raised over $1,000,000 towards St. Jude Children's Research Hospital.
1:44 PM – 24 Jun 2010

> Trump has two adult sons by his first wife Ivana. Donald Jr was born in 1977 and Eric followed in 1984. Both went to work at the Trump Organization. When Donald Trump handed over control of his companies and assets upon entering the White House in January 2017, Donald Jr and Eric were appointed as trustees.

Work is expected to begin today on my golf course in Scotland. It will be spectacular!
9:11 AM – 1 Jul 2010

Wishing everyone a wonderful Independence Day weekend. We have a lot to be thankful for.
8:41 AM – 2 Jul 2010

Due to popular demand, CNN will re-broadcast the Larry King Live show I hosted in June, in which I interview Larry. Monday July 5, 9 pm CNN
10:27 AM – 2 Jul 2010

The new edition of The Apprentice will be on Thursdays this fall at 10 pm ET---I'm putting people back to work!
9:52 AM – 6 Jul 2010

> Trump's belief that he can create work for people would be enormously magnified during the next five years.

It's going to get hotter in Las Vegas tonight! Watch the Miss Universe Pageant tonight on NBC at 9 p.m. I'm looking forward to being there!
8:55 AM – 23 Aug 2010

Congratulations to Miss Mexico, Jimena Navarrete, our new Miss Universe 2010, and congratulations to everyone for a fantastic show.
9:07 AM – 24 Aug 2010

> Miss Navarrete would remain loyal to Donald Trump even after he attacked Mexico during his presidential campaign, saying "Donald Trump has treated me super nicely, I'm still working with him until today, I have a contract with him."

Went to the Yankees game last night with Bill O'Reilly--we had a great time watching the Yankees win!
3:00 PM – 31 Aug 2010

> The conservative commentator and host of Fox News's flagship evening show *The O'Reilly Factor* was to prove a long-term supporter. O'Reilly is one of the handful of journalists Trump follows on Twitter. In April 2017 *The New York Times* revealed that O'Reilly and Fox had paid $13 million to settle harassment claims brought by five female employees.

I am very happy to have the civilian version of "The Apprentice" back on the air this fall. There will be excitement as well as opportunity.
3:52 PM – 14 Sep 2010

> In Trump's world, people are divided between celebrities and civilians.

Eric did a great job with his Eric Trump Foundation annual charity outing. I'm proud of him. http://bit.ly/c1y3c3
8:43 AM – 15 Sep 2010

> Eric suspended his charitable foundation in later 2016 amidst fears that donors might make contributions in order to gain special access to the White House. An Associated Press investigation alleged that the foundation had flouted charity standards, exaggerated its size and repeatedly directed payments to Donald Trump's golf clubs, which a spokesman described as "an oversight".

Tune in tonight at 10 pm on NBC for another exciting episode of The Apprentice -- and see the Dog Whisperer make an appearance.
10:10 AM – 30 Sep 2010

I'm honored to be presented the award of Doctor of Business Administration Honoris Causa from Robert Gordon University in Aberdeen, Scotland
8:40 AM – 6 Oct 2010

> The Robert Gordon University stripped Trump of his honorary doctorate in December 2015 after he called for Muslims to be banned from entering the USA. A spokesman said: "In the course of the current US election campaign, Mr Trump has made a number of statements that are wholly incompatible with the ethos and values of the university." The Scottish government had enjoyed a brief infatuation with Trump, overriding local objections to his golf course, but the relationship soon soured.

Scotland is beautiful and Trump Internatonal Golf Links-Scotland is progressing beautifully as well.
9:22 AM – 7 Oct 2010

An HR solutions company polled 1,000 employed adults to find out who would make ideal bosses...
12:48 PM – 14 Oct 2010

> Trump came third. Oprah Winfrey topped the poll followed by President Obama.

I'll be discussing a variety of topics tonight with Greta Van Susteren, 10 p.m. on Fox News. It will be the first of a two part series.
3:11 PM – 3 Nov 2010

> In his conversation with Van Susteren, Trump confided that he was thinking of running for President "for the first time in my life". This was not strictly true: Trump had also contemplated running for the Presidency in 1988, 2000 and 2004. Van Susteren has since moved from Fox to MSNBC but Trump still follows her on Twitter.

I'll be appearing on Larry King Live for his final show, Thursday night at 9 p.m., CNN. Larry's been on TV for 25 years...
3:55 PM – 14 Dec 2010

> Two weeks earlier Larry King had pulled off a coup by interviewing Vladimir Putin via satellite link from Moscow. Putin took the opportunity to tell the United States not to dabble in Russian politics. *The New York Times* said that: "Mr King… has long had a reputation for softball questions. So Mr. Putin's decision to appear on the program allowed his voice to be heard both in the United States and abroad while avoiding being challenged on contentious topics like his own grip on power and the limits on human rights and free speech in Russia." He was perhaps Trump's ideal interviewer.

Don't forget to watch Larry King tonight, CNN at 9 pm. He's a television legend and a great friend. It's going to be a fantastic farewell.

9:30 AM – 16 Dec 2010

2011

★ ★ ★ ★ ★

The birth of a new political language:
Trump discovers his voice

Don't forget to watch me tonight on Late Night with Jimmy Fallon, 12:35 a.m. on NBC. I'll be making a big announcement!
11:14 AM – 13 Jan 2011

> Rather than a tilt at the Presidency, the big announcement turned out to be the new cast for *Celebrity Apprentice*.

Be sure to watch Oprah today (4 pm on Channel 7), I'll be on with my entire family and it will be an entertaining hour
9:15 AM – 7 Feb 2011

> Trump's readiness to expose his whole family to Oprah Winfrey indicated he was getting serious about a run for the Presidency the following year. As long ago as 1988, Winfrey had questioned Trump on whether he would like to be President. Though his answer then was, "probably not", he predicted "I think I'd win… I'll tell you what: I wouldn't go in to lose."

It was great to appear on Piers Morgan Tonight last night as his first live guest. Piers won the Celebrity Apprentice and he's fantastic.
1:29 PM – 10 Feb 2011

> The fortunes of Piers Morgan and Donald Trump are closely linked. The British journalist had been sacked as editor of the *Daily Mirror* after publishing crudely faked photographs of British soldiers abusing Iraqi prisoners. To revive his career Morgan turned to America. He was the first winner of Trump's *Celebrity Apprentice*, before being chosen to replace Trump's friend Larry King as the presenter of CNN's flagship evening current affairs show. Piers Morgan is one of the forty-three accounts that Trump personally follows on Twitter.

Watch my speech at CPAC in Washington DC yesterday
http://www.youtube.com/watch?v=PR1b8yKxcAo
9:50 AM – 11 Feb 2011

The day after his appearance on the *Piers Morgan Show*, Presidential aspirant Trump gave a speech to the influential Conservative Political Action Conference (CPAC), arriving on stage accompanied by "For the Love of Money", the theme song to *The Apprentice*. Trump told a rapturous audience that he would "decide by June" whether to run for the Presidency.

Trump used this speech to align himself with the so-called "Birther Movement" that believes Barack Obama was born in Kenya, so making him ineligible to be US President:

"Our current President came out of nowhere. Came out of nowhere. In fact, I'll go a step further: the people that went to school with him, they don't even know him. They never saw him. They don't know who he is. It's crazy."

Check out ShouldTrumpRun....http://shouldtrumprun.com/
1:56 PM – 15 Feb 2011

The website was founded by Michael D. Cohen, Trump's personal lawyer. It was designed to gauge the public's interest in a potential Presidential run in 2012. Critics claimed that it violated campaigning rules.

Watch the latest From The Desk Of Donald Trump at http://bit.ly/f0kmi2 and read this article http://nydn.us/fpKQSY
5:48 PM – 17 Feb 2011

These portentous, pseudo-presidential video blogs featured Donald Trump speaking direct to camera about issues of the day.

Coming up in March: The "Comedy Central Roast of Donald Trump." March 15, mark your calendars. http://bit.ly/hYnA0E
12:36 PM – 28 Feb 2011

Before he appeared on this comedy programme, Trump declared that two subjects were off-limits: his past bankruptcies and any suggestion that he was not as rich as he said he was. He also tried unsuccessfully to censor jokes about his hair.

Trump grudgingly allowed the inclusion of "What's the difference between a wet raccoon and Donald Trump's hair? A wet raccoon doesn't have $7 billion", after the punchline total was upped from "$2 billion". (Trump had begun his negotiations with the writing team by insisting on "$10 billion".)

Watch as I humiliate a dais full of "talent." #TrumpRoast airs tonight at 10:30/9:30c on Comedy Central http://bit.ly/fugbyy
9:37 AM – 15 Mar 2011

Keep talking about me: use #TrumpRoast to tweet about how good I look on @ComedyCentral tonight at 10:30/9:30c http://bit.ly/hN3jow
3:28 PM – 15 Mar 2011

With #TrumpRoast, Trump uses a Twitter hashtag for only the second time.

@shouldtrumprun Hundreds of thousands of supporters have already gone to and joined the movement at shouldtrumprun.com Have you?
2:17 PM – 16 Mar 2011

The Should Trump Run Twitter account proved a dismal failure. Despite its ambitious claim that "We need to convince Donald Trump to run for President in 2012 and end all of the old rhetoric occurring in Washington", it secured little more than a thousand followers.

Check out my interview on @GMA http://abcn.ws/ib1t1c
10:47 AM – 17 Mar 2011

In this interview with *Good Morning America*, Trump returned to the subject of President Obama's birthplace: "Let me tell you, I'm a really smart guy. I was a really good student at the best school in the country. The reason I have a little doubt, just a little, is because he grew up and nobody knew him. If I got the nomination, if I decide to run, you may go back and interview people from my kindergarten. They'll remember me. Nobody comes forward. Nobody knows who he is until later in his life. It's very strange... The whole thing is very strange."

Plenty of people remember the young Barack Obama. It was, however, characteristic of Trump to allude to things being "strange" and the need to find out "what is really going on": with the unspoken implication that there is a conspiracy, a mystery.

The Comedy Central Roast of Donald Trump last week was the #1 highest rated Comedy Central Roast ever...it brought in 3.5 milion viewers
8:17 AM – 18 Mar 2011

I want to see people make lots of $$ and live better lives. I really think they can do that through TheTrumpNetwork http://trumpnetwork.com/
12:39 PM – 21 Mar 2011

The Trump Network claimed to be a "lucrative, groundbreaking opportunity... the first and only entrepreneurial opportunity of its kind being offered by Donald J. Trump" and "the greatest financial opportunity in America today!". It was actually a vitamin and nutritional supplement multi-level marketing scheme. The enterprise soon folded. Trump's claim to be altruistic in his business dealings is a theme common to many of his endeavours.

@oreillyfactor is having a poll, cast your vote for me at http://bit.ly/cxWgkp
9:25 AM – 3 May 2011

The Fox News poll revealed that viewers preferred Mitt Romney to Trump as their Republican candidate by 52 per cent to 48 per cent, though the state-by-state results revealed Trump had more support in the Rust Belt.

Guests are raving about our exclusive hotel mattress and so we've made it available for purchase!
2:23 PM – 13 May 2011

This has been a very difficult decision regarding the Presidential run and I want to thank all my twitter fans for your fantastic support.
1:47 PM – 16 May 2011

> The Tweet linked to Trump's full statement as released on Facebook:
>
> "After considerable deliberation and reflection, I have decided not to pursue the office of the Presidency. This decision does not come easily or without regret; especially when my potential candidacy continues to be validated by ranking at the top of the Republican contenders in polls across the country. I maintain the strong conviction that if I were to run, I would be able to win the primary and ultimately, the general election. I have spent the past several months unofficially campaigning and recognize that running for public office cannot be done half heartedly. Ultimately, however, business is my greatest passion and I am not ready to leave the private sector.
>
> "I want to personally thank the millions of Americans who have joined the various Trump grassroots movements and written me letters and e-mails encouraging me to run. My gratitude for your faith and trust in me could never be expressed properly in words. So, I make you this promise: that I will continue to voice my opinions loudly and help to shape our politician's [sic] thoughts. … I will not shy away from expressing the opinions that so many of you share yet don't have a medium through which to articulate."

Your most popular tweet answered, why I'm holding off on a Presidential bid… http://bit.ly/iF5pz6 #trumpvlog
12:26 PM – 9 Jun 2011

I've been visiting Trump Int'l Golf Links Scotland and the course will be unmatched anywhere in the world. Spectacular! http://t.co/O6fGgOs

1:13 PM – 21 Jun 2011

> Yet another Trump venture which is or will be the best, biggest and most popular the world has ever known. Or not. The Scots were never as keen as Trump was about their new golf course, which appears to have lost money every year since it opened in 2012.

Did my weekly phoner on Fox & Friends this morning... sounding off on issues of the day ... http://t.co/UaMWc6K

10:14 AM – 27 Jun 2011

> *Fox and Friends* is the Fox News breakfast show. For years Trump would give a phone-in interview every Monday. The close connection has continued into the White House, with the programme team granted privileged access. It is also an important source of news for Trump. Indeed many of his Tweets, even now as President, echo the talking points aired on the show.

Republicans should not negotiate against themselves again with @BarackObama in today's debt talks--First and foremost CUT,CAP and BALANCE.

11:17 AM – 7 Jul 2011

> Trump uses capital letters to emphasize a political point for the first time. The proposed "Cut, Cap and Balance Act" was a bill put forward by Republicans with Tea Party support to slash government spending.

THe Art of the Deal--"The best thing you can do is deal from strength, and leverage is the biggest strength you have." CUT, CAP and BALANCE.

11:18 AM – 7 Jul 2011

First mention on Twitter of his seminal 1987 book. Trump goes on to quote or mention *The Art of the Deal* 156 times. The book sold over a million copies. His ghostwriter Tony Schwartz would become a fierce critic of Candidate Trump, claiming that he had no attention span or any of the qualities normally associated with an ambitious politician.

If only @Obama was as focused on balancing the budget as he is on weakening Israel's borders then America would be on the path to solvency.
11:20 AM – 7 Jul 2011

America *was* on a path to prosperity, if not solvency. Obama's America Recovery and Reinvestment Act in 2009 had injected $787 billion into the economy, following a recession unprecedented since the war. By the time this Tweet was published the USA was well into a period of slow but steady growth, during which 3.7 million new private-sector jobs were created. The same year, President Obama presided over the injection of $62 billion into the ailing auto industry. The Federal Government expects to recover most of that investment from the industry's resultant increase in market share.

ObamaCare Tragedy Primed to Further Explode the Deficit http://t.co/wRxqlxA And @Obama transferred $500 billion from Medicare to fund it!
11:22 AM – 8 Jul 2011

Medicare was at the time almost broke. As a result of Obama's actions, Medicare probably won't go bust before 2030, and as a result 15 million people will have health insurance who wouldn't otherwise have done so. So not that much of a tragedy after all.

@macmiller "Donald Trump the Song" gets 16M hits on YouTube. Who wouldn't be flattered?
3:08 PM – 12 Jul 2011

What is better advice- "The Art of the Deal" or "Rules for Radicals"? I know which one @BarackObama prefers.
4:12 PM – 14 Jul 2011

> *Rules for Radicals: A Pragmatic Primer for Realistic Radicals* was published in 1971 by activist and writer Saul D. Alinsky. Alinsky's goal was to create a guide for future community organizers to use in uniting low-income communities or "Have-Nots", in order for them to gain social, political, legal and economic power.
>
> Hillary Clinton wrote a thesis on it and Obama was a disciple of Alinsky.

@BarackObama has sold guns to Mexican drug lords while his DOJ erodes our 2nd Amendment rights.
11:21 AM – 18 Jul 2011

> First critical mention of Mexico and a first reference to the right to bear arms as enshrined in the Second Amendment. Trump is tweeting here about a secret operation run by the US government, codenamed "Fast and Furious", that had inadvertently resulted in thousands of firearms ending up in the hands of criminals.

Obama, sadly, has no business or private sector background--- and it shows.
8:26 AM – 26 Jul 2011

> Shortly after Obama became President, US unemployment was around 10 per cent. During his Presidency, unemployment fell steadily, reaching 4.7 per cent at the end. Corporate profits more than doubled and the economy would gain jobs for 75 straight months, the longest stretch ever recorded. Increased support was made available to veterans, and homelessness among veterans was halved.

China has so much of our debt that they can't put us in default w/o killing themselves---US needs our toughest negotiator--- and fast!

8:42 AM – 27 Jul 2011

> Trump clearly believes that he is the negotiator he mentions.

Watch my wife Melania Trump tonight on @QVC at 1 a.m. So proud of her!

10:57 AM – 27 Jul 2011

> The future First Lady was allotted the graveyard slot on the home shopping network to push her line of jewellery.

People ask me every day to pose for pictures but the camera never works the first time--they are never prepared or maybe just very nervous!

3:09 PM – 27 Jul 2011

@BarackObama has not released his own debt plan yet. He's totally lost, ineffective, desperate. GOP has its best chance to make a great deal

3:37 PM – 28 Jul 2011

Watched Sean Hannity last night -- a great guy.

2:23 PM – 29 Jul 2011

> Fox News and national radio talk show host who has remained one of Trump's biggest defenders. The titles of his three published books perhaps best illustrate his political bent: *Let Freedom Ring: Winning the War of Liberty over Liberalism; Deliver Us from Evil: Defeating Terrorism, Despotism*; and *Liberalism, and Conservative Victory: Defeating Obama's Radical Agenda*. Trump follows Hannity on Twitter.

Ex-Presidential Pollster Pat Cadell says most voters sick of both parties and their failure.
10:43 AM – 30 Jul 2011

Why should we have any defense cuts in any deal? America must remain strong.
11:58 AM – 1 Aug 2011

All those politicians in Washington and not one good negotiator
8:33 AM – 3 Aug 2011

Wake Up America -- China is eating our lunch.
9:36 AM – 3 Aug 2011

> Over the summer of 2011, Donald Trump discovered the unique Twitter voice that would take him to the White House six years later.

America's debt officially became 100% of our GDP on @BarackObama's 50th birthday—coincidence?
12:44 PM – 4 Aug 2011

Obama Care is already having a devastating impact on our economy.
10:57 AM – 5 Aug 2011

The S&P downgrade is a direct result of @BarackObama's increased reckless budget spending and Obama Care.
He owns this.
10:12 AM – 8 Aug 2011

Congress should get back to Washington, but @BarackObama doesn't want to interrupt his vacation in Martha's Vineyard.
12:02 PM – 10 Aug 2011

It's easy to see why Americans are sick of career politicians and both parties.
10:36 AM – 12 Aug 2011

This is the message that would win Trump the Presidency.

Obama has no understanding of how to create jobs or opportunity. He believes in Government.
1:09 PM – 12 Aug 2011

@BarackObama played golf yesterday. Now he heads to a 10 day vacation in Martha's Vineyard. Nice work ethic.
12:36 PM – 15 Aug 2011

Unemployment is plaguing both Black and Hispanic youths. Very troubling.
1:41 PM – 15 Aug 2011

@BarackObama has a record low 39% Gallup approval rating. Why so high?
10:40 AM – 17 Aug 2011

According to Gallup, Trump's approval rating on 20 March 2017 was 35 per cent.

We spent over a billion on Libya and lead the way---why is Europe getting the oil?
10:57 AM – 23 Aug 2011

Let's not start celebrating over Libya until we see who takes over.
12:52 PM – 23 Aug 2011

As bad as Qaddafi was---what comes next in Libya will be worse---just watch.
2:24 PM – 23 Aug 2011

Britain and France had persuaded Obama to intervene against Muammar Gaddafi in Libya. Donald Trump consistently warned that chaos would follow the death of the Libyan leader. Events proved him right. His critique of the liberal interventionist consensus in Washington would help build his reputation as an honest voice.

Why did @BarackObama and his family travel separately to Martha's Vineyard? They love to extravagantly spend on the taxpayers' dime.
9:07 AM – 26 Aug 2011

In his first month as President, Trump's three visits to his Florida holiday home cost $11.3m., including the costs of his sons' business trips. This is only slightly less than the Obamas' total expenses over a full year.

More and more Americans seem fed up with both Parties----
I agree.
1:03 PM – 26 Aug 2011

If the UN unilaterally grants the Palestinians statehood, then the US should cut off all its funding. Actions have consequences.
11:03 AM – 30 Aug 2011

This line is repeated over the coming weeks. Trump positioned himself as an ardent defender of Israel. Later he would advocate moving the Israeli embassy to Jerusalem, and as President he abandoned the United States' longstanding commitment to the two-state solution.

Libya is being taken over by Islamic radicals---with @BarackObama's open support.
11:07 AM – 31 Aug 2011

China is happy to learn that @BarackObama plans to borrow another $300 Billion. @BarackObama is their favorite client.
12:23 PM – 8 Sep 2011

Want jobs? Slash corporate tax rate. Tax incentives for companies that create jobs in US. America will boom.
2:20 PM – 9 Sep 2011

Iran's nuclear program must be stopped – by any and all means necessary.
4:17 PM – 12 Sep 2011

> Trump was in general opposed to military adventures overseas. He makes an exception for Iran.

Had dinner with @RickPerry last night---great guy, straight shooter, impressive record.
8:52 AM – 15 Sep 2011

> The Governor of Texas had just announced his own run for the Republican candidacy. Perry's campaign would end in embarrassment when he failed to remember the name of one of the three agencies – Energy – he had promised to abolish as President. Perry is now Trump's Energy Secretary.

Can you imagine if @BarackObama had passed Cap and Trade?! Energy costs would be double from already record highs.
12:47 PM – 15 Sep 2011

Our next President must stop China's Rip-off of America.
10:02 AM – 21 Sep 2011

Australia is a beautiful country with terrific people who love America.
1:27 PM – 21 Sep 2011

> Donald Trump enjoying himself during a speaking tour. Relations with the US would sour after Trump's bad-tempered first call to Australian prime minister Malcolm Turnbull as President, in which Trump did his best to jettison President Obama's promise to take in just over a thousand Syrian refugees who were being held in an Australian detention camp.

The Iranians have just threatened to send warships to our coasts. They laugh at us. We can't allow them to develop nuclear weapons.
2:51 PM – 29 Sep 2011

A simplified tax code would spur economic growth and help create jobs. Unfortunately, Washington is incapable of simplifying anything.
3:27 PM – 29 Sep 2011

Everyone should boycott Italy if Amanda Knox is not freed---she is totally innocent.
11:12 AM – 30 Sep 2011

> Amanda Knox, an American citizen studying at Perugia University, had been convicted on questionable evidence of murdering her British student housemate Meredith Kercher.

Why is the UN condemning @Israel and doing nothing about Syria? What a disgrace.
12:07 PM – 6 Oct 2011

When will we stop wasting our money on rebuilding Afghanistan? We must rebuild our country first.
2:43 PM – 7 Oct 2011

> There is no idealism when it comes to Trump's foreign policy. He sees no point in the nation-building which George W. Bush, urged on by his ally Tony Blair, briefly attempted to achieve in Afghanistan and Iraq. To be fair to Trump, the West's attempts

to establish a functioning state in these two countries in the wake of the 2001 and 2009 invasions have completely failed.

A guy named @BobBeckel on FOX, their resident liberal, was not born with much of a brain.

9:06 AM – 11 Oct 2011

Beckel still appears on Fox News's popular roundtable discussion show *The Five*.

If the Prez wants to create jobs talk to some business people ---not liberal intellectuals.

12:44 PM – 11 Oct 2011

I don't want to be the only billionaire in America---I want all Americans to be rich.

1:31 PM – 11 Oct 2011

If the Wall Street protesters are upset about the economy then they should really be protesting @BarackObama at the White House.

12:06 PM – 14 Oct 2011

The Occupy Wall Street protest movement took control of a park in Lower Manhattan in September 2011, demanding among other objectives greater economic equality.

Why is @BarackObama always campaigning or on vacation?

12:43 PM – 17 Oct 2011

Happy to have passed 800,000 followers. Looking forward to passing 1M sooner than later.

2:37 PM – 17 Oct 2011

@BarackObama is holding Taiwan's request for 66 advanced F-16's. Wrong message to send to China.

9:16 AM – 18 Oct 2011

As President Elect, Trump would accept a call from the Taiwanese President unleashing a diplomatic row with China.

Iraq's government is treating us like fools. We should demand their oil.
3:07 PM – 18 Oct 2011

Bob Beckel, a commentator for FOX is bad for the @FoxNews brand: @BobBeckel is close to incompetent.
12:56 PM – 20 Oct 2011

Libya is adopting a more radical form of Sharia Law now under their new leadership. Is this what @BarackObama wanted?
3:42 PM – 24 Oct 2011

I only go on shows that get ratings, that's why I do @oreillyfactor, @hannityshow, and @gretawire. 'Your show @lawrence, like you, is a loser that will soon be off the air. @oreillyfactor killed you at 8PM.'
12:05 PM – 25 Oct 2011

Lawrence O'Donnell, presenter of *The Last Word* on MSNBC, had infuriated Trump by correctly predicting the exact date – 16 May – when Trump would abandon his Presidential ambitions. Trump would persist in claiming that his critics were losers, failing or incompetent, and continue to insist on his unique association with success.

Does @BarackObama ever work? He is constantly campaigning and fundraising--on both the taxpayer's dime and time---not fair!
1:10 PM – 25 Oct 2011

Please only respond by tweet @lawrence because like everyone else, I don't watch your show.
1:19 PM – 25 Oct 2011

The feud against Lawrence O'Donnell would continue for the next four years, and the list of Trump's enemies in the media would get much longer.

THe 2012 election is the most important in my lifetime. We must nominate a candidate who will win and will roll back @BarackObama's damage.
3:28 PM – 25 Oct 2011

I am happy to see the majority of the GOP candidates agree with me that the tax code must be simplified and the rates dropped.
2:16 PM – 26 Oct 2011

The US Air Force won the war in Libya to clear the way for Islamic Extremist control of Libya.
2:37 PM – 27 Oct 2011

David Cameron and Nicolas Sarkozy claimed the Libyan people had been liberated but Trump was already far ahead of them in predicting future chaos. Trump has consistently supported dictators across the Middle East.

The Al Qaeda flag is now flying over Benghazi. @BarackObama spent over $3Billion of our money for this?
2:17 PM – 1 Nov 2011

It snowed over 4 inches this past weekend in New York City. It is still October. So much for Global Warming.
2:43 PM – 1 Nov 2011

Egypt's Muslim Brotherhood just made its first visit to Hamas-led Gaza. Why did @BarackObama promote the "Arab Spring"?
10:46 AM – 2 Nov 2011

Iran's quest for nuclear weapons is a major threat to our nation's national security interests. We can't allow Iran to go nuclear.
11:34 AM – 4 Nov 2011

> At this point the US intelligence services were clear that Iran had no nuclear weapons programme.

China 'scorns' US cyber espionage charges--China does not respect us http://t.co/HwMz5NEa and feels Obama is a "dummy"
12:19 PM – 4 Nov 2011

> China had taken exception to a US report that it hacked American trade and technology secrets.

Mitt Romney did great in the debate last night.
11:21 AM – 10 Nov 2011

> Trump would become bitterly hostile to Romney after the Republican candidate's loss to Obama in 2012.

The Fed should not bail out the EU. Europe's financial mess is their problem, not our problem!
2:54 PM – 10 Nov 2011

> The European debt crisis erupted two years earlier, with Greece, Portugal and Spain worst affected. There has never been any serious suggestion that the United States Federal Reserve should intervene.

My new book, Time To Get Tough, comes out on December 5th. Pre-order on Amazon.com. It's the best book I've ever written.
9:46 AM – 16 Nov 2011

> According to a review in *Entertainment Weekly*, "Most of Donald Trump's new book, *Time to Get Tough: Making America No. 1 Again*, reads like a 190-page diatribe against the Obama presidency,

illegal immigration, and the people and media outlets who have dared to criticize him."

Made in America? @BarackObama called his 'birthplace' Hawaii "here in Asia." http://t.co/dQka2Plr

10:54 AM – 18 Nov 2011

Note Trump's use of inverted commas in order to cast doubt or suggest dishonesty. He would continue to claim for years, even after Obama released his birth certificate, that there was a mystery about the President's birthplace, thus questioning the legitimacy of his election.

Washington is simply incapable of any moderation because @BarackObama is such an extreme leftist. He must be defeated. #TImeToGetTough.

1:34 PM – 18 Nov 2011

Yesterday @BarackObama actually spent a full day in Washington. He didn't campaign, fund raise or play golf. Shocking.

12:09 PM – 22 Nov 2011

During the first ten weeks of his Presidency, Trump would visit his golf courses fourteen times.

I dictate my tweets to my executive assistant and she posts them. "Time is money"---The Art of the Deal.

9:01 AM – 23 Nov 2011

Rhona Graff served as Trump's loyal gatekeeper for over twenty-five years.

In my new book #TimeToGetTough I make a full financial disclosure detailing my net worth. http://t.co/A2DDoheG

10:05 AM – 23 Nov 2011

Trump claimed to be worth $7 billion. *Forbes* magazine questioned this figure, concluding he was probably worth less than $3 billion. Trump would later boast that he was worth over $10 billion. The true figure will never be known until Donald Trump follows the example of previous US Presidents and releases his full tax return. This is unlikely to happen.

In order to get elected, @BarackObama will start a war with Iran.
2:48 PM – 29 Nov 2011

The banks were bailed out by us. They should start lending to private entrepreneurs. The banks are slowing American growth.
3:14 PM – 29 Nov 2011

Newly released emails prove that scientists have manipulated data on global warming. The data is unreliable. http://t.co/DdW3Hsvn
1:25 PM – 30 Nov 2011

Trump links this Tweet to an article in the *Wall Street Journal* by the British journalist James Delingpole, who later found a home at Breitbart News. Climate change sceptics, often linked to major coal and oil corporations, make a fetish of scientific uncertainty even though the vast majority of experts agree that the human contribution to global warming is profoundly important.

Met @newtgingrich at Trump Tower today. He's a big thinker.
12:02 PM – 5 Dec 2011

At this point in the contest Gingrich was well ahead of Romney in Gallup's daily tracking poll.

First there was the Declaration of Independence, then there

was the Constitution. Now there is #TimeToGetTough.
Available today.
1:04 PM – 5 Dec 2011

> This Tweet suggests that the Declaration of Independence and
> the United States Constitution were little more than trailers for
> Trump's masterpiece.

President Reagan put it best: "Welfare's purpose should be to
eliminate, as far as possible, the need for its own existence."
2:28 PM – 6 Dec 2011

> Trump's first mention of Ronald Reagan. He would go on to
> reference the Republican President more than a hundred times.

"The Architect" @KarlRove is directly responsible for losing both
houses & @BarackObama becoming President. Ignore him.
1:44 PM – 7 Dec 2011

> Trump detested the political strategist Karl Rove and the
> Republican Establishment he represented.

Be sure to stop by Trump Tower today -- I'll be signing copies
of my new book "Time To Get Tough" from 11 am to 2 pm.
9:16 AM – 9 Dec 2011

@BarackObama has accumulated more debt in 3 years than
the first 42 Presidents combined. He is simply out of control.
4:52 PM – 12 Dec 2011

> There is a glaring contradiction between Trump's obsession with
> reducing the size of the national deficit and his determination
> to spend huge sums on infrastructure while cutting taxes.

Thousands of e-mails from folks urging me to seek the
Americans Elect Presidential nomination.
10:22 AM – 14 Dec 2011

Americans Elect wanted to break the two-party system by running an independent candidate chosen by online primaries. It got nowhere.

#noratings @Lawrence will soon be off tv- bad ratings- he has a face made for radio.
10:55 AM – 15 Dec 2011

The feud with Lawrence O'Donnell continues.

If speeches and memoirs created jobs then @BarackObama would be Ronald Reagan.
1:31 PM – 15 Dec 2011

"I believe this book will rock a lot of people. Don't just read #TImeToGetTough but share it with your friends and family!" -RushLimbaugh
1:27 PM – 16 Dec 2011

Rush Limbaugh, a right-wing radio show host, remains one of Trump's key cheerleaders.

Congratulations to my son Eric for making the Forbes 30 under 30 list. He's done a great job! http://t.co/YDElKzG6
4:36 PM – 19 Dec 2011

Dummies left Iraq without the oil--not believable!
9:38 AM – 20 Dec 2011

What a shock! The U.S. Capitol Christmas tree pays homage @BarackObama but failed to mention Jesus.
3:12 PM – 20 Dec 2011

Trump's notable lack of conventional religious piety and his well-publicized affairs and divorces have not deterred him from attacking his opponents' failure to demonstrate their loyalty to Christian practices. Donald Trump was brought up as a member of Norman Vincent Peale's Reformed Church, regularly attending his Marble Collegiate Church in Manhattan. Peale was a celebrity pastor whose books sold millions, notably *The Power of Positive Thinking* (1952). Peale interpreted Christianity as a cult of success, and he preached the cultivation of an absolute self-confidence. "Any fact facing us, however difficult, even seemingly hopeless, is not so important as our attitude toward that fact," Peale wrote. "A confident and optimistic thought pattern can modify or overcome the fact altogether." It is hard not to conclude that the young Trump absorbed these lessons only too well.

In order to preserve my options and guarantee that @BarackObama is defeated, I changed my voter registration to independent.
1:45 PM – 27 Dec 2011

> Trump seems here to be keeping open the possibility that he may still run as a third party or independent candidate.

Govt. collapsing in Iraq only 2 weeks after withdrawal of our troops. Sadly, I called this one and please remember, I alone called it.
2:38 PM – 27 Dec 2011

China hacked the U.S. Chamber of Commerce and now has the information of all 3 million members. China keeps taunting us because they do not respect our leader #TimeToGetTough
4:06 PM – 27 Dec 2011

What a convenient mistake: @BarackObama issued a statement for Kwanza but failed to issue one for Christmas. http://t.co/DodG53Rx
11:02 AM – 28 Dec 2011

> Kwanza is a celebration of African heritage in African-American culture, observed from 26 December to 1 January each year.

I predicted the 9/11 attack on America in my book "The America We Deserve" and the collapse of Iraq in @TimeToGetTough.
11:49 AM – 29 Dec 2011

The Mar-a-Lago Club has the best meatloaf in America. Tasty. http://t.co/3GS8TRgM
1:23 PM – 29 Dec 2011

I like Russell Brand, but Katy Perry made a big mistake when she married him. Let's see if I'm right---I hope not.
3:44 PM – 29 Dec 2011

> Trump's obsession with commenting on celebrity marriages and affairs would continue for some years. He had experience in these matters: his very public infidelity with Marla Maples while married to Ivana, the mother of his three eldest children, fed tabloid gossip in New York for nearly two years in the early nineties.

I play golf to relax. My company is in great shape. @BarackObama plays golf to escape work while America goes down the drain.
1:12 PM – 30 Dec 2011

The Washington Establishment will never rein in government spending, waste, fraud and abuse. A great thinker and outsider is needed.
2:03 PM – 30 Dec 2011

> The identity of the great thinker is modestly veiled here.

2012

★ ★ ★ ★ ★

"Let's take a closer look at that birth certificate"

Celebrity Apprentice continues to be a top ten trend on twitter this morning http://t.co/Xd69CFKu

2:28 PM – 4 Jan 2012

"If other countries benefit from our armed forces protecting them, those countries should pay for the protection." #TimeToGetTough

2:01 PM – 6 Jan 2012

Our Marines are sent to kill the Taliban not coddle them. USMC should be praised not investigated. Semper Fi !

12:39 PM – 13 Jan 2012

> Trump issued this Tweet in the wake of the publication of a video that appeared to show US Marines urinating over the corpses of several Taleban fighters. The defence secretary Leon Panetta condemned the video as "utterly deplorable". However, Trump calls for the Marine Corps to be praised rather than investigated. Trump ends with the motto of the US Marine Corps, *semper fidelis*, which translates as "always faithful".

Rick Perry--a good man, a great family and a patriot.

2:37 PM – 19 Jan 2012

> Perry had pulled out of the race for the Republican candidacy, but would later re-emerge, after a stint on *Dancing with the Stars*, as a member of Trump's cabinet.

"While Obama is obsessed with "green collar jobs," blue collar workers aren't buying it." #TimeToGetTough http://amzn.to/xdUxyN http://bit.ly/wNYhAc

11:27 AM – 23 Jan 2012

My daughter Ivanka thinks I should run for President. Maybe I should listen. http://t.co/QW78vJja

11:26 AM – 25 Jan 2012

In an interview with HollywoodLife.com Ivanka Trump said "I do think he'd make a good President, I think he'd be phenomenal!"

"People are smart. They know you can't be "for" jobs but against those who create them. It doesn't work."
#TimeToGetTough
12:04 PM – 25 Jan 2012

Trump has used the word "smart" in nearly 400 of his Tweets.

@BarackObama gave 1% of his income to charity from 2000 through 2004 http://t.co/C3rtWcoT I guess he only likes spending our money.
3:20 PM – 26 Jan 2012

This information cited by Trump was correct. Between 2000 and 2004 the Obamas earned $1.2 million before tax but gave away only $10,770. However, according to *Forbes* magazine they gave away $1.1 million while earning $10.8 million before tax while in the White House. Trump's failure to release his tax return means that it is impossible to say how much Donald Trump gives to charity. The *Washington Post's* David A. Fahrenthold telephoned more than 420 charities with a connection to Trump. Fahrenthold reported that for the period 2008–2015 he could find only one personal gift from Trump, to the Police Athletic League of New York City, in 2009. It was worth less than $10,000.

The GOP primary is getting very nasty. The candidates need to remember that @BarackObama is the main target. He must not be reelected.
2:42 PM – 30 Jan 2012

The Islamists are taking over Egypt through the election. http://t.co/QczymGts Why did @BarackObama force Mubarak out? He was an ally.
3:39 PM – 30 Jan 2012

Congratulations to @MittRomney for an impressive win in Florida. He performed well under pressure.
9:58 AM – 1 Feb 2012

I will be making a major announcement tomorrow (Thursday, February 2) at 12:30 pm at Trump International Hotel & Tower, Las Vegas, Nevada. I will be arriving this evening at approximately 11:30 pm. The announcement will pertain to the Presidential race. All media welcome.
5:41 PM – 1 Feb 2012

Watch my endorsement of @MittRomney. http://t.co/AdV6ruj3
4:30 PM – 2 Feb 2012

"So, I speak badly of China, but I speak the truth and what do the consumers in China want? They want Trump." #TimeToGetTough
12:44 PM – 6 Feb 2012

> Trump had long been trying to break into the Chinese market. He finally succeeded in March 2017 after his Presidential victory when the Chinese government granted Trump thirty-eight trademarks in the country.

Not the world, only your tiny group of viewers--the world doesn't care about you. @lawrence You're too stupid to know what more than 7 billion dollars is--and that's low. The recent press conference was not in a casino, try some research for a change. Why don't you try radio but that won't work either, and stop lying to your few viewers. Maybe you should try going back to 8 pm--but Ed Schultz is much better. Your ratings are so pathetic you must have an "in" at msnbc. See your psychiatrist immediately, you need help.
1:20 PM – 6 Feb 2012

> When it came to pursuing his vendetta against MSNBC's Lawrence O'Donnell, Trump was unable to contain himself to

Twitter's usual 140 characters. He employed a Tweet-expanding facility in order to express his full scorn, a technique he would continue to use from time to time.

The Prayer Breakfast was used by @BarackObama to say that the Bible commands higher income taxes. That's not the way it is!
3:23 PM – 6 Feb 2012

Trump's first mention of the Bible. He uses it to justify lower taxes.

I believe @BarackObama is manipulating the jobless numbers http://t.co/4EO1W6cK
2:04 PM – 7 Feb 2012

Employment had just dropped for the fifth consecutive month to 8.3 per cent, the lowest figure in three years.

I endorsed @MittRomney not because I agree with him on every issue but because he will get tough with China.
3:23 PM – 7 Feb 2012

Many, many people are disappointed I didn't run third party-- but I won't risk @BarackObama benefiting from a split in the anti-Obama vote
4:00 PM – 7 Feb 2012

Many people have been asking me to answer questions. You can ask me questions at any time. #TrumpQandA
11:03 AM – 8 Feb 2012

Trump's responses didn't exactly set Twitter alight:

@IanBQueen In answer to your question, my favorite thing to do is spending time with my family.
2:03 PM – 8 Feb 2012

@Miss_Drax My first job was working for and with my father, Fred C. Trump.

2:07 PM – 8 Feb 2012

@GrimeyGatsby I only require four hours of sleep per night.

2:39 PM – 8 Feb 2012

> Trump's habit of tweeting very late at night and in the small hours of the morning suggests that this answer is probably true.

@Misterglorious I wear suits from the Donald J. Trump Signature Collection.

11:02 AM – 9 Feb 2012

> Like his wife Melania and daughter Ivanka, Trump has his own fashion line, specializing in business attire. He rarely missed a chance to urge his followers to support it. This would lead to problems.

@IvankaTrump's @CNN interview with @piersmorgan discussing @ApprenticeNBC, the economy and politics http://t.co/tMvQdmEN

11:32 AM – 10 Feb 2012

> In a single Tweet Donald Trump promotes his daughter Ivanka, his ally Piers Morgan and his TV show *The Apprentice*.

Whitney Houston was a great friend and an amazing talent. We will all miss her and send our prayers to her family.

11:05 AM – 13 Feb 2012

Honored to have passed 1 million twitter followers. We are making America #1 again. #TimeToGetTough

12:44 PM – 13 Feb 2012

> It had taken Trump almost three years to reach this milestone.

He links the fortunes of his Twitter account with those of the country itself.

@BarackObama's budget funds the "Arab Spring" with $800B and the Muslim Brotherhood in Egypt $1.3B in military aid. He loves radical Islam.

2:45 PM – 14 Feb 2012

Trump mistakenly added three noughts to the $800 million of economic aid to countries swept by revolutions. The $1.3 billion of military aid to Egypt is correct.

Old Post Office Building in DC will be a world-class Trump property. Honored to be doing this historic building-- Washington will be proud.

11:47 AM – 16 Feb 2012

Trump had secured a lease from the government on the property opposite the White House. This arrangement would later prove controversial.

Weakness is very dangerous: @BarackObama is going to unilaterally disarm our nuclear arsenal. America keeps the world safe!

4:29 PM – 16 Feb 2012

The more I get to know @MittRomney the more I like him. He has the judgment and private sector experience America needs in the White House.

10:05 AM – 22 Feb 2012

@CelebApprentice is having wonderful ratings once again. @IvankaTrump & @DonaldJTrumpJr. I am very proud of this season.

12:35 PM – 22 Feb 2012

Rev. Graham made a critical point. @BarackObama has turned a blind eye to the Christians being persecuted in Muslim countries. Iran continues to theaten us while going nuclear. Iran has just issued execution orders for a Christian pastor. http://bit.ly/zsgjuu
2:51 PM – 22 Feb 2012

Donald Trump courting the Evangelical lobby.

It is time to get out of Afghanistan. We are building roads and schools for people that hate us. It is not in our national interests.
2:34 PM – 27 Feb 2012

I loved being a surrogate on behalf of @MittRomney. I am glad I was able to help him win.
12:27 PM – 29 Feb 2012

Trump claiming credit for Romney's success in the early primaries. Later he would show utter contempt for Romney.

Today will be a Super Tuesday for @MittRomney -- he will win over 220 delegates from states across every region. He will be the nominee.
12:20 PM – 6 Mar 2012

Coincidence? More than half of @BarackObama's 47 biggest fundraisers have been given administration jobs. http://t.co/JJqEe6tM
9:56 AM – 9 Mar 2012

Trump's own cabinet would include many key donors to his campaign.

When I was 18, people called me Donald Trump. When he was 18, @BarackObama was Barry Soweto. Weird.
10:34 AM – 12 Mar 2012

@MittRomney has won the most delegates, received the most votes and won the most states. The primary is over. Time to defeat @BarackObama.

3:36 PM – 13 Mar 2012

The day after @BarackObama blocks a Texas voter photo ID law, @JamesOkeefeIII exposes more dead people getting ballots http://t.co/hTCMSDP5

3:55 PM – 13 Mar 2012

> In this early attack on alleged Democratic ballot rigging, Trump relies on a Breitbart News report by the far-right activist James O'Keefe. Voter fraud is in fact almost non- existent in the US. However Trump (and some states with Republican majorities) insist that it is a threat and use this to justify restrictive ID laws. This could be seen as an attempt to make it more difficult for black, poor and immigrant voters to exercise their democratic right. Ironically, it would be a Trump supporter who committed the first case of voter fraud in the 2016 election. Terri Lynn Rote, fifty-five, cast two votes in Des Moines, Iowa explaining she had done so because of her fear "the polls are rigged". A *Washington Post* investigation would find only a handful of further cases, nearly all of which involved Republican voters. In March 2017, it emerged that Trump's chief strategist Steve Bannon was the subject of a criminal investigation into voter registration fraud. It appeared that Bannon was registered to vote at a vacant house in Florida, due for demolition, while owning a house in California but staying regularly in New York and Washington, DC.

I'm not a hunter and don't approve of killing animals. I strongly disagree with my sons who are hunters, but they acted legally and did what lots of hunters do.

1:56 PM – 15 Mar 2012

> Eric and Donald Jr faced damaging allegations of cruelty after photographs were circulated on the internet showing them

standing next to a dead elephant, crocodile, a kudu and holding a leopard. The images went viral.

Why does @BarackObama always have to rely on teleprompters?
1:39 PM – 19 Mar 2012

I am deeply disturbed by what I have read in the case of @TrayvonMartin. I support a full investigation and justice.
10:14 AM – 20 Mar 2012

> The seventeen-year-old Trayvon Martin, an African-American, had been shot dead by George Zimmerman, a neighbourhood watch volunteer, in Sanford, Florida. Zimmerman would be charged with Martin's murder but was acquitted on self-defence grounds even though Martin was unarmed. This incident helped to inspire the Black Lives Matter campaign. Donald Trump is taking the side of justice for the dead teenager.

@MittRomney should consider Gov McDonnell of VA, Gov Christie of NJ and Senator Rubio of FL for VP. Really good men doing a really good job.
12:29 PM – 20 Mar 2012

> Governor Christie would later be ditched as the head of Trump's transition team after a power struggle with Trump's son-in-law Jared Kushner, and Trump would launch contemptuous attacks on Marco Rubio when he became his rival for the 2016 Republican candidacy.

Happy Birthday to my legendary friend Aretha Franklin.
12:57 PM – 22 Mar 2012

> Aretha Franklin, the so-called "Queen of Soul", sang at President Obama's 2009 inauguration. She was absent from Trump's inauguration in 2017.

He @BarackObama is caught on tape making election promises to @MedvedevRussiaE on missile defense and national security http://t.co/I6mCEnUn

11:43 AM – 26 Mar 2012

> President Obama had been captured on tape promising the Russian President Medvedev "more flexibility" on missile defence. Trump himself would be accused of secret deals with Russia.

He @BarackObama received an early endorsement from the Soviet newspaper Pravda over @MittRomney http://bit.ly/GVXkYr The Soviet oligarch has spoken!

1:12 PM – 29 Mar 2012

A study says @Autism is out of control--a 78% increase in 10 years. Stop giving monstrous combined vaccinations immediately. Space out small individual shots--small babies can't handle massive doses. Get smart--and fast--before it is too late.

9:25 AM – 30 Mar 2012

> Concern surrounding a perceived link between vaccines given to children and the development of autism stems in part from a report by the disgraced former doctor, Andrew Wakefield, published in *The Lancet* in 1998. In 2010 Wakefield's report was found to be fraudulent and he was struck off the British medical register. Andrew Wakefield, who continues to peddle anti-vaccine theories and now lives in Texas, was a guest at Trump's Inauguration Ball.

America's competitors love @BarackObama. @MedvedevRussiaE says @BarackObama has been "the best 3 years" for Russia http://t.co/LM6y8wNl

11:16 AM – 2 Apr 2012

"Money was never a big motivation for me, except as a way to keep score. The real excitement is playing the game." #TheArtofTheDeal
2:01 PM – 3 Apr 2012

My twitter account is now reaching more people than the New York Times--not bad. And we're only going to get better!
11:14 AM – 4 Apr 2012

@BarackObama doesn't believe in the Supreme Court or its power--I thought he was a constitutional lawyer. Why won't @BarackObama release his grades and various other standard application facts--could he be hiding something?
1:28 PM – 4 Apr 2012

> Obama had attacked Supreme Court judges for "judicial activism" over their opposition to his Affordable Care Act. Donald Trump here sides with the judiciary and continues to push his theory that Obama is concealing information that might disqualify him from the Presidency.

"Look, if we can make chopsticks in America and sell them to the Chinese, we can compete on hundreds of other fronts as well."TimeToGetTough
8:16 AM – 12 Apr 2012

It's Thursday, how much $ has @BarackObama wasted today?
12:39 PM – 12 Apr 2012

Many many people are thanking me for what I said about @autism & vaccinations. Something must be done immediately.
11:00 AM – 13 Apr 2012

> Trump's support for a discredited and damaging hypothesis

seems to be based on a general predisposition to accept conspiracy theories aired on his favoured radio and TV shows.

One of the simplest joys of life is golf. A great game to both play and watch.
12:13 PM – 13 Apr 2012

I have captured the smell of success. Meet me and the new "Success" @Macys Herald Square April 18 5:30pm, first 100 customers get my new book.
9:41 AM – 17 Apr 2012

Trump promotes both his new brand of cologne and latest book at Macy's department store in New York.

Yesterday was @BarackObama's favorite day of the year--he collects our taxes to redistribute.
9:12 AM – 18 Apr 2012

In 1995 Trump had declared a $916 million loss on his income tax return, a tax deduction so substantial that some calculated it could have allowed him to legally avoid paying any income taxes for up to eighteen years.

Not only are wind farms disgusting looking, but even worse they are bad for people's health. They should be outlawed and allowed only in heavily industrialized areas.
1:30 PM – 23 Apr 2012

"I'm loyal to people who've done good work for me."
#TheArtofTheDeal
7:47 AM – 24 Apr 2012

He @BarackObama believes that the War on Terror is over http://t.co/de0ax99Y Who does he think won?
9:18 AM – 26 Apr 2012

@rupertmurdoch is a superb businessman and a world class CEO.He has built a tremendous empire and is certainly "fit" to run his corporation.

12:50 PM – 1 May 2012

> Rupert Murdoch, owner of Fox News, remains one of Donald Trump's closest allies. The future of Murdoch's business empire was in the balance after his newspaper, *The News of the World*, was shown to have hacked the phone of murdered schoolgirl Milly Dowler as well as others, including numerous politicians and celebrities. In April 2012 a parliamentary report into this scandal had concluded that Mr Murdoch was not a "fit person" to exercise stewardship of a major international company. Murdoch would later reward Trump's loyalty at this time of crisis by throwing the weight of his media behind Trump's Presidential campaign.

Bad move-@BarackObama released $147M in aid to the Palestinians http://t.co/ZGf87eCQ That money is going to Hamas.

1:53 PM – 1 May 2012

> Trump volunteered no serious evidence to support his claim.

In the 1920's people were worried about global cooling--it never happened. Now it's global warming. Give me a break!

3:13 PM – 4 May 2012

> Trump shares his scepticism about climate change with much of the right of the Republican Party.

The election result in France is very disappointing. The Europeans have to embrace austerity in order for their economy to fully recover.

1:56 PM – 7 May 2012

> The Socialist François Hollande had defeated the incumbent Nicolas Sarkozy in the Presidential election.

V.P.....really!

2:28 PM – 8 May 2012

> This Tweet linked to an ABC report speculating that Mitt Romney could chose Trump as Vice President running mate. Trump warmed to the idea. Michael Cohen, his special counsel at the Trump Organization, was quoted: "If the opportunity presents itself where Mr Trump is offered the position of Vice President, I suspect he would seriously consider it."

Joe Biden called America "the Problem" vis a vis Iran http://t.co/T1cPLiZn He never wastes an opportunity to say something stupid.@JoeBiden

2:06 PM – 9 May 2012

> Trump couldn't resist making a dig at the serving Vice President who was in favour of a deal that would severely limit Iran's access to nuclear material that might be turned into a bomb.

Welcome to the new reality. @BarackObama is now letting China buy US banks http://t.co/i1C02ub2 The US government is selling us out.

10:18 AM – 10 May 2012

Procter and Gamble is relocating its beauty headquarters from Cincinnati to Asia--what are we doing?!

1:30 PM – 11 May 2012

@Cher should stop with the bad plastic surgery and nasty statements about good people running for office. I can't stand her computer enhanced voice or music.

3:20 PM – 11 May 2012

> Trump was responding to a hostile Tweet from Cher: "If ROMNEY gets elected I don't know if I can breathe same air as Him & his Right Wing Racist Homophobic Women Hating Tea Bagger Masters."

The TIME Magazine cover showing late age breast feeding is disgusting--sad what TIME did to get noticed. @TIME
9:13 AM – 14 May 2012

> Trump's visceral dislike of images of women that don't conform to ideas of sanitized glamour would come under scrutiny during his later Presidential bid.

I hope Mark Zuckerberg signs a prenup with his current girlfriend- perhaps soon to be wife. Otherwise, she can walk away with 9 billion.
10:58 AM – 15 May 2012

Seems hard to believe that @Facebook could be worth that much--be careful if you invest. And Mark Zuckerberg--get a pre-nup.
11:21 AM – 18 May 2012

> Facebook shares had that day been floated on the market at $38. As of March 2017 they were worth $142 a share.

Let's take a closer look at that birth certificate. @BarackObama was described in 2003 as being "born in Kenya."
http://t.co/vfqJesJL
2:31 PM – 18 May 2012

> Trump's source for his latest slur against Barack Obama was WorldNetDaily. This website provided a diet of conspiracy theories, end-of-the-world predictions, and outlandish attacks on President Obama. Obama had released his birth certificate and all parties other than Trump and hardline birther conspirators agreed that the document was in order.

Rapper @MacMiller's song, "Donald Trump", now has 57 million hits--- I created another star--- where's my cut?
10:14 AM – 22 May 2012

Who would you like to see on next season of #CelebrityApprentice? Let us know- everyone wants to be on it.
11:12 AM – 22 May 2012

I wonder if @BarackObama ever applied to Occidental, Columbia or Harvard as a foreign student. When can we see his applications? What do they say about his place of birth.
3:34 PM – 22 May 2012

> Trump had no intention of letting go of this conspiracy theory, which was by then unsustainable. It would be another four years before he grudgingly admitted he was wrong.

Welcome to Twitter, @melaniatrump!
2:59 PM – 23 May 2012

Lolo Jones, our beautiful Olympic athlete, wants to remain a virgin until she gets married--she is great. @Followlolo
8:35 AM – 24 May 2012

> Lori Susan "Lolo" Jones is an American hurdler and bobsledder.

"Do not go where the path may lead, go instead where there is no path and leave a trail." Ralph Waldo Emerson
10:25 AM – 24 May 2012

> Emerson was a nineteenth-century philosopher and essayist who advocated self-reliance. Trump would frequently quote him, though he seems never to have absorbed Emerson's reverence for nature. Emerson was also a passionate abolitionist, which sits oddly with Trump's declared admiration for Andrew Jackson, the racist seventh President of the USA.

"Attitude is a little thing that makes a big difference." -- Winston Churchill
3:11 PM – 24 May 2012

Trump has a weakness for Churchill quotes, having cited the British wartime prime minister in over thirty Tweets.

.@BarackObama is practically begging @MittRomney to disavow the place of birth movement, he is afraid of it and for good reason.
10:37 AM – 29 May 2012

Trump's attempt to rebrand the "birther" movement as "place of birth movement" didn't gain traction.

"For what is the best choice, for each individual, is the highest it is possible for him to achieve." Aristotle
8:17 AM – 30 May 2012

Perhaps @BarackObama's biggest shortcoming as President is he failed to unite the country.
10:49 AM – 30 May 2012

Everybody is raving about the Trump Home Mattress by @SertaMattresses. If you are looking for a mattress, go buy this one--http://bit.ly/Nf4taF You'll love it!
1:19 PM – 30 May 2012

It was an honor to be with @MittRomney the night he clinched the nomination. He will defeat @BarackObama and be a tremendous POTUS.
3:29 PM – 30 May 2012

Thank you to the @nydailynews for a very nice story-http://t.co/ckRwPXLB
9:56 AM – 1 Jun 2012

The tabloid *New York Daily News* had published an article titled "Romney's got a true friend in Trump".

Just cancelled my subscription to @USATODAY. Boring newspaper with no mojo--must be losing a fortune. Founder @AlNeuharth has always been a lightweight---just like his paper.
12:21 PM – 5 Jun 2012

> Donald Trump was responding to an article in the national newspaper *USA Today* titled "Trump is a clown who hurts Romney".

.@BillClinton was very nice to me, as I am to him, on the Piers Morgan Show (CNN). He is loyal to his friends. @piersmorgan
10:10 AM – 6 Jun 2012

The Miss USA Pageant #MissUSA was a big ratings hit for @nbc--NBC won the evening. Thank you, Donald.
10:43 AM – 6 Jun 2012

> In this Tweet Donald Trump thanks himself for having delivered top ratings to NBC.

"He who knows when he can fight and when he cannot, will be victorious." -- Sun Tzu
2:09 PM – 8 Jun 2012

Typical--@BarackObama's Press Secretary deflects any criticism of Obama's constant celebrity visits by attacking me. My great honor.
3:35 PM – 8 Jun 2012

With almost 1.3 million followers and rising really fast, everyone is asking me to critique things(and people). Finally, I will be a critic.
11:41 AM – 11 Jun 2012

Today is my birthday. My wish is for our country to be great and prosperous again.
11:39 AM – 14 Jun 2012

Today's announcement by @BarackObama on immigration was done for reelection. He is using the office of the presidency as a campaign tool.
1:24 PM – 15 Jun 2012

I'll be on @foxandfriends on Monday at 7:30 AM. Always interesting. Tune in!
3:04 PM – 15 Jun 2012

Putin has no respect for our President --- really bad body language.
5:14 PM – 19 Jun 2012

> Putin had rebuffed President Obama's request to work with the United States to depose Bashar al-Assad as President of Syria.

The Amateur! First @BarackObama was caught bowing to the Saudi King but now the President of Mexico! http://t.co/f0CFiUS9
2:36 PM – 20 Jun 2012

> Note Trump's fascination with body language and looking strong. The future President links here to the Weasel Zippers website, which prides itself on "scouring the bowels of the internet".

SHOCK - @BarackObama's people are sending paid political organizers to heckle at @MittRomney events http://t.co/TdZTHk2v
3:05 PM – 20 Jun 2012

I look forward to playing golf with President @BarackObama someday.
3:34 PM – 20 Jun 2012

Sometimes there is justice. A Chinese military newspaper was hacked. http://t.co/CgZyoszb
1:51 PM – 22 Jun 2012

The Islamists have won. Just as I predicted, the Muslim
Brotherhood has taken over Egypt. @BarackObama never
should have abandoned Mubarek.

12:31 PM – 25 Jun 2012

> Mohamed Morsi, leader of the Egyptian Freedom and Justice
> Party (Muslim Brotherhood), had won the Egyptian national
> elections. Trump does not think democracy is desirable in
> the Middle East if there is ever a chance of Islamist politicians
> coming to power.

It is terrible that @BarackObama did not appoint an
independent counsel to investigate the national security leaks.
No accountability.

2:24 PM – 27 Jun 2012

Wow, the Supreme Court passed @ObamaCare. I guess
@JusticeRoberts wanted to be a part of Georgetown society
more than anyone knew.

11:23 AM – 28 Jun 2012

> The Chief Justice John G. Roberts Jr, a conservative-leaning
> judge, had sided with liberal colleagues in upholding Obama's
> health care reforms. He justified his decision as follows: "the
> Constitution permits such a tax, it is not our role to forbid it, or
> to pass upon its wisdom or fairness". This would not be Trump's
> last attack on a judge whose decisions he disliked.

Obamacare will bankrupt our country and lead to socialized
medicine. We must all focus now on electing @MittRomney
this November.

2:41 PM – 28 Jun 2012

Justice Roberts turned on his principles with absolutely
irrational reasoning in order to get loving press from the
Washington establishment. He should be ashamed of himself.

11:53 AM – 29 Jun 2012

Happy to have just passed 1.3M Twitter followers. Love communicating with everyone daily.
3:51 PM – 2 Jul 2012

Is it legal for @BarackObama to make campaign donor calls from Air Force One? http://t.co/TJM5NNVT Obama is always fundraising on our dime.
9:04 AM – 3 Jul 2012

> Within a month of assuming the Presidency, Trump would use Air Force One as the backdrop to a campaign rally held in an airport hangar in Florida, and use the plane to make regular visits to his private club in Palm Beach.

Degenerate former Congressman Anthony Weiner is trying to make a comeback. He is a sick & perverted man that New York does not want or need.
11:38 AM – 3 Jul 2012

> A year earlier, Democratic New York Congressman, Anthony Weiner, was forced to resign after accidentally tweeting lewd pictures of himself to followers. Weiner was married to Huma Abedin, Hillary Clinton's deputy chief of staff at the State Department and longtime confidante. Weiner's further antics would play a key role in determining the outcome of the 2016 election.

As I anticipated, Justice Roberts made the cover of Time Magazine etc. The liberal media now loves him-- he should be ashamed.
3:13 PM – 6 Jul 2012

> Trump's first use of the term "liberal media".

Keep an eye on Anthony Weiner. Weasels are hard to get rid of.
5:07 PM – 6 Jul 2012

What a coincidence?! @BarackObama's campaign logo uses the same font as Cuban communist propaganda posters. http://t.co/EAvn6KPU

10:59 AM – 11 Jul 2012

Almost daily more discrepancies in @BarackObama's biography continue to arise. Who is this guy?

3:19 PM – 11 Jul 2012

> The evidence-free hints that Obama's biography was faked were a constant feature of Trump's communications during this period.

Have we ever had a POTUS before @BarackObama who earned over 1/3 of his income from foreign sources and paid taxes to another country?

12:29 PM – 12 Jul 2012

> As *Time* magazine reported on the eve of Trump's inauguration, Trump "appears to own or control more than 500 businesses in some two-dozen countries around the world".

America's Olympic uniforms are manufactured in China. Burn the uniforms!#U.S.OlympicCommittee

12:06 PM – 13 Jul 2012

> Items from Trump's own branded line of business clothing, including shirts, are made in China, Bangladesh, Honduras and Vietnam.

Happy 94th birthday to Nelson Mandela!

12:49 PM – 18 Jul 2012

"Show me someone without an ego, and I'll show you a loser." --How To Get Rich

8:46 AM – 19 Jul 2012

Some really dumb blogger for failing @VanityFair, a magazine whose ads are down almost 18% this year, said I wear a hairpiece --- I DON'T!
5:17 PM – 19 Jul 2012

Who else could take 16 vacations, play over 100 rounds of golf and hold over 300 fundraisers while serving as POTUS besides @BarackObama--& not one jobs meeting.
9:18 AM – 23 Jul 2012

The polling numbers for 2012 are very interesting--will Americans ultimately want their leaders to be 'likeable' or 'competent'?
12:48 PM – 31 Jul 2012

Another example of @BarackObama's diplomatic triumphs-- he gave the Queen of England an iPod filled with his speeches.
1:24 PM – 31 Jul 2012

You pick it!
#1. Anybody that says anything derogatory about @BarackObama is labeled stupid, insane, or something worse than that. The liberal media doesn't want to know the truth!
#2. Anything said against the President--whether it's the truth or not--is viewed as blasphemy by the media. It's clear that the liberal media does not want the truth included in their mix.
#3. The liberal media has made it clear that nothing derogatory can be said about the President. It's also obvious that the truth is of no interest to them.
3:02 PM – 31 Jul 2012

An 'extremely credible source' has called my office and told me that @BarackObama's birth certificate is a fraud.
3:23 PM – 6 Aug 2012

> This slur, never substantiated, was retweeted more than twenty thousand times.

71

I have founded and run one of the largest real estate empires in the world. I employ thousands of people. Why am I the enemy?
1:42 PM – 7 Aug 2012

A 'confidential source' has called my office and told me that @BarackObama has added over $6T to the new national debt & ruined US credit.
2:38 PM – 7 Aug 2012

I am honored that @BarackObama has featured my plane in one of his attack ads. It was made in America!
2:46 PM – 7 Aug 2012

Have you been to the @TrumpGrill in the Trump Tower Atrium? Best meatloaf in the City--my mother's famous recipe. 212.836.3249
9:39 AM – 9 Aug 2012

Trump handily gives the phone number for bookings.

Just letting China know in advance that the USA will win the medal count in the Olympics. Even with your cheating you can't beat us.
2:37 PM – 9 Aug 2012

The worst Olympic cheats in 2012 were the Russians.

The failing New York Daily News knowingly incorrectly reported that I wanted to speak at the Republican National Convention—wrong!
9:20 AM – 10 Aug 2012

Trump uses "failing" as an attack adjective in nearly 150 Tweets.

SUN newspaper/Scotland reports that "Tourism jump is thanks to Trump." 8,000 visitors in one month from 20 countries http://t.co/ZC0boYWu
10:50 AM – 10 Aug 2012

The *Sun* newspaper is owned by Trump's longtime supporter Rupert Murdoch. It is possible that some of the tourists visiting Scotland that August – a major tourist destination long before Trump was born – were visiting his golf course.

Today I am working on my 'big surprise' for the @RNC convention. Everyone will love it.

1:08 PM – 14 Aug 2012

Lightweight reporter Alex Pareene @pareene is known as a total joke in political circles. Hence, he writes for Loser Salon. @Salon

1:33 PM – 15 Aug 2012

It is easy to see why Trump was angry with Alex Pareene. The online reporter had correctly anticipated Trump's lovingly prepared stunt for the Republican National Convention. Pareene's extremely rude article read as follows:

"Donald Trump, an oft-bankrupt make-believe mogul clown with a television show where he pretends to fire America's saddest former celebrities, is one of the Republican Party's most prominent national figures, because he is on TV and people have heard of him. So, after flirting with a pretend presidential run in late 2011, he became a very important Mitt Romney Supporter, helping with fundraising and robocalls and so on. Also Donald Trump believes, and frequently says, on television, that the president was secretly born in Kenya and that his birth certificate is a fraud and that he's a secret Muslim who got into Harvard Law even though he's an idiot thanks to affirmative action and that Bill Ayers secretly ghost-wrote the president's first memoir. And he will have a special surprise at the Republican National Convention later this month!

"Last week, Trump said, 'I was asked to speak at the RNC but said no,' which is Trump Code for 'I begged them to let me speak and someone thought that was probably a bad idea,' but to allow him to save face he claimed that he 'will be doing something much bigger – just watch!'

"So maybe that's the surprise? I mean it's a surprise that the Republican Party is actively embracing Donald Trump, a widely hated fraud who subscribes to an entire host of insane and racist conspiracy theories about the president's background, but not really a 'big surprise'.

"The real surprise is almost definitely just going to be some idiotic video where Trump 'fires' an Obama impersonator."

Chelsea Clinton will be very successful in the world of politics. She's always been a great person--a winner. With parents like hers, she will be a major success.
8:19 AM – 16 Aug 2012

One of the hardest jobs in politics must be cleaning up after @JoeBiden gaffes. I feel sorry for his spokespeople.
9:31 AM – 16 Aug 2012

Certain Internet sites are like a bad epidemic that won't go away---others are terrific
2:25 PM – 16 Aug 2012

Jeffrey Robinson's #TrumpTower has it all. The ultra rich, powerful, and beautiful. It's your summer must-read.
7:00 AM – 17 Aug 2012

Billed as "The sexiest novel of the decade", *Trump Tower* is still displayed prominently in the gift store at Trump Tower. One critic described the erotic thriller as "incredibly sexist" and pointed to dialogue such as: "Come on, you're a shoo-in... Two white guys and a great-looking minority girl with perfect boobs? No contest."

It's amazing how many people still come up to me to thank me for 'The Art of The Deal.' The book has changed a lot of lives.
8:05 AM – 22 Aug 2012

Today we just passed 1.4 million twitter followers..
11:09 AM – 23 Aug 2012

Massive combined inoculations to small children is the cause for big increase in autism….
2:22 PM – 23 Aug 2012

> Trump continues to support a theory that has been comprehensively debunked on both sides of the Atlantic. Andrew Wakefield, the author of the theory, has tried to sue his critics and the *British Medical Journal* for defamation both in the US and UK. His case has been thrown out by the courts.

A hurricane will be coming to Tampa. My @RNC convention surprise hits Monday night!
7:55 AM – 24 Aug 2012

I am proud of the Tea Party. These great patriots have accomplished so much in strengthening our country in only 3 short years.
2:05 PM – 24 Aug 2012

.@DineshDSouza's '2016: Obama's America' is expanding to over 1,000 theaters this weekend. Will be highest grossing documentary in 2012. !!
2:40 PM – 24 Aug 2012

> This film was described by *Entertainment Weekly* as "nothing more than an insidious attempt to dishonestly smear the President by giving intellectual cover to the worst in subterranean conspiracy theories and false, partisan attacks". In 2016 D'Souza would release the equally provocative *Hillary's America: The Secret History of the Democratic Party*.

One point I made last night and will continue to push is that the @GOP can't be pollitically correct. We must fight fire with fire.
2:16 PM – 27 Aug 2012

.@ariannahuff is unattractive both inside and out. I fully
understand why her former husband left her for a man -
he made a good decision.
9:54 AM – 28 Aug 2012

> Ariana Huffington is the founder of the Huffington Post website.
> This Tweet was "liked" over seven and a half thousand times.
> Trump was learning that there was a mass audience for this kind
> of abuse.

It's Thursday and again I ask--how much money is China
stealing from us?
8:03 AM – 30 Aug 2012

The dummies left Iraq (and Libya) without the oil!
12:33 PM – 30 Aug 2012

> The effect on the Middle East, and world politics more generally,
> if the US had confiscated the oil supplies of countries it invaded
> can easily be imagined.

It's Friday, how many advertisers dropped @HuffPost today?
7:56 AM – 31 Aug 2012

Very good speech by @MichelleObama--and under great
pressure--Dems should be proud!
10:09 AM – 5 Sep 2012

> This was a rare moment of generosity to his opponent's wife.
> Notoriously, Melania's speech to the GOP Convention in
> 2016 would plagiarize Michelle Obama's speech to the 2008
> Democratic National Convention. Trump's loyal ghostwriter
> Meredith McIver would take the blame on that occasion.

Why does US doping agency destroy an American icon,
@lancearmstrong, for events that took place years ago
in France?
10:24 AM – 5 Sep 2012

.@lancearmstrong, revise your decision to quit--go back
and fight.
10:28 AM – 5 Sep 2012

> Lance Armstrong's systematic use of doping to achieve his
> remarkable results in cycling races was exposed in a series of
> articles and books, notably by the *Sunday Times* reporter David
> Walsh.

Almost every T.V. show is asking me to go on--especially the
@Late_Show. It's simple--I get the ratings!
12:59 PM – 5 Sep 2012

The Democrats dropped all references to God from their
platform. Not good!
2:17 PM – 5 Sep 2012

> Only his third Tweet to mention God, but the frequency would
> rocket during his Presidential campaign as Trump courted the
> Evangelical vote.

Bill Clinton did a great job last night--the Democrats are lucky
to have him. Do you really believe he likes @BarackObama?
8:51 AM – 6 Sep 2012

Why has Barack Obama repeatedly told inconsistent stories
about his religious background? http://t.co/ywQEJZok
Who is he?
8:42 AM – 11 Sep 2012

> Trump turns his fire from Obama's birthplace to claims that he
> is a secret Muslim. Note the date.

On this solemn day of remembrance we can all take joy
in the fact that Bin Laden's last sight was a Navy SEAL
pulling the trigger.
12:44 PM – 11 Sep 2012

Obama will go down as the worst President in history on many topics but especially foreign policy.
2:46 PM – 12 Sep 2012

This is all about American weakness and an incompetent President.
8:14 AM – 13 Sep 2012

Wake Up America! See article: "Israeli Science: Obama Birth Certificate is a Fake" http://t.co/f7esUdSz
10:40 AM – 13 Sep 2012

> Trump here provides a link to FreedomOutpost.com, an extreme right-wing news site.

I keep getting great feedback on new #TRUMP cologne 'Success.' Exclusively available at @Macy's http://t.co/8YMD9fQH And best shirts & ties
2:49 PM – 13 Sep 2012

I hate @USAToday's redesign--the logo is terrible. Lightweight Al Neuharth must've had something to do with this. No wonder paper is failing.
10:32 AM – 14 Sep 2012

> Trump claimed he had cancelled his subscription to USA Today three months earlier.

Hey @KimKardashian--I hear you are undecided in the election. I can explain why you should vote for @MittRomney.
7:57 AM – 17 Sep 2012

> The reality TV star Kim Kardashian would later publicly support Hillary Clinton in the 2016 campaign.

Kate Middleton is great--but she shouldn't be sunbathing in the nude--only herself to blame.
1:03 PM – 17 Sep 2012

> The Duchess of Cambridge had been photographed by zoom-lensed paparazzi while on a private holiday in rural France.

@rdowns I never went bankrupt. Enemies love to say I did. Didn't happen.
9:37 AM – 18 Sep 2012

> According to the fact-checking organization, PolitiFact, Trump has filed for Chapter 11 bankruptcy protection six times.

I really like Chelsea Clinton--an amazing young woman. She got the best of both parents. (@IvankaTrump agrees)
10:54 AM – 21 Sep 2012

The Emmys are all politics, that's why, despite nominations, The Apprentice never won--even though it should have many times over.
2:36 PM – 24 Sep 2012

English taxpayers should stop subsidizing the destruction of Scotland by paying massive subsidies for ugly wind turbines.
9:09 AM – 26 Sep 2012

Does Madonna know something we all don't about Barack? At a concert she said "we have a black Muslim in the White House."
1:08 PM – 27 Sep 2012

I hope the @RNC is ready for a Third Party if they blow this election because that is what they will face. They must fight hard.
1:15 PM – 27 Sep 2012

> Trump is here setting himself up to run in 2016.

A resort in Arizona is using sewage to make snow.
Environmentalists are going crazy--I won't be skiing in that snow.
1:49 PM – 27 Sep 2012

It's amazing how different all of the polling results are--not
an exact science.
1:31 PM – 28 Sep 2012

The Chinese are now hacking White House computers.
Why not? They already own the place.
1:55 PM – 2 Oct 2012

Under Obama, Iran has taken over Iraq, Al Qaeda has taken
over Libya, the Muslim Brotherhood now controls Egypt.
Worst foreign policy ever.
2:24 PM – 2 Oct 2012

The cheap 12 inch sq. marble tiles behind speaker at UN
always bothered me. I will replace with beautiful large marble
slabs if they ask me.
8:37 AM – 3 Oct 2012

> The Trump aesthetic is often a matter of size and glitter. His
> fondness for shiny new marble, reflective glass, gilding, crystal
> and velvet is on display in Trump Tower and in his luxury
> hotels, which owe much to the opulent taste of the French
> Second Empire.

I'm always amazed when I travel to my foreign properties.
Seeing the Trump brand across 4 continents proves that
excellence can be universal.
2:29 PM – 3 Oct 2012

Happy to have just passed 1.5M followers on twitter. We
picked up over 14,000 yesterday alone. It's great to speak to
everyone daily.
10:31 AM – 4 Oct 2012

Trump had been mentioned by Barack Obama during the Presidential debate the evening before.

Congratulations to Michelle and Barack Obama on their 20th anniversary.
10:43 AM – 4 Oct 2012

More than 70M people watched the Presidential Debate. A new record. See what happens when I am so prominently mentioned (just kidding)!
3:38 PM – 5 Oct 2012

The public is about to learn a lot more information on Barack Obama and his true background in the coming weeks…
5:06 PM – 9 Oct 2012

> This information was never forthcoming. Trump often hinted darkly at revelations that would justify his unsustainable allegations.

I enjoy meeting tourists in #TrumpTower. People travel from across the world to see the five-level Atrium & waterfall.
3:40 PM – 10 Oct 2012

Why does Barack Obama's ring have an arabic inscription? http://t.co/upa00265 Who is this guy?
3:11 PM – 11 Oct 2012

British PM Cameron is making a fool of himself by wasting billions of pounds on unwanted & environment destroying Scottish windmills.
7:52 AM – 12 Oct 2012

> His campaign against the Scottish government's wind-farms was long-running and ineffectual.

I have never seen a thin person drinking Diet Coke.
1:43 PM – 14 Oct 2012

.@MittRomney's poll numbers are looking really good. One more great debate performance and it will be a total knockout.
8:40 PM – 14 Oct 2012

Obama will be trying very hard at next debate- he doesn't want to lose the Boeing.
9:24 PM – 14 Oct 2012

> Air Force One is a Boeing 747.

Lots of response to my comment on Diet Coke-let's face it, it doesn't work- just makes you hungry.
11:22 AM – 15 Oct 2012

I turned down going to the debate tonight so that I could do live tweets to my many followers.
9:08 AM – 16 Oct 2012

> Trump signals here that he will be providing a live Twitter commentary on the second Presidential debate.

.@rupertmurdoch is absolutely right, it will be a nightmare for @Israel if Obama is re-elected.
9:27 AM – 16 Oct 2012

> This is the first time Trump directs a Tweet at his ally, Rupert Murdoch, using his Twitter handle. Murdoch joined Twitter in December 2011, embracing the freedom of the medium for a few years before dropping it, following his marriage to Jerry Hall in March 2016. Some of Murdoch's final Tweets supported Trump's campaign for the Republican nomination.

Diet Coke tweet had a monster response--dammit, I wish the stuff worked.
10:37 AM – 16 Oct 2012

It's amazing--my weekly scheduled interviews on @foxnews and @CNBC draw the highest ratings. And they get bigger week by week--thanks folks!
12:01 PM – 16 Oct 2012

The Coca Cola company is not happy with me--that's okay, I'll still keep drinking that garbage.
12:47 PM – 16 Oct 2012

Getting ready to watch the debate--- as they say "let's get ready to rumble"!
7:46 PM – 16 Oct 2012

.@MittRomney looks much stronger and much more Presidential!
8:25 PM – 16 Oct 2012

Obama keeps saying that he will do something--- but why hasn't he done it? It's all talk.
8:26 PM – 16 Oct 2012

Obama is looking rhetorical and weak. @MittRomney is looking strong and sharp.
8:43 PM – 16 Oct 2012

PM Obama weak on immigration. All words, no action. He's been Prez 4 years.
9:12 PM – 16 Oct 2012

Obama keeps namedropping Bill Clinton-- he is no Bill Clinton.
9:12 PM – 16 Oct 2012

Obama better than last time, but again, @MittRomney wins. Good night. #debate
9:50 PM – 16 Oct 2012

Do you believe Barack Hussein Obama (aka Barry Soetoro) looked like a president last night? I don't!
9:16 AM – 17 Oct 2012

Polls are starting to look really bad for Obama. Looks like he'll have to start a war or major conflict to win. Don't put it past him!
9:30 AM – 17 Oct 2012

My twitter has become so powerful that I can actually make my enemies tell the truth.
10:06 AM – 17 Oct 2012

My twitter followers will soon be over 2 million--& all the "biggies." It's like having your own newspaper.
10:07 AM – 17 Oct 2012

Robert Pattinson should not take back Kristen Stewart. She cheated on him like a dog & will do it again--just watch. He can do much better!
1:47 PM – 17 Oct 2012

> Trump's comment on this Hollywood relationship – Stewart and Pattinson were stars of the popular *Twilight* series about beautiful young vampires – was perhaps informed by his own serial infidelity. As ever Trump's voyeuristic and impertinent comments generated a massive response with over twenty thousand Retweets.

Lots of response to my Pattinson/Kristen Stewart reunion. She will cheat again—100% certain--am I ever wrong?
9:27 AM – 18 Oct 2012

Robert I'm getting a lot of heat for saying you should dump Kristen- but I'm right. If you saw the Miss Universe girls you would reconsider.
11:21 AM – 18 Oct 2012

.@BetteMidler talks about my hair but I'm not allowed to talk about her ugly face or body --- so I won't. Is this a double standard?
10:57 AM – 28 Oct 2012

While @BetteMidler is an extremely unattractive woman, I refuse to say that because I always insist on being politically correct.
10:59 AM – 28 Oct 2012

> New Yorker Bette Midler didn't like Trump's building plans. She tweeted that Trump deserved "to be held down and his hair cut off" for being "architect of the ruination of the West Side".

I never fall for scams. I am the only person who immediately walked out of my 'Ali G' interview
12:44 PM – 30 Oct 2012

> Trump had actually spoken for seven minutes before terminating the interview, according to Ali G creator Sacha Baron Cohen.

I will start reviewing various political reporters etc & websites as to their professionalism & fairness—many people asking for this.
9:46 AM – 2 Nov 2012

> Trump issued this threat following widespread criticism that he had gone too far in suggesting that Obama was not born in America. In a blaze of publicity he had offered "to donate $5 million to charity if President Obama releases his college records and applications, along with his passport records and applications", setting a deadline a week before the election.

Thank you to @piersmorgan for your nice statement about me in the @HollywoodReporter http://t.co/3Kii0xLN
10:33 AM – 5 Nov 2012

> Piers Morgan, as so often, stood up for Donald Trump. He

told the *Hollywood Reporter*: "He's the personification of brash, successful America Incorporated. The guy, whether you like him or not, is a brilliant self-publicist, a brilliant businessman. He's a billionaire; he's very proud of his country. Now I don't think everything he does is necessarily a good idea." Morgan insisted that "Donald is always welcome on my show. It doesn't mean I always give him an easy time."

Tomorrow's election will have historic repercussions for our country. Make America strong again. Vote for @MittRomney.

4:19 PM – 5 Nov 2012

The concept of global warming was created by and for the Chinese in order to make U.S. manufacturing non-competitive.

2:15 PM – 6 Nov 2012

This notorious utterance, cited in evidence that Trump believes climate change is a "hoax" created by China, has been retweeted almost 105,000 times.

Very dangerous pattern developing across country by Obama supporters. Detroit poll watcher was threatened with gun http://t.co/XfJiqT6G

2:28 PM – 6 Nov 2012

More reports of voting machines switching Romney votes to Obama. Pay close attention to the machines, don't let your vote be stolen

2:56 PM – 6 Nov 2012

Claims of voter fraud would be a consistent undercurrent in Trump's later campaign for the Presidency. No evidence has ever been produced to show that tampering with voting machines or impersonation has affected the electoral process in recent times.

Do we still want a President who bows to the Saudis and lets
OPEC rip us off? Make America strong, vote for @MittRomney.
4:16 PM – 6 Nov 2012

> This was Trump's last Tweet promoting Romney. The
> Republican candidate would that evening concede he had lost.

Well, back to the drawing board!
11:18 PM – 6 Nov 2012

> Obama had won both the Electoral College (332 to 206) and the
> popular vote (65,915,795 to 60,993,504).

We can't let this happen. We should march on Washington
and stop this travesty. Our nation is totally divided!
11:29 PM – 6 Nov 2012

Lets fight like hell and stop this great and disgusting injustice!
The world is laughing at us.
11:30 PM – 6 Nov 2012

Our nation is a once great nation divided!
11:43 PM – 6 Nov 2012

The electoral college is a disaster for a democracy.
11:45 PM – 6 Nov 2012

More votes equals a loss … revolution!
11:30 PM – 6 Nov 2012

He lost the popular vote by a lot and won the election.
We should have a revolution in this country!
11:39 PM – 6 Nov 2012

> These last two Tweets calling for "revolution" were subsequently
> deleted. This is hardly surprising as the Tweets could plausibly
> be interpreted as advocating armed insurrection. And Obama

had in fact won the popular vote by a significant margin. NBC news host Brian Williams was quick to draw attention to these incendiary Tweets. He told viewers that "Donald Trump – who has driven well past the last exit to relevance and peered into something closer to irresponsible here – is tweeting tonight". Williams said that he was reluctant to tell viewers their content but added: "It is out there and getting an airing tonight – you may as well know about it."

Trump was quick to respond:

Brian--Thanks dummy--I picked up 70,000 twitter followers yesterday alone. Cable News just passed you in the ratings. @NBCNightlyNews

12:14 PM – 7 Nov 2012

It is telling that Trump does not challenge Brian Williams's substantial point that he was acting irresponsibly by disputing the result of the election. Instead Trump attempted to squash his critics by boasting about the number of his Twitter followers.

Brian, if I'm "well past the last exit to relevance" how come you spent so much time reading my tweets last night? @NBCNightlyNews

12:20 PM – 7 Nov 2012

Aberdeen tourism is booming because of my great Scottish golf club.

12:05 PM – 10 Nov 2012

There is no readily available information which suggests any unusual increase in tourism in the area at that or any other relevant time, and no suggestion that the tourists visiting Aberdeenshire were attracted there by the Trump Links.

Trump International Golf Links was just rated one of the greatest courses in the world. Virtually all reviews are saying the same thing.
12:06 PM – 10 Nov 2012

> These reviews have proved hard to trace.

The people of Scotland love Trump International Golf Links.
12:06 PM – 10 Nov 2012

> If so they're very quiet about it, but then Scotland can be a reserved and discreet nation. Perhaps the people of Scotland really do love the golf links.
>
> The Munros don't. For thirty-five years the Munros have owned a cottage with access to the shore, and a view of the sea for ten miles to a distant lighthouse. Now all they see is the tall earth wall Trump built to hide their property from his. Their access to the shore across a public road is chained up, and security staff lurk in 4x4s to observe the doings of the hapless Munros.
>
> Nor does Michael Forbes. He's the man who refused to sell what Trump described as his "pigsty of a home" in the middle of the Trump estate. Nor do the local council, whose objections to the tycoon's plans were overruled by the Scottish Government. Nor do David and Moira Milne, who when Trump visited in June 2016 flew a Mexican flag from the roof of their home, a former coastguard station overlooking Trump's clubhouse.

Karl Rove is now making excuses for his total wasting of $400M—not one win—(the Republicans better get smart next time)…
4:04 PM – 3 Dec 2012

… Time for the Republicans to find someone new—and better.
4:04 PM – 3 Dec 2012

How could Michael Forbes get Scot of the Year when he lost—badly—to me & Andy Murray, a true Scot, who won the U.S. Open & Olympic gold?

3:46 PM – 4 Dec 2012

> Aberdeenshire farmer Forbes was a noisy campaigner against Trump's golf course. He and his elderly mother refused to sell their property. Forbes featured heavily in Anthony Baxter's documentary about Trump's Scottish venture *You've been Trumped*.

We are getting rid of all Glenfiddich garbage alcohol from Trump properties.

12:24 PM – 5 Dec 2012

> Forbes had won the "Glenfiddich Spirit of Scotland" Award.

How can George Osborne reduce UK debt while spending billions to subsidize Scotland's garbage wind turbines that are destroying the country?

2:50 PM – 6 Dec 2012

> Alan Sugar, presenter of the UK version of *The Apprentice*, unwisely intervened at this point by tweeting to Trump 'The Scottish don't want you!' Trump hit back:

.@Lord_Sugar If you think ugly windmills are good for Scotland you are an even worse businessman than I thought…

3:56 PM – 6 Dec 2012

…. to do The Apprentice but I approved you anyway. Without my show you'd be nothing!

4:07 PM – 6 Dec 2012

> Sugar replied that "the ugly windmills will bring more revenue and green power to Scotland than your golf project… Shut up and argue with Obama."

@Lord_Sugar--Keep working hard so I make plenty of $ with your show...
4:22 PM – 6 Dec 2012

... and many others. Drop to your knees, Sugar, and say thank you, Mr. Trump.
4:54 PM – 6 Dec 2012

Dopey @Lord_Sugar—Look in the mirror and thank the real Lord that Donald Trump exists. You are nothing!
5:08 PM – 6 Dec 2012

If the Republicans ever want to win a presidential election in the next 30 years they must get rid of @KarlRove. He is useless.
5:55 PM – 10 Dec 2012

I hate hearing after all of the hard work that @MittRomney never wanted to become President.
2:54 PM – 27 Dec 2012

2013

★ ★ ★ ★ ★

"The Russians are playing a
very smart game"

The party of the year in Palm Beach was the New Year's Eve celebration at the Mar-a-Lago Club--it was amazing. http://t.co/3GS4mh7C
12:01 PM – 2 Jan 2013

Wow, I have just exceeded 2 million followers--and in such a short time!
10:38 AM – 14 Jan 2013

Lance Armstrong is now going to admit guilt—can that be possible after many years of denying? Just go away Lance.
2:32 PM – 14 Jan 2013

> Trump supported Armstrong up to this point. Perhaps the admission of fault is seen by Trump as the unforgivable weakness.

I wish President @BarackObama the best of luck in his second term...
1:39 PM – 21 Jan 2013

> Obama had just been sworn in for his second term as President.

President Obama's inaugural had record low ratings. What does that portend?
3:19 PM – 25 Jan 2013

> Second term swearing-in broadcasts never command the same viewing figures as initial inaugurations. In fact, Obama's tally of 20.6 million in 2013 was the most for a second swearing-in since that of Bill Clinton in 1997. Trump's 2017 inauguration would be viewed by 30.6 million, down by 18 per cent on the 38 million who watched Obama take the office for the first time in 2009.

Lots of people are asking whether or not I should have run for President—stay tuned for the answer.
3:27 PM – 25 Jan 2013

Little @MacMiller, you illegally used my name for your song "Donald Trump" which now has over 75 million hits.
3:45 PM – 31 Jan 2013

Little @MacMiller, I want the money not the plaque you gave me!
3:50 PM – 31 Jan 2013

Little @MacMiller, I'm now going to teach you a big boy lesson about lawsuits and finance. You ungrateful dog!
4:03 PM – 31 Jan 2013

> Trump never went ahead with his threat to sue.

"Donald Trump dedicates second Scottish golf course to beloved mother Mary" http://t.co/jVyGduGK via @MailOnline
1:51 PM – 4 Feb 2013

> Donald Trump named his second golf course in Scotland after his mother Mary MacLeod who had emigrated to America from the Isle of Lewis in the Outer Hebrides in 1930.

Wise words from my father: "Know everything you can about what you're doing." Fred C. Trump
10:38 AM – 5 Feb 2013

> Frederick Christ Trump was the son of a Bavarian immigrant, listed as "Friedr. Trumpf" in his 1885 immigration papers. It is thought the family name was originally Drumpf.

Wise words from my mother: "Trust in God and be true to yourself." Mary MacLeod Trump
10:40 AM – 5 Feb 2013

Re: immigration. Do the Republicans not realize that Dems will get 100% of 11 million votes no matter what they do?
9:48 AM – 6 Feb 2013

Immigration reform really changes the voting scales for the Republicans—for the worse!
9:49 AM – 6 Feb 2013

Happy 102nd birthday to President Ronald Reagan. Every day that passes, Reagan's presidency looks better and better.
1:52 PM – 6 Feb 2013

Obama can kill Americans at will with drones but waterboarding is not allowed—only in America!
9:50 AM – 7 Feb 2013

It's okay but why do the haters (& losers) want to follow me on twitter?? Get a life!
1:39 PM – 12 Feb 2013

> Trump is starting to understand that not all of his followers are fans.

Republicans must be careful with immigration—don't give our country away.
11:02 AM – 21 Feb 2013

> Both of Trump's parents came from immigrant stock.

My Twitter has been seriously hacked--- and we are looking for the perpetrators.
12:00 PM – 21 Feb 2013

> The hackers only managed to tweet two lines of verse from the rapper Lil' Wayne and Wil.i.Am's song "Scream and Shout", "These hoes think they classy? Well that's the class I'm skippin", before Trump regained control.

Twitter will soon be irrelevant if lowlifes are so easily able to hack into accounts.
1:57 PM – 21 Feb 2013

Big response to my Tea Party statement-remember they were never fully energized by Romney campaign and will have far more power with time.

7:50 AM – 24 Feb 2013

I'm saying that the Tea Party, perhaps by another name, will soon have another big moment- and will be a major factor in victory!

8:33 AM – 24 Feb 2013

Trump continues to position himself for a run in 2016.

By popular demand, I will be tweeting on the very tainted Academy Awards tonight!

1:36 PM – 24 Feb 2013

Here we go with the Oscars!

8:33 PM – 24 Feb 2013

I don't like the opening even a little bit!

8:50 PM – 24 Feb 2013

Very tacky set!

8:59 PM – 24 Feb 2013

Lincoln never sounded like that!

9:40 PM – 24 Feb 2013

Trump here takes issue with Daniel Day-Lewis's Oscar-winning portrayal. Nobody can claim to know exactly what Lincoln sounded like because there is no recording of his voice. Day-Lewis was praised for skilful use of contemporary accounts and making use of the insight of historians to inform his performance.

The Oscar broadcast is really boring - where is the glamour and beauty?

11:30 PM – 24 Feb 2013

I've had enough of this - good night!
12:07 AM – 24 Feb 2013

I'll be doing Fox and Friends this morning at seven.
3:04 AM – 25 Feb 2013

The media is so in the tank for Obama that it is amazing—
the funny thing is, he can't stand them!
12:22 PM – 25 Feb 2013

WHY CAN'T THE MEDIA TELL THE TRUTH - WE WOULD ALL
BE SO MUCH BETTER OFF!
6:03 PM – 15 Mar 2013

> Trump vexed by the reception to his speech at CPAC. The
> *Washington Post* called it a "rambling" speech which "combined
> dire predictions about the GOP's future with boasts about his
> own career".

.@rushlimbaugh is right—the Republicans lost because they
weren't conservative enough—or tough enough.
8:51 AM – 19 Mar 2013

Be weak on immigration and ensure Democratic victory.
8:51 AM – 19 Mar 2013

I don't like seeing the Pope standing at the checkout counter
(front desk) of a hotel in order to pay his bill. It's not Pope-like!
10:46 AM – 19 Mar 2013

Why do the losers & haters always say I wear a "wig" when
they know I don't. Like it or not, it's all mine—just ask
Barbara Walters.
4:41 PM – 20 Mar 2013

> At Trump's invitation, Barbara Walters had tugged his hair
> during an interview two years earlier in order to check it was

real. Though the hair stayed on, she said afterwards, "I still think it's a hairpiece."

Now AP is banning the term "illegal immigrants" What should we call them? 'Americans'?! This country's political press is amazing!
3:12 PM – 3 Apr 2013

I have gotten to know many Spanish speaking people as the owner of Trump National Doral in Miami. They are smart, hard working and great.
10:57 PM – 4 Apr 2013

Congratulations to @IvankaTrump and Jared on the big news. I will have yet another grandchild this fall!
12:38 PM – 11 Apr 2013

It is terrible that neither Obama, Biden nor Kerry attended Lady Thatcher's funeral. They would all run to Muslim Brotherhood Morsi's.
2:05 PM – 17 Apr 2013

Sexting Pervert @anthonyweiner has returned to twitter. Parents of all underage girls should BLOCK him immediately!
3:22 PM – 23 Apr 2013

"@backupwraith: i firmly believe that @realDonaldTrump is the most superior troll on the whole of twitter. that is all."A great compliment!
3:05 AM – 24 Apr 2013

Trump takes the accusation of being a troll as a compliment.

I have many great people but also an amazing number of haters and losers responding to my tweets-why do these lowlifes follow - nothing to do!
3:34 AM – 24 Apr 2013

Wow, I'm at 2,200,000 followers but I'd love to get rid of the haters & losers—they're such a waste of time!
11:50 AM – 25 Apr 2013

The Time Magazine list of the 100 Most Influential People is a joke and stunt of a magazine that will, like Newsweek,soon be dead. Bad list!
10:54 PM – 26 Apr 2013

Trump had not made the cut.

Wow, I just found out that in a major poll of its readers the @NewYorkObserver voted me #1 on the "power 100" list in NY……
12:29 PM – 1 May 2013

The *New York Observer* was owned by Trump's son-in-law, Jared Kushner. In April 2016, it would be one of the few US newspapers to endorse Trump's candidacy for president. Kushner, who lacked any experience of government, was propelled into a senior position in the White House in early 2017. He has a dizzying portfolio ranging from domestic policy to international diplomacy.

"@Heaveenly: @realDonaldTrump how does it feel to have 2.1 million followers" Great - like owning The New York Times without the lo$$es! .
8:04 PM – 7 May 2013

Benghazi. Obama lied. Our people died.
3:16 PM – 13 May 2013

Amazingly @AnthonyWeiner is going to run. The cure rate for his problem is 0. Lots of other things will come out.
2:15 PM – 22 May 2013

Weiner, the New York politician and husband of Hillary

Clinton's key aide, had just confirmed his candidacy for the Mayoral election. He had made headlines with his "sexting" and further scandal would indeed follow.

"@coolz36: @realDonaldTrump you would make this country great again if you ran for president" No, only if I WON-then it would be great again

11:06 AM – 26 May 2013

I've done the largest house sale in U.S. history by selling a Palm Beach mansion for $100M, $60M more than I paid. I love real estate.

3:28 PM – 5 Jun 2013

Trump here refers to the sale of Maison de L'Amitié in 2008. The beachside property had languished on the market for two years and so observers were surprised when billionaire Dmitry Rybolovlev struck a deal with Trump. It is believed that Rybolovlev, who once sported a bulletproof vest, never set foot in the property.

We should stay the hell out of Syria, the "rebels" are just as bad as the current regime. WHAT WILL WE GET FOR OUR LIVES AND $ BILLIONS?ZERO

7:33 PM – 15 Jun 2013

I met a Trump Twitter hater last night (well known). As he came near me he nervously said, "Mr. Trump, it is an honor to meet you sir!" Nice

9:45 PM – 18 Jun 2013

The Miss Universe Pageant will be broadcast live from MOSCOW, RUSSIA on November 9th. A big deal that will bring our countries together!

10:00 PM – 18 Jun 2013

Do you think Putin will be going to The Miss Universe Pageant in November in Moscow - if so, will he become my new best friend?
10:17 PM – 18 Jun 2013

> Putin didn't attend the pageant. But Trump was evidently very taken with the idea of being his friend, as later events would show.

"@athompson362: Why did I quit following @realDonaldTrump? Twitter is boring without him. I'm back for good!" Everybody comes back!
11:02 PM – 18 Jun 2013

I like doing this once a month for the haters & losers (and as they know)-I don't wear a "wig". Some may not like my hairstyle, but all mine
7:39 PM – 29 Jun 2013

"@realDonaldTrump is a great entrepreneur, fantastic business man,a terrible politician. Best wishes, by the way" @MarcoCompagno You are probably correct, I am too honest to be a good politician!
11:26 AM – 8 Jul 2013

I wonder if traitor Edward Snowden will be attending the Miss Universe Pageant in Moscow on November 9th.
6:30 AM – 13 Jul 2013

> Edward Snowden, an American computer contractor and former CIA employee, was responsible for arguably the most important leak of intelligence information in United States history. Snowden had been granted asylum in Russia.

Perhaps Miss USA can lure Snowden back?
6:38 AM – 13 Jul 2013

I would invite Edward Snowden to be a judge at the Miss Universe Pageant in Moscow but would be concerned that he would sell results early!
5:36 PM – 13 Jul 2013

"One thing I've learned about the press is they're always hungry for a good story, the more sensational the better." - Art of the Deal
2:27 PM – 18 Jul 2013

> Trump was notorious for feeding stories, particularly to the Page Six gossip column of Murdoch's *New York Post* and *People* magazine. Sometimes he would phone up with stories, including details of his marital problems, taking care to disguise his voice and pretending to be his own public relations man, one "John Barron".

"@jcalcat: @realDonaldTrump give me a good reason why I shouldn't unfollow you" Because you can't live without.me or my extreme knowledge!
5:10 AM – 24 Jul 2013

"@ryan211: @realDonaldTrump Hey Donald is this actually you tweeting or just an assistant?" ME!
6:07 AM – 26 Jul 2013

"@_olliesdaddy: @realDonaldTrump is there anyone that loves you more than yourself?" Probably not!
6:20 PM – 28 Jul 2013

"@TheOtherRosie: @realDonaldTrump @kmcs1957 Do you have someone you would trust to run your businesses while you were president?" My kids!
6:35 PM – 28 Jul 2013

My motto is: 'Never give up.' I follow this very strictly. I do not let problems and challenges stop me; they are normal.
9:36 AM – 16 Aug 2013

So, lets get this right. Steve Jobs dies and leaves his wife everything-billions of dollars. Now his wife has a boyfriend (lover). Oh Steve!
7:42 AM – 19 Aug 2013

The hatchet job in @NYMag about Roger Ailes is total bullshit. He is the ultimate winner who is surrounded by a great team. @FoxNews
10:09 AM – 21 Aug 2013

> Roger Ailes, founder and CEO of Fox News, would later be forced to relinquish control of the channel after multiple claims of sexual harassment against female employees.

I hope the NY tax payer appreciates the millions Schneiderman is about to waste on a small case. I will litigate to victory.
3:05 PM – 26 Aug 2013

> Eric Schneiderman, as New York Attorney General, accused Trump of "defrauding consumers out of $40 million with [his] sham 'University'... No matter how rich or popular you are, no one has [the] right to scam hard working New Yorkers; anyone who does will be held accountable." Schneiderman would doggedly pursue Trump over the coming years, and Trump would use his Twitter account to direct personal abuse at Schneiderman.

There has been a systematic targeting of the Tea Party by the Obama administration. Now Schneiderman goes after me. No coincidence.
10:33 AM – 27 Aug 2013

I have a dream that our country will be great again! #DreamDay
8:32 AM – 28 Aug 2013

> Trump marks the fiftieth anniversary of Dr Martin Luther King's speech on racial equality.

Josh8J4 "@realDonaldTrump I have a dream that you will be president to make this country great again. #USA" Thank you.
1:11 PM – 28 Aug 2013

Remember, all these 'freedom fighters' in Syria want to fly planes into our buildings
1:57 PM – 28 Aug 2013

> Trump was quick to spot how Al Qaeda had emerged as a powerful force in the Syrian uprising.

President Obama's weakness and indecision may have saved us from doing a horrible and very costly (in more ways than money) attack on Syria!
5:48 AM – 1 Sep 2013

It is truly amateur hour at the White House - and this is why we should not be doing the "war thing" right now!
5:57 AM – 1 Sep 2013

"@mguarino64: @realDonaldTrump " How would you treat the Syria situation if president ?" I'd let them all fight with each other-focus on US!
6:09 AM – 1 Sep 2013

> Trump's first important foreign policy decision as President was to launch an air strike on Sharyat airfield in Western Homs, Syria, on 7 April 2017.

Congratulations to @PiersMorgan on winning @BritishGQ TV Personality Of The Year. Piers deserves his success!
11:17 AM – 4 Sep 2013

"@FSUSteve: @realDonaldTrump Why do you think you're so polarizing?" Because I like to be-it often times brings out the truth!
11:20 PM – 4 Sep 2013

Tell Congress to straighten out the many problems of our country before trying to be the policemen to the world. Make America great again!

6:22 AM – 5 Sep 2013

While everyone is waiting and prepared for us to attack Syria, maybe we should knock the hell out of Iran and their nuclear capabilities?

7:43 AM – 5 Sep 2013

My shirts, ties and suits are selling great @Macy's because they are the best and most stylish at a really reasonable price - thanks!

6:08 PM – 7 Sep 2013

"@JimSlickatshort: @realDonaldTrump We really don't need your shirts, damn we need your brains! Get involved in politics!" Thanks!

6:26 PM – 7 Sep 2013

The Russians are playing a very smart game. In the meantime they are buying lots of time for Syria and making U.S. look foolish. Dangerous!

6:09 PM – 10 Sep 2013

This new Russian strategy guarantees victory for the Syrian government-and makes Obama and U.S. look hopelessly bad. President in trouble!

6:25 PM – 10 Sep 2013

> With the United States threatening air strikes in response to Syrian dictator Bashar al-Assad's alleged use of chemical weapons, Russian Foreign Minister Sergey Lavrov proposed an alternative plan to avert a US attack. He suggested that Syria should place its chemical weapons under international control and then destroy them. Trump was well ahead of the game in grasping that Russian intervention was likely to secure victory for the regime.

Putin is having such a good time. Our President is making him look like the genius of all geniuses. Do not fear,we are a NATION OF POTENTIAL

8:11 AM – 11 Sep 2013

> *The New York Times* had just published an article by Putin under the title "A plea for caution from Russia".

My friend Larry King @kingsthings asked me to do an interview with him—he was always great to me—& I agreed. Watch tonight 9 PM on RTV.

12:23 PM – 3 Oct 2013

> After parting ways with CNN, Larry King had found a new home: Russia Today (RT), the Russian government's English-language news channel. King had previously served on the advisory board of a pro-Kremlin television station in Georgia, and in 2012 he moderated the alternative presidential debate hosted by RT. RT's publicity for that event declared: "In response to widespread blackout from both the mainstream media and political establishment alike, RT is honored to be presenting a platform for the major third-party candidates also vying for the White House this election year to debate."
>
> RT summarized Trump's 2013 interview with King: "American business icon Donald Trump talks with Larry King about the government shutdown, Obamacare, President Obama, Putin, Hillary Clinton, and lack of leadership from Congress. He calls for Republicans to unify and raises the possibility of running himself in 2016."

Angela Merkel is doing a fantastic job as the Chancellor of Germany. Youth unemployment is at a record low & she has a budget surplus.

1:01 PM – 3 Oct 2013

While the Pres. of Iran tweets sweet nothings to Obama he forbids the Iranians to use twitter. Very revealing.
2:18 PM – 4 Oct 2013

> Hassan Rouhani had begun using Twitter in May, using his first Tweet to announce his run for the presidency. He was elected the following month.

"We build too many walls and not enough bridges." - Isaac Newton
3:11 PM – 7 Oct 2013

"@sandersandrew: @realDonaldTrump Donald you are a true American hero. I can't wait to celebrate Trump day in the future." Wow, nice.
7:48 AM – 17 Oct 2013

> Not so outlandish as it seems. Trump issued a proclamation on 20 January 2017 to mark his inauguration day a "National Day of Patriotic Devotion".

"@phickeyma: When I come home from work my Twitter page is filled with Donald Trump tweets…Love reading them…So Bold & Truthful."
5:36 PM – 18 Oct 2013

> Trump loved to retweet messages from his followers, thus forging a personal bond with voters. In the election year of 2016 Retweets would come to form approximately half of his Twitter output.

THE ROLLOUT OF OBAMACARE IS A TOTAL DISASTER AND AN EMBARRASSMENT TO OUR COUNTRY. THE WORLD IS WATCHING AND LAUGHING.$635,000,000 WEBSITE!
4:41 PM – 19 Oct 2013

First Titanic sunk on its maiden voyage.Next the Hindenburg
explodes on its first flight to America.Now we suffer the
ObamaCare rollout!

12:19 PM – 25 Oct 2013

> The Hindenburg had undertaken a season of successful
> crossings of the Atlantic before the disaster.

Isn't it amazing that the U.S. and NSA can listen to the highly
protected phone conversations of world leaders but can't
get O's records!

2:18 PM – 26 Oct 2013

"@willfitz94: @realDonaldTrump How do you have time to tweet
everyone when your so busy?" When I like people, I find time!

2:10 AM – 27 Oct 2013

Fact – all the countries complaining about us spying on them
spy on us. They just don't get caught—stupid!

1:07 PM – 29 Oct 2013

ObamaCare is a disaster and Snowden is a spy who should
be executed-but if he could reveal Obama's records,I might
become a major fan

5:48 PM – 30 Oct 2013

Looking forward to attending the GREAT Rev. @BillyGraham's
birthday party tonight--there's nobody like him!

1:14 PM – 7 Nov 2013

"Read the Bible. Work hard and honestly. And don't complain."
– Rev. @BillyGraham

3:43 PM – 7 Nov 2013

> The famous evangelist was ninety-five years old. Graham had
> been a strong supporter of Richard Nixon in the 1960s and
> thrown his weight behind Mitt Romney in 2012.

I'm in Moscow for Miss Universe tonight - picking a winner is very hard, they are all winners. Total sellout of arena. Big night in Russia!
8:47 AM – 9 Nov 2013

I was just given a great tour of Moscow - fantastic, hard working people. CITY IS REALLY ENERGIZED! The World will be watching tonight!
9:21 AM – 9 Nov 2013

I just got back from Russia-learned lots & lots. Moscow is a very interesting and amazing place! U.S. MUST BE VERY SMART AND VERY STRATEGIC.
9:44 PM – 10 Nov 2013

ObamaCare is on LIFE SUPPORT - it will soon be DEAD ON ARRIVAL - A bad concept that was incompetently administered!
6:44 AM – 13 Nov 2013

Maybe some of the dead voters who helped get President Obama elected can be brought back to life after signing up for ObamaCare.
5:16 AM – 18 Nov 2013

> Trump continued to insist, despite lacking any evidence, that Democrats had used the votes of dead people to win the election for Obama.

@RSPBScotland RSPB IS A TOTAL JOKE-They went for bird chopping wind turbines in @Aberdeenshire and fought me on bird friendly golf course!
7:18 AM – 29 Nov 2013

> Trump takes aim at Royal Society for the Protection of Birds.

My ties, shirts and cufflinks have never been more beautiful-THE BEST-available at Macy's!
7:42 AM – 29 Nov 2013

Nelson Mandela and myself had a wonderful relationship--
he was a special man and will be missed.
http://t.co/GVziRpWbkB

5:17 PM – 5 Dec 2013

> Trump's reaction to the death of Nelson Mandela is the most
> repulsive example of Donald Trump's ghoulish habit of
> claiming a strong connection with famous people when they
> die. There is no evidence at all that Trump enjoyed a "wonderful
> relationship" with Nelson Mandela. They had little in common.
> John R. O'Donnell, former president of Trump Plaza Hotel
> and Casino, said that Donald Trump once remarked: "laziness
> is a trait in blacks". By contrast, Nelson Mandela, arguably the
> greatest person of the twentieth century, stood for human
> freedom and racial equality.

It always seems impossible until it is done. --Nelson Mandela

5:38 PM – 5 Dec 2013

Ice storm rolls from Texas to Tennessee - I'm in Los Angeles
and it's freezing. Global warming is a total, and very
expensive, hoax!

10:13 AM – 6 Dec 2013

Just read @PiersMorgan's book "Shooting Straight" and
whether you love him or hate him (I'm in the first category),
it is terrific.

11:12 AM – 9 Dec 2013

> Another example of the Trump–Morgan mutual promotion
> society in action.

How amazing, the State Health Director who verified copies
of Obama's "birth certificate" died in plane crash today.
All others lived

4:32 PM – 1 Dec 2013

The paranoid attitude in American politics in full bloom. The official, Loretta Fuddy, had a faulty life vest and an irregular heartbeat, and died of stress while in the water.

I hope you all are looking at the Donald J. Trump Signature Collection of ties, shirts & cufflinks @Macys—great for Christmas & holidays.

3:41 PM – 12 Dec 2013

Wow, it's snowing in Isreal and on the pyramids in Egypt. Are we still wasting billions on the global warming con? MAKE U.S. COMPETITIVE!

7:32 PM – 14 Dec 2013

Every fall of snow becomes an argument against global warming. Trump has remained silent during heatwaves and droughts.

We should be focusing on beautiful, clean air & not on wasteful & very expensive GLOBAL WARMING bullshit! China & others are hurting our air

5:07 AM – 15 Dec 2013

Prime Minister @David_Cameron is very foolish in giving @AlexSalmond so much money to build wind turbines which r destroying Scotland.

11:40 AM – 17 Dec 2013

"@josh_hlbrk: @realDonaldTrump If you keep tweeting Macy's advertisements, I will unfollow you." No you won't, you're stuck.

8:25 AM – 19 Dec 2013

Enough about my ties etc. @Macys, but they are doing really big numbers - people love them (and @Macys loves Trump)!

9:16 AM – 19 Dec 2013

I'd like to wish all of my friends--and even my many enemies--
a very Merry Christmas and Happy New Year.
1:12 PM – 24 Dec 2013

The new Pope is a humble man, very much like me, which
probably explains why I like him so much!
10:37 AM – 25 Dec 2013

Donald Trump would later call Pope Francis "disgraceful" for
questioning his faith.

2014

★ ★ ★ ★ ★

"I WOULD BUILD A BORDER FENCE LIKE YOU HAVE NEVER SEEN BEFORE"

Just hit a million on Facebook- http://t.co/FDv4aLoomz
10:36 AM – 6 Jan 2014

In politics, and sometimes in life, FRIENDS COME AND GO, BUT ENEMIES ACCUMULATE!
9:28 AM – 11 Jan 2014

Watching Gates on @seanhannity - looks like he got hit by a truck! Why didn't Obama get him, and others,to sign a confidentiality agreement?
11:02 PM – 14 Jan 2014

> Donald Trump is famous for imposing a non-disclosure agreement (NDA) on everyone he does business with. According to Salon.com, "His wives have all signed prenuptial agreements compelling their silence, and he has threatened to yank alimony to keep it that way. Unsurprisingly, Trump also forced Miss Universe contestants to sign contracts denying them the right to criticize him publicly or reveal anything they learned about him."
>
> He is also reported to have used this mechanism to silence members of his campaign and transition teams.

I hope we never find life on another planet because if we do there's no doubt that the United States will start sending them money!
6:34 AM – 16 Jan 2014

Happy Anniversary to my wonderful wife @MELANIATRUMP -- a truly great decision by me! http://t.co/eO9ei1njWv
1:59 PM – 22 Jan 2014

Just received a wonderful letter from a new father who bought his son his first book, The Art of the Deal. Great parent!
3:46 PM – 29 Jan 2014

> The book's ghostwriter Tony Schwartz claimed in an interview

with the *New Yorker* that he [Schwartz] wrote "every word" of the book. "Donald Trump made a few red marks when I handed him the manuscript, but that was it," he said in another interview. "I feel a deep sense of remorse that I contributed to presenting Trump in a way that brought him wider attention and made him more appealing than he is."

Wow, honored to just pass 2.5M followers on @twitter. Thanks to all my followers. We are going to have a great year together.
3:54 PM – 29 Jan 2014

How does frumpy & little read @nytimes editorial writer Gail Collins keep her job? She is totally irrelevant! @nytimescollins
8:55 AM – 6 Feb 2014

> Collins had dismissed Trump's electoral appeal: "Honestly, somebody is always better than nobody. Except possibly when we are talking about Donald Trump."

My new club on the Atlantic Ocean in Ireland will soon be one of the best in the World - and no-one will be looking into ugly wind turbines!
8:24 AM – 14 Feb 2014

The Irish government is too smart to destroy their beautiful coastline w/ bird-killing, ugly wind turbines. @AlexSalmond @AberdeenCC
10:30 AM – 14 Feb 2014

> Trump's organization would cite the threat of climate change in its application to build a 2.8km-long wall to protect erosion-hit dunes beside his Doonbeg golf links in Co. Clare from rising sea levels. The plan for a wall was, however, dropped in December 2016 after resistance from locals.

A dishonest slob of a reporter, who doesn't understand my sarcasm when talking about him or his wife, wrote a foolish & boring Trump "hit"
11:34 PM – 14 Feb 2014

How come discredited reporter @mckaycoppins refused to write that the events in New Hampshire, Buffalo and N.Y. were all record breakers!
4:38 PM – 16 Feb 2014

> McKay Coppins had written an article for BuzzFeed entitled "36 hours on the fake campaign trail with Donald Trump". Trump told Coppins when asked what he thought of Twitter trolling: "I do love provoking people. There is truth to that. I love competition, and sometimes competition is provoking people. I don't mind provoking people. Especially when they're the right kind of people." On his relationship with journalists, Trump stated, "If I am treated unfairly, I will go after that reporter." Coppins asked, "Are you going to come after me when this article comes out?" Trump answered, "Maybe."

Amazing story in @BreitbartNews about the sleazebag blogger Coppins who fabricated nonsense about me for irrelevant @BuzzFeed. CONGRATS!
8:14 PM – 18 Feb 2014

> Trump hits back at McKay Coppins through Breitbart. The article was titled "Exclusive—Trump: 'Scumbag' Buzzfeed blogger ogled women while he ate bison at my resort". McKay's marriage survived this attempt at character assassination.

Ben Smith (is that really his last name?) of @BuzzFeed is a total mess who probably got his minion Coppins to do what he didn't want to do?
8:20 PM – 18 Feb 2014

I wonder how much money dumb @BuzzFeed and even dumber Ben Smith looooose each year? They have zero credibility - totally irrelevant and sad!

9:10 PM – 18 Feb 2014

> Ben Smith, as BuzzFeed Editor-in-Chief, would go on to publish a thirty-five page dossier containing unverified allegations about Donald Trump's ties to Russia in January 2017.

Isn't it crazy, I'm worth billions of dollars, employ thousands of people, and get libeled by moron bloggers who can't afford a suit! WILD.

8:14 AM – 19 Feb 2014

Do you think that very dumb reporter(blogger) McKay Coppins has apologized to his wife for his very inappropriate behavior while in Florida?

7:41 PM – 23 Feb 2014

> Trump continues to persecute the BuzzFeed reporter.

I'll be playing golf tomorrow in Palm Beach at the number one rated golf course in the State of Florida, Trump International Golf Club.

8:45 AM – 28 Feb 2014

New York Magazine just named the most influential "tweeters" in N.Y. and one Donald Trump was #2 after ESPN. Actually, I'm easily #1!

6:17 AM – 4 Mar 2014

What do you think Obama will do when Putin seizes Alaska?

6:33 AM – 4 Mar 2014

Actually Putin doesn't want Alaska because the Environmental Protection Agency will make it impossible for him to drill for oil!

7:24 AM – 4 Mar 2014

Putin has become a big hero in Russia with an all time high popularity. Obama, on the other hand, has fallen to his lowest ever numbers. SAD

9:00 PM – 21 Mar 2014

I believe Putin will continue to re-build the Russian Empire. He has zero respect for Obama or the U.S.!

9:03 PM – 21 Mar 2014

The situation with Russia is much more dangerous than most people may think - and could lead to World War III. WE NEED GREAT LEADERSHIP FAST

6:23 AM – 22 Mar 2014

Via @BreitbartNews by @rwildewrites: "TRUMP: 'I WOULD BUILD A BORDER FENCE LIKE YOU HAVE NEVER SEEN BEFORE'" http://t.co/4xeMNWrSb8

3:42 PM – 14 Apr 2014

> Significantly, Trump's first explicit mention on Twitter of a border fence between the United States and Mexico was reported in Breitbart.

The way President Obama runs down the stairs of Air Force 1, hopping & bobbing all the way, is so inelegant and unpresidential. Do not fall!

7:23 PM – 22 Apr 2014

Putin has shown the world what happens when America has weak leaders. Peace Through Strength!

2:37 PM – 28 Apr 2014

> Trump had yet to embrace the narrative of Putin as an ally in the war of civilizations. Ronald Reagan also used "Peace Through Strength" as a campaign slogan.

Via @BBCNews: "US property tycoon Donald Trump confirms Turnberry buy"

3:51 PM – 1 May 2014

> Trump is happy to use a BBC report to tell his followers of his purchase of Turnberry, the famous Scottish golf course which regularly hosts the British Open.

China will now pass our economy this year, way ahead of projections. Pres. Obama – China's greatest asset!

8:17 AM – 2 May 2014

Are you allowed to impeach a president for gross incompetence?

5:23 AM – 4 Jun 2014

BREAKING NEWS: Obama has just made a trade with Russia. They get Florida, California & our gold supply. We get borscht & a bottle of vodka.

11:14 AM – 5 Jun 2014

The Miss U.S.A. pageant will be amazing tonight. To be politically incorrect, the girls (women) are REALLY BEAUTIFUL. NBC at 8 PM.

10:17 AM – 8 Jun 2014

Manufacturing is now less than 9% of US GDP. The Rust Belt, heart of our country's factory sector, has been destroyed by our leaders.

2:00 PM – 19 Jun 2014

> In this Tweet Trump maps his route to the White House in 2016.

If only the illegals were Tea Party members then Obama would get them out of the country immediately.

8:16 AM – 9 Jul 2014

Mexico is allowing many thousands to go thru their country & to our very stupid open door. The Mexicans are laughing at us as buses pass by.
2:24 PM – 10 Jul 2014

My @BreitbartNews' @biggovt editorial: "A COUNTRY THAT CANNOT PROTECT ITS BORDERS WILL NOT LAST" http://t.co/hYA9V8KaX8
2:27 PM – 11 Jul 2014

> Trump chooses Breitbart as the forum in which to air his views on the border situation with Mexico.

Many people have said I'm the world's greatest writer of 140 character sentences.
3:50 PM – 21 Jul 2014

Obama wanted Putin to reset. Instead, Putin laughed at him and reloaded.
3:51 PM – 21 Jul 2014

Obama should work on a ceasefire in Chicago as well as Gaza.
2:36 PM – 30 Jul 2014

> Trump would make much of Chicago's appalling murder rate during his campaign, implying the violence there was typical of American cities.

If Obama resigns from office NOW, thereby doing a great service to the country—I will give him free lifetime golf at any one of my courses!
4:22 PM – 10 Sep 2014

They should have rebuilt the two buildings of the World Trade Center exactly as they were, except taller and stronger. A better statement!
7:35 AM – 11 Sep 2014

I wonder if I run for PRESIDENT, will the haters and losers vote
for me knowing that I will MAKE AMERICA GREAT AGAIN?
I say they will!
5:52 PM – 26 Sep 2014

I will be releasing the full interview with a guy named Baxter
@antbaxter only to show the bias and stupidity of him and
@BBCWorld. Clowns!
7:06 PM – 28 Sep 2014

> Anthony Baxter, director of *You've Been Trumped*, had just
> released a new documentary. *A Dangerous Game* probed the
> environmental cost of luxury golf resorts, including two
> developed by the Trump Organization. Trump had agreed to be
> interviewed but became angry when challenged.

Every time I speak of the haters and losers I do so with
great love and affection. They cannot help the fact that
they were born fucked up!
7:21 PM – 28 Sep 2014

Fact--Obama does not read his intelligence briefings
nor does he get briefed in person by the CIA or DOD.
Too busy I guess!
3:15 PM – 30 Sep 2014

> Trump would controversially refuse to take regular classified
> intelligence briefings when he became President.

Something very important, and indeed society changing, may
come out of the Ebola epidemic that will be a very good thing:
NO SHAKING HANDS!
12:14 PM – 4 Oct 2014

> Trump claims to be a "germophobe", using hand sanitizers
> after shaking hands with members of the public and for years
> refusing the traditional handshake in business dealings. He was

reluctant to shake hands with German Chancellor Angela Merkel in March 2017 but clung on to the hand of Canadian Prime Minister Justin Trudeau for much longer than courtesy demanded.

In a little reported event, China has just overtaken the United States as the NUMBER ONE World economic power! Great going Washington!

6:25 AM – 9 Oct 2014

Congratulations to @piersmorgan on his new position as Editor-at-Large for the United States of @MailOnline! My Apprentice champ!

3:01 PM – 9 Oct 2014

Morgan had left CNN the previous month, not long after his show *Piers Morgan Live* was axed.

Obama won't send troops to fight jihadists, yet sends them to Liberia to contract Ebola. He is a delusional failure.

3:49 PM – 9 Oct 2014

"I've never seen anything like it, everything he touches turns to gold!" So nice, a quote by Fred C.Trump about his son Donald (me!).

5:04 AM – 11 Oct 2014

I watched Russell Brand @rustyrockets on the @jimmyfallon show the other night—what the hell do people see in Russell—a major loser!

3:50 PM – 16 Oct 2014

Brand had described Trump as a "bit daft": "It's not like he's a person who's a super guy or anything. He's just good at hungry hippo, and we live in hungry hippo land."

Thank you Piers for the wonderful article and, also, great writing. @piersmorgan http://t.co/LZzoDjSlez

1:01 PM – 17 Oct 2014

> Piers Morgan had loyally come to Trump's defence against Russell Brand with an article in the *Mail Online*.

An interesting cartoon that is circulating. http://t.co/OPG2R2ytkr

11:29 AM – 22 Oct 2014

> Donald Trump drew attention to a poorly drawn cartoon depicting the founding fathers at a desk with the caption "I keep thinking we should include something in the Constitution in case the people elect a fucking moron."

Just out - the POLAR ICE CAPS are at an all time high, the POLAR BEAR population has never been stronger. Where the hell is global warming?

4:15 AM – 29 Oct 2014

> According to the *New Scientist* magazine, the area of the world's oceans covered by floating sea ice in January 2017 was "the smallest recorded since satellite monitoring began in the 1970s". The *New Scientist* added that "it is also probably the lowest it has been for thousands of years". In the same month, Trump's administration drew up plans to slash expenditure on NASA's climate monitoring programmes.

Very excited for @LaraLeaYunaska and @EricTrump's wedding this weekend.

4:20 PM – 3 Nov 2014

> Donald Trump's new daughter-in-law, Lara Lea Yunaska, was a producer for CBS's entertainment gossip show *Inside Edition*.

Happy Thanksgiving - I hope everyone can get together to
MAKE AMERICA GREAT AGAIN! It won't be easy, nothing is,
but it can be done.
9:54 PM – 26 Nov 2014

.@Newsmax by @melaniebatley: "Donald Trump Tells Why
He's Eyeing the White House.I'll Tell You Why He Could Win."
http://t.co/0Vv6VUqjxo
2:32 PM – 4 Dec 2014

> Trump here links to an interview in which he signals he was
> "going to take a very serious look" at running for the White
> House in 2016. He explained: "The reason that I'm looking at
> it very strongly this time is I'm so sick and tired of politicians.
> I am so sick and tired of watching these politicians who are all
> talk and no action… I have an instinct for things. I think the
> country is ready for someone who gets it. I think the country
> is ready for somebody who can take it to greatness again…
> I've been popular with a large group of people for a long period
> of time. Part of it is the success, part of it is what I say, and
> part of it is that they feel that I'm not somebody who can be
> ripped off and they're tired of being ripped off as a country."
>
> The report asserted that Trump's grassroots network
> included "his 2.4 million followers on Twitter".

THE LAST THING THIS COUNTRY NEEDS IS ANOTHER BUSH!
3:04 PM – 16 Dec 2014

> Jeb Bush, the former Florida Governor and second son of
> George H. W. Bush, had just become the first Republican
> candidate to throw his hat in the ring for the Presidential race.

So many people think I will not run for President.Wow,
I wonder what the response will be if I do. Even the haters
and losers will be happy!
6:52 PM – 24 Dec 2014

Merry Christmas to all - have a fantastic day, year and life! The World, with great leadership, will become a much more beautiful place!

9:59 PM – 24 Dec 2014

Where's the electability? Jeb is losing to HRC by 13 points. A Bush will never beat a Clinton. Wake up @GOP!

4:24 PM – 30 Dec 2014

2015

★ ★ ★ ★ ★

"Let's Make America Great Again!"

The Mar-a-Lago Club was amazing tonight. Everybody was there, the biggest and the hottest. Palm Beach is so lucky to have best club in world

2:02 AM – 1 Jan 2015

"@ericleebow: @realDonaldTrump Hope you finally run for President. That should be your new year's resolution."
Good thought!

2:11 AM – 1 Jan 2015

My condolences and prayers to the victims of the terrorist attack in Paris.

4:55 PM – 7 Jan 2015

> On the morning of 7 January, Al Qaeda terrorists attacked the offices of the French satirical magazine *Charlie Hebdo*, killing twelve people including the editor and several cartoonists. It is thought they carried out the atrocity on the grounds that *Charlie Hebdo* had repeatedly published cartoons of the Prophet Muhammad.

Why does Obama continue to release the worst of the worst from Gitmo?! Look at Paris and wake up!

4:56 PM – 7 Jan 2015

> Donald Trump was swift to exploit the *Charlie Hebdo* tragedy for political purposes. "The worst of the worst" was a phrase used by George W. Bush to justify incarcerating terrorist suspects without trial in Guantánamo Bay. Many of the inmates had no connection with either the Taleban or Al Qaeda.

Isn't it interesting that the tragedy in Paris took place in one of the toughest gun control countries in the world?

5:29 PM – 7 Jan 2015

Almost no news organizations are showing the "satirical" pictures. Gee, I wonder why? The media is usually so brave!

8:00 PM – 7 Jan 2015

Remember, @foxandfriends at 7:00 A.M. and Celebrity
Apprentice at 8:00 P.M. Enjoy!

10:55 PM – 11 Jan 2015

Charlie Hebdo reminds me of the "satirical" rag magazine Spy
that was very dishonest and nasty and went bankrupt. Charlie
was also broke!

9:10 AM – 14 Jan 2015

> *Spy* was a satirical magazine that repeatedly targeted Trump
> in the 1980s. Among other epiphets it had labelled him a
> "short-fingered vulgarian", "Well-fed condo hustler", "Debtor-
> adulterer", "Forbes 400 dropout", "Flyaway-haired mogul"
> and "Shuttle-owning dilettante-megalomaniac". When Trump
> Tower was unveiled, *Spy* described it as a "Ghastly new glass-
> and-steel penis substitute".

If the morons who killed all of those people at Charlie Hebdo
would have just waited, the magazine would have folded -
no money, no success!

9:13 AM – 14 Jan 2015

"@VladimirRussia7: @realDonaldTrump Oh,How I respect you-
a billionaire,a family man,and a TV Star!" Thanks.

3:00 AM – 17 Jan 2015

> Donald Trump was to retweet five gushing messages of
> support from a mysterious individual with the Twitter
> handle @ValdimirRussia7 within the space of a month. The
> @ValdimirRussia7 account no longer exists.

"AIR FORCE TRUMP: AHEAD OF 2016, THE DONALD
SLAMS ROMNEY, BUSH IN SOUTH CAROLINA"
http://t.co/DIMQdF1nxC via @BreitbartNews by @mboyle1

8:19 PM – 19 Jan 2015

> Trump again links to a Breitbart report. This concerned an

interview given by Donald Trump onboard his jet en route to a Tea Party gathering. In it Trump rubbished Mitt Romney, saying, "He ran against a failed President and he lost. Now it's time for somebody else." He added that "I think Hillary can be beaten. And I can beat her."

Via @DMRegister by @WilliamPetroski: "Trump: I can make America great again" http://t.co/
3:34 PM – 24 Jan 2015

Trump links to a report in the *Des Moines Register* of his speech at the Iowa Freedom Summit, a beauty contest for Republican hopefuls. Trump told a cheering audience: "I know what needs to be done to make America great again. We can make this country great again. The potential is enormous and I am seriously thinking of running for President."

Via @BreitbartNews: "DONALD TRUMP AT SUMMIT: OBAMACARE A 'FILTHY LIE,' CAN BUILD 'A BEAUTY' OF A BORDER FENCE" http://t.co/ubqpHOogl8
8:52 AM – 25 Jan 2015

Breitbart news gave a racier account of Trump's speech.

Word is that @NBCNews is firing sleepy eyes Chuck Todd in that his ratings on Meet the Press are setting record lows. He's a real loser!
10:48 AM – 25 Jan 2015

Apprentice = big hit. Miss Universe = Big hit. I always get big ratings. If I hosted Meet the Press instead of Sleepy Eyes,a smash! @NBCNews
9:21 AM – 27 Jan 2015

Trump loved to mock Chuck Todd, the host of NBC's *Meet the Press*. Trump's attacks did the presenter no harm. As of March 2017 the ratings for Chuck Todd's show exceed those of all its rival

Sunday political shows, beating CBS, ABC and Fox News in total viewers and the key younger demographic valued by Trump.

Wow, I have always liked the @nypost but they have really lied when they covered me in Iowa. Packed house, standing O, best speech! Sad.
8:45 AM – 28 Jan 2015

I guess Rupert Murdoch and the @nypost don't like Donald Trump. Such false reporting about my big hit in Iowa. Even my enemies said "bull."
9:04 AM – 28 Jan 2015

Trump falls out with Murdoch whose *New York Post* had given the thumbs down to the Iowa speech. The *Post* disliked its anti-immigrant tone and concluded that "Trump is a fool".

I will take full credit for Mitt Romney dropping out of the race— looks like he won't be endorsing Trump any time soon.
2:06 PM – 30 Jan 2015

Are all the illegals pouring into our country vaccinated? I don't think so. Great danger to U.S.
11:44 AM – 3 Feb 2015

We're worried about waterboarding as our enemy, ISIS, is beheading people and burning people alive. Time for us to wake up.
10:34 AM – 4 Feb 2015

Worst graphics and stage backdrop ever at the Oscars. Show is terrible, really BORING!
11:02 PM – 22 Feb 2015

The Oscars are a sad joke, very much like our President. So many things are wrong!
12:26 AM – 23 Feb 2015

The talks between the U.S. and Iran are going on forever, WORLD'S LONGEST NEGOTIATION. Obama has no idea what he is doing - incompetent!

6:35 PM – 23 Feb 2015

The evening news broadcasts must stop talking about weather—boring and too many other topics.

11:26 AM – 24 Feb 2015

The Mexican legal system is corrupt, as is much of Mexico. Pay me the money that is owed me now - and stop sending criminals over our border

7:47 PM – 24 Feb 2015

So many people are angry at my comments on Mexico—but face it—Mexico is totally ripping off the US. Our politicians are dummies!

10:30 AM – 25 Feb 2015

"Donald Trump ready to end @ApprenticeNBC for White House run" http://t.co/hN3gHZFVFX via via @dcexaminer by @eScarry

6:03 PM – 27 Feb 2015

> Donald Trump makes the ultimate sacrifice in order to run for the Presidency.

Via @BreitbartNews by @mboyle1:"Donald Trump Slams Liberals In 'Dishonest Press': 'I'm Going To Start Naming Names'" http://t.co/7uzPNPJ9vK

10:49 PM – 1 Mar 2015

> Trump ratchets up his attack on the press, retweeting a Breitbart article that reported on a meeting between Trump and his Tea Party supporters from which the mainstream press had been excluded. According to Breitbart, Trump told them "I'm going to start naming names because it really is incredible how dishonest the press is."

"Americans are hungry to feel once again a sense of mission and greatness." – Pres. Ronald Reagan
2:47 PM – 25 Mar 2015

"Donald Trump launches new men's fragrance-- "Empire" -- @Macys "Because every man has his own empire to build'" http://t.co/LBk4Xlr1FO
3:06 PM – 25 Mar 2015

Politicians are all talk and no action. Washington can only be fixed by an outsider. Let's make America great again! http://t.co/jEgR6jSQ5J
3:57 PM – 2 Apr 2015

> Trump provides a link to what would become his official campaign website.

Many journalists are honest and great - but some are knowingly dishonest and basic scum. They should.be weeded out!
10:42 PM – 6 Apr 2015

I will be speaking at the NRA event today in Nashville. Many friends will be there.
6:59 AM – 10 Apr 2015

> The National Rifle Association (NRA) is one of the most powerful lobbies in the United States. Trump courted it very successfully. He rarely displays interest in guns or hunting though he does possess a concealed weapons licence which permits him to carry a handgun about his person. Trump promised to back NRA demands to prevent background checks and permit ownership of assault rifles. The organization would fill his campaign coffers with over $30 million.

The NRA in Nashville today was amazing. Packed house and standing ovation for Trump. THANKS!
10:11 PM – 10 Apr 2015

"@dalley5: I got the tingle up my leg when you spoke! The common sense was to die for…we need somebody that will really fix this!"

10:19 PM – 10 Apr 2015

"@gabriellebragg4: How do I find out where @realDonaldTrump is giving speeches at? Because I really want to go to one."

10:47 PM – 10 Apr 2015

"@sarzitron: The best part about @realDonaldTrump running for president will be @HillaryClinton losing. I hate her so much."

3:07 PM – 12 Apr 2015

> Hillary Clinton had that morning announced she was seeking the Democratic nomination. She told Twitter followers, "I'm running for President. Everyday Americans need a champion, and I want to be that champion. – H"

Marco Rubio should pick a location that has working air conditioning next time - especially when in Miami - proper plan. Sweating profusely!

9:30 PM – 13 Apr 2015

> Donald Trump's way of acknowledging that one of his key rivals has declared his run for the Republican nomination. Rubio was favoured by much of the media and political Establishment. He would be eaten alive by Trump.

"@WingsUnchained: @RealDonaldTrump is not a professional liar like politicians. I was watching Cruz, but Donald also has my attention now."

7:19 AM – 15 Apr 2015

> Senator Ted Cruz, then the Republican Right's preferred candidate, had been the first major figure to announce his candidacy on 23 March.

I do what I do out of pure enjoyment. Hopefully, nobody does it better. Theres a beauty to making a great deal. It's my canvas.
6:43 PM – 17 Apr 2015

Just returned from New Hampshire where the crowd was great-and got a beautiful standing ovation! Wonderful people who truly love the U.S.A.
8:38 PM – 18 Apr 2015

How does failed writer and pundit like @stephenfhayes, with no success and little talent, get away with criticizing candidates.
8:48 AM – 20 Apr 2015

> Stephen Hayes, writer for the right-wing *Weekly News*, had described Trump as "a conservative of convenience" and a "clown".

"@MSJACKIEWOW: @realDonaldTrump NOBODY TRUMPS TRUMP WHEN IT COMES TO TWEETS…HOLY SH@T UR THE TWEET MASTER…GREAT JOB".
10:00 PM – 20 Apr 2015

Wow, Hillary and Bill are in deep trouble, but don't worry, my fellow Republicans will let them off the hook. All talk, no action.
9:59 AM – 21 Apr 2015

> Rupert Murdoch's *New York Post* had run a splash on the speaking fees Bill Clinton had levied while Hillary was at the State Department. The revelations came from a book by Peter Schweizer, Breitbart News's Senior Editor-at-Large. *Clinton Cash: The Untold Story of How and Why Foreign Governments and Businesses Helped Make Bill and Hillary Rich*, was published by Murdoch's HarperCollins. The book helped to cast doubt on the Clintons' probity. *Time* wrote that "allegations are presented as questions rather than proof" but that "the book's dark suggestions reflect the growing problem Clinton faces in her run for the White House in 2016 as more and more details of the foundation's

fundraising activities present the appearance of impropriety and lack of transparency during her time as Secretary of State".

I'm a conservative, but the weakness of conservatives is that they destroy each other, whereas liberals unite to win.
3:15 PM – 21 Apr 2015

I want to negotiate my own, and much better, trade deals for our country. MUST INCLUDE CURRENCY MANIPULATION (and more). DO NOT LET PASS!
3:46 PM – 22 Apr 2015

Do you notice that the polling establishment doesn't put me in polls, but put in folks who hardly register. MAKE AMERICA GREAT AGAIN!
8:00 AM – 23 Apr 2015

It is time for DC to protect the American worker, not grant amnesty to illegals. Let's Make America Great Again! https://t.co/u25yl5T7E8
1:30 PM – 23 Apr 2015

"@bean1227: @realDonaldTrump When are you announcing run #PresidentTrump !?" Stay tuned!
9:23 AM – 25 Apr 2015

I don't know if Hillary will be able to run, she is a walking time bomb!
10:24 AM – 25 Apr 2015

Will be interviewed on @foxandfriends at 7:00 - 5 minutes. Then I head to New Hampshire, great people!
6:57 AM – 27 Apr 2015

During this appearance on Fox News, Trump focused his concern on allegations against Bill and Hillary's organization, the Clinton Foundation. The Foundation accepted money from Saudi Arabia and other countries during the time Hillary was Secretary of State. Trump accused her of "bribery. 100%". Trump then introduced what was to become a campaign rally staple: "This isn't about voters – this is about jail time." His followers got the message.

"@blayne_troy: @foxandfriends Mr. Trump calls it like it is. HRC should be investigated, prosecuted and put in federal prison."
7:40 AM – 27 Apr 2015

Billions of dollars spent on Baltimore and it's still a total mess. Leadership is needed, not dollars. Our whole country is going to hell!
9:21 AM – 1 May 2015

This was a precursor to the remarkably bleak theme that would dominate Trump's Inauguration Address, defined by its macabre reference to "American carnage".

If the working, proud and productive people of our country don't start exerting their authority and views, the U.S. as we know it is doomed!
9:49 AM – 1 May 2015

Baltimore had a really tough night - only great leadership can solve the many inner-city problems facing our country. Jobs, jobs, jobs!
12:34 AM – 2 May 2015

Baltimore had seen rioting following the death in police custody three weeks earlier of African-American Freddie Gray, with protests also taking place around the country, adding impetus to the Black Lives Matter movement.

The racial divide in our country is almost at an all-time high - and getting worse every time you turn on the television.
5:53 AM – 2 May 2015

Throughout 2015 the United States was shaken by protests about police shootings of African-Americans. It is not entirely clear whether Trump is saying that black protests (often with considerable support from white people) about police shootings were evidence of worsening race relations, or whether he was hinting that the divide was unbridgeable.

I am the only one that knows how to build cities - pols are all talk and no action. Our cities need help, and fast. They are crumbling!
3:34 PM – 3 May 2015

If elected, I will undo all of Obama's executive orders.
I will deliver. Let's Make America Great Again!
https://t.co/u25yl5T7E8
2:09 PM – 4 May 2015

I am thrilled to share that the Trump Home furniture collection by @doryainteriors, just opened a new showroom in Toronto with @arteriorsto. The collection looks amazing!
2:11 PM – 5 May 2015

"There can be no liberty unless there is economic liberty." – The Iron Lady Margaret Thatcher
3:07 PM – 5 May 2015

I was proud to be one of Ronald Reagan's earliest supporters. Like Reagan, it's time to Make America Great Again!
http://t.co/toq7Ddalco
1:09 PM – 12 May 2015

Reagan repeatedly promised to "make America great again" during his 1980 Presidential campaign. He, too, used it as a slogan on campaign merchandise and in speeches on the stump.

The only one to fix the infrastructure of our country is me -
roads, airports, bridges. I know how to build, pols only know
how to talk!
10:12 PM – 12 May 2015

> Trump had never built infrastructure on this scale. He had
> spent his career developing hotels, clubs and apartment blocks,
> not highways or great bridges.

I am the BEST builder, just look at what I've built. Hillary can't
build. Republican candidates can't build. They don't have
a clue!
7:23 AM – 13 May 2015

Going to New Hampshire, all sold out crowds. People want
real change - POLS WILL NEVER MAKE OUR COUNTRY
GREAT AGAIN!
8:07 AM – 14 May 2015

Via @UnionLeader by @tuohy: "Trump inches closer to a
decision" http://t.co/Hgp2LW9Ucj
1:02 PM – 15 May 2015

I am in Iowa today, great STATE, fantastic PEOPLE! Many
speeches, big crowds - all sold out! MAKE AMERICA
GREAT AGAIN!
7:27 AM – 16 May 2015

"@carrillo_pete: @realDonaldTrump @TheBrodyFile -I'm all
aboard the Trump Train. I know it won't derail. ☒"
4:48 PM – 16 May 2015

> First use of the "Trump Train" phrase that would become the
> collective term, as well as much-used hashtag, for Trump's
> supporters.

Jeb Bush gave five different answers in four days on whether or not we should have invaded Iraq. He is so confused.Not presidential material!

8:04 PM – 1 May 2015

Marco Rubio was a complete disaster today in an interview with Chris Wallace @FoxNews concerning our invading Iraq.He was as clueless as Jeb

8:11 PM – 17 May 2015

I laugh when I see Marco Rubio and Jeb Bush pretending to "love" each other, with each talking of their great friendship. Typical phony pols

8:54 PM – 17 May 2015

I would like to wish everyone, including all haters and losers (of which, sadly, there are many) a truly happy and enjoyable Memorial Day!

3:26 PM – 24 May 2015

The middle-class has become the new poor in this country and our incompetent politicians are unable to do anything about it.They don't care!

6:58 PM – 25 May 2015

.@AnnCoulter's new book-- "Adios, America! The Left's Plan to Turn Our Country into a Third World Hellhole"-- is a great read. Good job!

4:20 PM – 26 May 2015

> The writer and polemicist Ann Coulter was also admired by David Duke, leader of the Ku Klux Klan, who told *Esquire*, "If you really look at what she says, if you read her books, it's very close to what I've been saying."

Wow, the economy is really bad! GROSS DOMESTIC PRODUCT down 0.7% in 1st. quarter - and getting worse. I TOLD YOU SO! Only I can fix.

5:17 PM – 29 May 2015

Was in Iowa yesterday-great people. Record crowds at both speeches. Something big is happening. Pols are all talk. Make America great again!

1:33 AM – 5 Jun 2015

Amazing NH poll released! We are getting ready to Make America Great Again! http://t.co/gdRpkRwySd

7:32 PM – 8 Jun 2015

> The Gravis Marketing poll put Trump in fourth position – Jeb Bush was far ahead on 21 per cent.

I am really happy that Hillary made her speech right under Trump World Tower!

11:43 AM – 13 Jun 2015

> Clinton had launched her campaign with a large rally of supporters in bright sunshine on the southern tip of Roosevelt Island, with the view of the Manhattan skyline in the background.

Remember, politicians are all talk and no action - they will never be able to MAKE OUR COUNTRY GREAT AGAIN! Controlled by lobbyists & donors

3:43 PM – 13 Jun 2015

> Even in his initial wave of appointments in December 2016, Trump would grant cabinet positions to six of his biggest donors: Small Business administrator for Linda McMahon, who gave $7.5 million; Education Secretary for Betsy DeVos, $1.8 million (contributed by the DeVos family); Deputy Commerce Secretary for Todd Ricketts, $1.3 million

(contributed by his parents); Treasury Secretary for Steven Mnuchin, former Goldman Sachs executive, $425,000; Labor Secretary for Andrew Puzder, $332,000 and Commerce Secretary for Wilbur Ross, who donated $200,000. Lobbyists and Wall Street bankers would be brought in to fill other key roles.

Tomorrow will be a really big day for America. MAKE AMERICA GREAT AGAIN!

6:12 AM – 15 Jun 2015

It is almost time. I will be making a major announcement from @TrumpTowerNY at 11AM. Follow on social media! #MakeAmericaGreatAgain

8:04 AM – 16 Jun 2015

I am officially running for President of the United States. #MakeAmericaGreatAgain https://t.co/Ct0lNu7kz0

10:57 AM – 16 Jun 2015

The linked photograph showed Trump surrounded by family members in the Trump Tower lobby.

Today I officially declared my candidacy for President of the United States. Watch the video of my full speech- https://t.co/gonTk0o9Dt

2:15 PM – 16 Jun 2015

Many of the cheering supporters were later revealed to be actors hired for the day. Trump attacked Mexican immigrants in his speech: "They are not our friend, believe me. But they're killing us economically. The US has become a dumping ground for everybody else's problems… When Mexico sends its people, they're not sending their best… They're bringing drugs. They're bringing crime. They're rapists. And some, I assume, are good people."

The tragedy in South Carolina is incomprehensible. My deepest condolences to all.

11:58 AM – 18 Jun 2015

> A white gunman had entered the Emanuel African Methodist Episcopal Church in Charleston killing nine parishioners before fleeing. The perpetrator, Dylann Roof, a twenty-one-year-old white supremacist, was later sentenced to death.

Hillary Clinton reaches new low. #TrumpVlog
https://t.co/kgmQ2jVF6b

9:42 AM – 19 Jun 2015

> Hilary Clinton had linked Trump's attack on Mexican immigrants to the church massacre in South Carolina.

I like Mexico and love the spirit of Mexican people, but we must protect our borders from people, from all over, pouring into the U.S.

8:15 PM – 19 Jun 2015

Mexico is killing the United States economically because their leaders and negotiators are FAR smarter than ours. But nobody beats Trump!

8:54 PM – 19 Jun 2015

Druggies, drug dealers, rapists and killers are coming across the southern border. When will the U.S. get smart and stop this travesty?

9:22 PM – 19 Jun 2015

Who would you rather have negotiating for the U.S. against Putin, Iran, China, etc., Donald Trump or Hillary? Is there even a little doubt?

7:57 PM – 20 Jun 2015

Sadly, I will no longer be doing @foxandfriends at 7:00 A.M. on Mondays. This is because I am running for president and law prohibits. LOVE!

5:31 AM – 22 Jun 2015

I want to thank Elizabeth, Steve, Brian and all of the great folks of @foxandfriends for the long and successful run we had together. NICE!

5:39 AM – 22 Jun 2015

"Hillary Clinton Dominates the Pack in Fake Twitter Followers" http://t.co/e16f6FM8uQ

9:39 AM – 22 Jun 2015

Trump retweeted an article highlighting research that stated 35 per cent of Clinton's then 2.3 million followers were fake. By contrast, Trump's 2.6 million followers were 90 per cent real people.

In subsequent analyses, these results would be reversed. In April 2016 a study found that 8 per cent of his followers were fake, compared to 7 per cent for Clinton. By February 2017 20 per cent of Trump's followers were deemed "egg avatars" or inactive compared to 16 per cent of Clinton's. The *Daily Beast* investigated Trump's followers, concluding that not all of them "are human": "Throughout the 2016 presidential campaign, automated networks of social-media bots spread erroneous information to potential voters – often to the benefit of Trump. According to a new memo compiling data from the election by a team of researchers including Oxford University Professor Philip Howard, automated pro-Trump activity outnumbered automated pro-Hillary Clinton activity by a 5:1 ratio by Election Day."

It would later be claimed that Russian influence was one of the reasons for the explosion in Trump's Twitter following. In an article for Rupert Murdoch's online magazine HeatStreet, Louise Mensch alleged that "Trump has two categories of support on Twitter. Alt-right trolls, and Russian bot accounts pretending to be patriotic Americans. In many cases, these two groups cross over. The alt-right contains actual humans, such as @prisonplanet, and many, many bots… It is not that Donald Trump does not have widespread support. He does; even at his current polling lows, his support includes millions of Americans. It is, rather, that Trump's supporters are incredibly unlikely to use Twitter. Broadly speaking, Trump's real supporters aren't on Twitter – and Trump's Twitter supporters aren't real."

My daughter, Ivanka, will be representing me today at the opening of our campaign office in Manchester, NH #MakeAmericaGreatAgain!

2:20 PM – 24 Jun 2015

My message, MAKE AMERICA GREAT AGAIN, is beginning to take hold. Bring back our jobs, strengthen our military and borders, help our VETS!

9:16 PM – 24 Jun 2015

We have to bring back and cherish the middle class - once the backbone and true strength of the U.S.A. It can happen!

10:17 PM – 24 Jun 2015

I'll be in Iowa tonight making a speech to a record setting crowd. The word is getting out, MAKE AMERICA GREAT AGAIN!

12:41 PM – 27 Jun 2015

A great article by @NolteNC spelling out the truth on Mexico, trade, the border & illegals. Thank you @BreitbartNews http://t.co/oJnV2OXcEc

3:09 PM – 27 Jun 2015

For all of those who want to #MakeAmericaGreatAgain, boycott @Macys. They are weak on border security & stopping illegal immigration.

12:00 PM – 1 Jul 2015

Trump had enjoyed a long and profitable connection with the New York department store that stocked his branded products. However, Macy's was appalled by Trump's attack on Mexicans in his launch speech and issued a press release: "In light of statements made by Donald Trump, which are inconsistent with Macy's values, we have decided to discontinue our business relationship with Mr. Trump and will phase-out the Trump menswear collection, which has been sold at Macy's since 2004."

.@Macys stock just dropped. Interesting. So many people calling to say they are cutting up their @Macys credit card. Thank you!
10:09 AM – 2 Jul 2015

Wow, Huffington Post just stated that I am number 1 in the polls of Republican candidates. Thank you, but the work has just begun!
6:22 AM – 3 Jul 2015

Thx to all the people who called to say they are cutting their @Macys credit card as a protest against illegal immigrants pouring into US
12:14 PM – 6 Jul 2015

We have got to take our country back. It's time!
9:48 PM – 6 Jul 2015

I will be in California this weekend making a speech for Clint Eastwood. Then to Arizona and Vegas. Big crowds. Discussing illegals & more!
6:22 AM – 8 Jul 2015

"EXCLUSIVE — DONALD TRUMP ON THE GOP PRIMARY: 'IF I WIN, I WILL BEAT HILLARY'" http://t.co/wlz13nYels via @BreitbartNews by Katie McHugh
4:14 PM – 9 Jul 2015

Trump gives another exclusive interview to Breitbart.

Today I will be rallying with with 15,000 patriots in Arizona for border security! Let's Make America Great Again! https://t.co/u25yl5T7E8

11:48 AM – 11 Jul 2015

I will not be able to attend the Miss USA pageant tomorrow night because I am campaigning in Phoenix. Wishing all well!

7:56 PM – 11 Jul 2015

A turning point: politics wins over pageants.

Thank you Piers. https://t.co/uH6h74qShv

3:18 PM – 15 Jul 2015

Piers Morgan had praised Trump's decision making.

"@UncleLouie Clearly Trump gets social media. His tweets are everywhere & no sugar coating, he keeps it real. Wish all candidates did that"

4:02 PM – 15 Jul 2015

Via @BreitbartNews by Steve Bannon: "'TIME TO GET TOUGH': TRUMP'S BLOCKBUSTER POLICY MANIFESTO" http://t.co/rrRd7AkFED

1:35 PM – 16 Jul 2015

A rare reference to Steve Bannon, then executive chairman of Breitbart News and today Trump's strategy chief in the White House. Bannon praised Trump's bestselling *Time to Get Tough* as a "penetrating, serious, and detailed enunciation of his political philosophy and policy views". Bannon added that Trump's book "clearly lays out serious policy solutions to vexing U.S. problems. Welfare reform, cyberwarfare, energy, illegal immigration and crime, taxes, healthcare, national defense – you name it, Trump offers his plans, often including specific bills and amendments. Best of all, Trump does it all in his refreshingly blunt and authentic voice – the very voice now resonating with a citizenry fed up with the Political Class and its conceits."

Leaked emails from Steve Bannon published by the *Daily Beast* would later suggest that by the summer of 2015 Bannon was already acting clandestinely as Trump's campaign manager. In one of the emails he told a colleague that Breitbart was "Trump-Central".

The ever dwindling @WSJ which is worth about 1/10 of what it was purchased for, is always hitting me politically. Who cares!
9:25 AM – 20 Jul 2015

The *Wall Street Journal* is owned by Rupert Murdoch's News Corporation.

"@insuradude: @foxandfriends @foxnation tell your owner Murdoch we are turning Fox off if he keeps belittling @realDonaldTrump. No Fox!"
7:29 PM – 21 Jul 2015

Murdoch had tweeted that Trump was "wrong" on immigration: "When is Donald Trump going to stop embarrassing his friends, let alone the whole country?"

Boycott @Macys, no guts, no glory. Besides, there are far better stores!
9:57 PM – 22 Jul 2015

While I'm beating my opponents in the polls, I'm also beating lobbyists, special interests & donors that are supporting them with billions.
3:22 PM – 28 Jul 2015

I truly LOVE all of the millions of people who are sticking with me despite so many media lies. There is a great SILENT MAJORITY looming!
8:58 AM – 29 Jul 2015

I look forward to the debate on Thursday night & it is certainly my intention to be very nice & highly respectful of the other candidates.

2:46 PM – 30 Jul 2015

The event in Cleveland Ohio would be the first in the series of twelve Republican Presidential debates, and nine forums, between the candidates for the Republican Party's nomination.

It came out that Huma Abedin knows all about Hillary's private illegal emails. Huma's PR husband, Anthony Weiner, will tell the world.

10:50 AM – 3 Aug 2015

Huma Abedin was vice chair of Hillary Clinton's campaign, having previously worked closely with her at the State Department. Clinton was under investigation for having used an unsecured private server at her home for dealing with emails during her time as Secretary of State. Abedin was married to Anthony Weiner, the contents of whose laptop, seized by the FBI after further sexting adventures, would later help turn the race against Clinton.

I really enjoyed the debate tonight even though the @FoxNews trio, especially @megynkelly, was not very good or professional

2:53 AM – 7 Aug 2015

Kelly, one of the moderators of the debate, put the following brutal question to Donald Trump: "You've called women you don't like 'fat pigs', 'dogs', 'slobs' and 'disgusting animals'… Your Twitter account has several disparaging comments about women's looks. You once told a contestant on *Celebrity Apprentice* it would be a pretty picture to see her on her knees. Does that sound to you like the temperament of a man we should elect as President?"

.@FoxNews you should be ashamed of yourself. I got you the highest debate ratings in your history & you say nothing but bad…
3:35 PM – 7 Aug 2015

So many "politically correct" fools in our country. We have to all get back to work and stop wasting time and energy on nonsense!
7:29 AM – 8 Aug 2015

> Trump was under attack for his reaction to Megyn Kelly's line of questioning. Hardly surprising: he told CNN, "She gets out and she starts asking me all sorts of ridiculous questions. You could see there was blood coming out of her eyes, blood coming out of her wherever. In my opinion, she was off base."

It amazes me that other networks seem to treat me so much better than @FoxNews. I brought them the biggest ratings in history, & I get zip!
2:42 PM – 9 Aug 2015

Roger Ailes just called. He is a great guy & assures me that "Trump" will be treated fairly on @FoxNews. His word is always good!
10:35 AM – 10 Aug 2015

> Roger Ailes, founder and CEO of Fox News. *The New York Times* reported that Ailes told senior executives that Rupert Murdoch, the channel's owner, asked him if Fox could "back off the Trump coverage". *The New York Times* said that Ailes reassured his staff that they should continue covering Trump "the way he [Ailes] wanted to".

My official #MakeAmericaGreatAgain hat is now available online. To shop please visit http://t.co/3zYilYWs87 --- it is selling fast!
2:46 PM – 11 Aug 2015

First mention of the red baseball cap emblazoned with "Make America Great Again". It became the symbol of Trump's campaign.

Now that I started my war on illegal immigration and securing the border, most other candidates are finally speaking up.
Just politicians!
4:22 PM – 22 Aug 2015

Jeb Bush just talked about my border proposal to build a "fence." It's not a fence, Jeb, it's a WALL, and there's a BIG difference!
7:39 AM – 25 Aug 2015

Congrats everyone--we topped 4 million today on Twitter--and heading up fast!
1:41 PM – 1 Sep 2015

Hillary Clinton made a speech today using the biggest teleprompter I have ever seen. In fact, it wasn't even see through glass, it was black
4:36 PM – 5 Sep 2015

Hillary said such nasty things about me, read directly off her teleprompter…but there was no emotion, no truth. Just can't read speeches!
4:42 PM – 5 Sep 2015

Congrats to my friend @Schwarzenegger who is doing next season's Celebrity Apprentice. He'll be great & will raise lots of $ for charity.
11:39 AM – 14 Sep 2015

I hope Arnold S. does well with the Apprentice because he is a nice guy and also, because I get a big percentage of the profits!
10:18 PM – 15 Sep 2015

Trump's relationship with Schwarzenegger would sour.

Just announced that in the history of @CNN, last night's debate was its highest rated ever. Will they send me flowers & a thank you note?
12:17 PM – 17 Sep 2015

GIVE AMERICA BACK ITS DREAM! -- Donald J. Trump
2:08 PM – 18 Sep 2015

I am attracting the biggest crowds, by far, and the best poll numbers, also by far. Much of the media is totally dishonest. So sad!
7:56 PM – 20 Sep 2015

I am having a really hard time watching @FoxNews.
9:00 PM – 21 Sep 2015

Do you ever notice that lightweight @megynkelly constantly goes after me but when I hit back it is totally sexist. She is highly overrated!
9:00 PM – 22 Sep 2015

> "Highly overrated" is a familiar phrase in Trump's lexicon. He would later apply it to Meryl Streep and the cast of *Hamilton*. The overrated figures he criticizes usually enjoy a spike in popularity after his assaults.

Just remember, the birther movement was started by Hillary Clinton in 2008. She was all in!
9:16 PM – 22 Sep 2015

> Hillary Clinton never lent credibility to the birther movement. Nevertheless Trump would continue to claim that Democratic opponents of Obama had exploited the theory that he had been born outside of America. Trump, having failed to provide any evidence to support his theory, was now preparing to climb down and looking for a plausible scapegoat.

.@FoxNews has been treating me very unfairly & I have therefore decided that I won't be doing any more Fox shows for the foreseeable future.
11:02 AM – 23 Sep 2015

> Stonewalling media requests and withholding media access: a staple Trump tactic.

Despite the establishment and the media's best efforts, the people are speaking loudly and clearly. Thank you to my amazing supporters!
11:24 AM – 24 Sep 2015

Hope we all enjoy @60Minutes tomorrow night. I do believe they will treat me fairly!
6:25 PM – 26 Sep 2015

"@Apipwhisperer: @MarkPavelich @gentlemanirish @60Minutes EXCELLENT WATCHING PUTIN'S BRILLIANCE AND TRUMP'S. @CBS I LOVED THE INTERVIEWS."
9:30 PM – 27 Sep 2015

> The CBS network's iconic current affairs programme *60 Minutes* presented viewers with two interviews. The first, with Trump "on top, in his Fifth Avenue penthouse in Manhattan"; the second, a "rare – and surprising" interview with the Russian President: "Putin invited us to meet him at his state residence outside Moscow where we found him characteristically confident and combative".

Wow, the ratings for @60Minutes last night were their biggest in a year--- very nice!
5:00 PM – 28 Sep 2015

"@Tea4Freedom: Pastor Robert Jeffres accurately gushes about Donald Trump http://t.co/iRcAPKF7yZ" Pastor Jeffres is a great guy!
8:50 AM – 2 Oct 2015

Trump calls Pastor Jeffress a "great guy". Jeffress was the leader of the politically powerful First Baptist Church in Dallas. Jeffress has attacked Islam as an "evil, evil religion" that promotes paedophilia. He claims that Catholicism – the religion of Mike Pence, Steve Bannon and a number of Trump's Irish American supporters – represents "the genius of Satan". He says that homosexuals are "miserable" pursuers of a "filthy" lifestyle, adding that gay marriage is "paving the way" for the Antichrist. Jeffress (the Tweet misspelt his name) would preach at a private service for Trump and his family just before he took the oath of office.

Bush and Rubio are finally attacking each other, as I knew they would, in order to be the last "establishment" man standing against me. Great

6:16 AM – 3 Oct 2015

'The goal is to be the winner': Donald Trump's campaign is for real. Via The Guardian http://t.co/7yP6iW2srp

2:07 PM – 8 Oct 2015

The *Guardian* earns a Retweet. For the most part, Donald Trump retweets outlets which reinforce rather than challenge his world view.

Just leaving Las Vegas. Unbelievable crowd! Many Hispanics who love me and I love them! https://t.co/t7hzDV9wEr

4:04 PM – 8 Oct 2015

I was so happy when I heard that @Politico, one of the most dishonest political outlets, is losing a fortune. Pure scum!

6:49 PM – 8 Oct 2015

Everybody's talking about my doing twitter during the likely very boring debate tonight. @realDonaldTrump #DemDebate

10:09 AM – 13 Oct 2015

Trump telling his followers that he will be "live tweeting" the first debate of the Democratic Primary.

All are very scripted and rehearsed, two (at least) should not be on the stage.
8:48 PM – 13 Oct 2015

Sorry, there is no STAR on the stage tonight!
9:02 PM – 13 Oct 2015

Like her or not, Hillary did what she had to do in the debate last night—get through it. Her opponents were very gentle and soft!
9:55 AM – 14 Oct 2015

#DemDebate was really boring but had a lot of fun live tweeting and picked up by far the most followers.
9:57 AM – 14 Oct 2015

> The day before the debate Trump had gained a relatively meagre 4,785 followers. On the day of the debate, galvanized by his tweeting, he added 153,085 followers.

The debate last night proved that Hillary is running against the "B" team. She won't be so lucky when it comes to me!
11:31 AM – 14 Oct 2015

Signing my tax return…. http://t.co/XJfXeaORbU
12:13 PM – 15 Oct 2015

> The photograph of Trump at his desk with a stack of papers three foot high would be the closest the American electorate ever got to seeing his tax return before election day.

.@HillaryClinton is on the front page of the @nytimes waving to 200 people in New Hampshire. My crowd next door was 5,000 people – no pic!
9:47 AM – 17 Oct 2015

Good news for those that want to Make America Great Again - I am winning every poll in every STATE and NATIONAL - and by big numbers! Thanks

6:50 PM – 17 Oct 2015

Remember, official campaign merchandise (hats, apparel etc.) can only be bought at https://t.co/SXUUL7I8vp. Be careful, don't get ripped-of

12:08 PM – 23 Oct 2015

> The price of the official red baseball caps was $25. The military camouflage print version was $30. The "Red Cap Collectable Ornament" for Christmas trees was $99.

Thanks, @PiersMorgan. You're great!

10:32 PM – 28 Oct 2015

> After the third Republican debate in Boulder, Colorado, Morgan tweeted: "Trump's a fantastic debater. Don't know why others even bother taking him on. Like goading a 3-ton bull."

While in politics it is often smart to send out false messages, one thing is clear: That Hillary does not want to run against TRUMP.

7:00 PM – 1 Nov 2015

Saturday Night Live has some incredible things in store tonight. The great thing about playing myself is that it will be authentic! Enjoy

12:34 PM – 7 Nov 2015

> Hillary Clinton had been invited to appear as a guest on NBC's popular comedy sketch show a month before. Donald Trump, by contrast, was asked to host the whole show, a role usually reserved for Hollywood's A-list. Trump rose to the occasion. He had learnt the power of self-parody. One sketch, titled 'White House 2018', portrayed 'President Trump' surrounded by cabinet members, including his daughter, Ivanka, played by Ivanka Trump – now a fixture in the real Trump White House.

Thanks Piers. Greatly appreciated. @piersmorgan
https://t.co/2mlMzNRMOc

3:43 PM – 9 Nov 2015

> Trump retweeted Piers Morgan's glowing review of *Saturday Night Live* in the *Mail Online*: "Donald Trump made me laugh with him and at him" – "he nailed it".

Marco Rubio is a total lightweight who I wouldn't hire to run one of my smaller companies - a highly overrated politician!

10:35 PM – 9 Nov 2015

President Obama said "ISIL continues to shrink" in an interview just hours before the horrible attack in Paris. He is just so bad! CHANGE.

8:39 AM – 14 Nov 2015

> More than 120 people were killed in a series of co-ordinated attacks by Islamic State terrorists in Paris on 13 November, including a massacre at the Bataclan Theatre during a concert by an American rock band. Trump uses this tragedy to attack Obama.

When will President Obama issue the words RADICAL ISLAMIC TERRORISM? He can't say it, and unless he will, the problem will not be solved!

9:18 AM – 15 Nov 2015

> Trump repeatedly attacked both Barack Obama and Hillary Clinton for not using the term "radical Islamic terrorism". There was a good reason for their failure to do so. Clinton and Obama both refused to blame all Muslims for violent acts carried out by tiny groups such as Al Qaeda and Islamic State. By contrast, Trump has consistently sought to suggest that Islam itself is the problem, rather than the abuse of one of the world's great faiths by a handful of violent men. Both Donald Trump and his chief strategist, Steve Bannon, believe that Islam is an enemy ideology and Al Qaeda and ISIS are acting in the

name of all Muslims. This belief underlies many of the policies which Donald Trump has promoted after entering the White House, such as the attempt to ban citizens from certain Muslim countries from entering the US, and calls to declare the Muslim Brotherhood a terrorist organization.

Wow, @Macys shares are down more than 40% this year. I never knew my ties & shirts not being sold there would have such a big impact!

1:47 PM – 16 Nov 2015

The vendetta against the department store continued.

Will be landing in Knoxville, Tennessee shortly - tremendous crowd expected. It's all very simple, we want to #MakeAmericaGreatAgain!

4:47 PM – 16 Nov 2015

Refugees from Syria are now pouring into our great country. Who knows who they are - some could be ISIS. Is our president insane?

8:54 AM – 17 Nov 2015

The United States, a country of 318.9 million people, had accepted just over two thousand Syrian refugees.

Eight Syrians were just caught on the southern border trying to get into the U.S. ISIS maybe? I told you so. WE NEED A BIG & BEAUTIFUL WALL!

8:11 AM – 19 Nov 2015

Everyone is now saying how right I was with illegal immigration & the wall. After Paris, they're all on the bandwagon.

11:30 AM – 19 Nov 2015

So nice when media properly polices media. Thank you @BreitbartNews. https://t.co/IGUh57zOJz

10:26 AM – 21 Nov 2015

Breitbart had launched a vigorous defence of Trump after *The New York Times* accused him of planning to introduce a register of Muslims.

When you do your Christmas shopping remember how disloyal @Macys was to the subject of illegal immigration. #BoycottMacys #DumpMacys

1:45 PM – 23 Nov 2015

I LIVE IN NEW JERSEY & @realDonaldTrump IS RIGHT: MUSLIMS DID CELEBRATE ON 9/11 HERE! WE SAW IT! https://t.co/1SksZU9qlj

7:22 PM – 25 Nov 2015

Trump retweets a link to a story from the right-wing website Infowars that Muslims in New Jersey celebrated the destruction of the Twin Towers on September 11, a theory that Trump also believes. Infowars is run by Alex Jones, a conspiracy theorist who has also asserted that the Sandy Hook massacre of twenty primary school children in 2012 was staged in order to discredit the gun lobby. He has also suggested US government complicity in the 9/11 attacks. Jones is an enthusiastic advocate of the theory that there is a link between vaccination and autism, for which Trump has shown considerable sympathy. The Infowars website sells crank medicines, including the Infowars Life Survival Shield X-2 Nascent Iodine. In February 2017, Jones would claim that the new President was still telephoning him for advice. This statement was not disputed by the White House.

I do not know the reporter for the @nytimes, or what he looks like. I was showing a person groveling to take back a statement made long ago!

4:40 PM – 26 Nov 2015

Trump had mimicked the physical actions of a disabled reporter who had challenged Trump's claims that Muslims celebrated on

9/11. Trump told a rally "Now the poor guy, you gotta see this guy," before contorting his right arm into a crooked pose and pulling a face in an apparent impersonation. The reporter, Serge Kovaleski, has a congenital joint condition that affects the movement in his arms. Kovaleski later insisted that he and Trump knew each other well. He told *The New York Times* how he and Trump had met many times and were "on a first name basis for years".

The truth continues to come out after 14 years. A truth that many in the media did not want to tell. #Trump2016
https://t.co/AtuacgxOW1

9:20 PM – 1 Dec 2015

Trump directed his followers to a Breitbart report titled "9 pieces of documentation that vindicate Trump's claims of 9/11 Muslim celebrations".

I beat Hillary in the new @FoxNews Poll head to head. SHE HAS NO STRENGTH OR STAMINA, both of which are needed to MAKE AMERICA GREAT AGAIN!

3:19 PM – 2 Dec 2015

I consider my health, stamina and strength one of my greatest assets.The world has watched me for many years and can so testify-great genes!

7:19 AM – 3 Dec 2015

As a presidential candidate, I have instructed my long-time doctor to issue, within two weeks, a full medical report-it will show perfection

8:08 AM – 3 Dec 2015

"@FieldRoamer: America's most reliable bellwether county has fallen for @realDonaldTrump https://t.co/KkNnQDiLfb"
Great story, thanks!

3:53 PM – 6 Dec 2015

After spending months attacking the Politico website, Trump was suddenly happy to promote its (well-researched) report on his appeal to blue-collar voters.

Just put out a very important policy statement on the extraordinary influx of hatred & danger coming into our country. We must be vigilant!

4:47 PM – 7 Dec 2015

Statement on Preventing Muslim Immigration: https://t.co/HCWU16z6SR https://t.co/d1dhals0S7

5:32 PM – 7 Dec 2015

The statement read:

"Donald J. Trump is calling for a total and complete shutdown of Muslims entering the United States until our country's representatives can figure out what is going on. According to Pew Research, among others, there is great hatred towards Americans by large segments of the Muslim population. Most recently, a poll from the Center for Security Policy released data showing '25% of those polled agreed that violence against Americans here in the United States is justified as a part of the global jihad' and 51% of those polled, 'agreed that Muslims in America should have the choice of being governed according to Shariah'. Shariah authorizes such atrocities as murder against non-believers who won't convert, beheadings and more unthinkable acts that pose great harm to Americans, especially women. Mr. Trump stated, 'Without looking at the various polling data, it is obvious to anybody the hatred is beyond comprehension. Where this hatred comes from and why we will have to determine. Until we are able to determine and understand this problem and the dangerous threat it poses, our country cannot be the victims of horrendous attacks by people that believe only in Jihad, and have no sense of reason or respect for human life. If I win the election for President, we are going to Make America Great Again.' – *Donald J. Trump*"

The "Center for Security Policy" cited in the report was founded by Frank Gaffney Jr, an anti-Muslim campaigner who is now an influential force in the White House.

I told you @TIME Magazine would never pick me as person of the year despite being the big favorite They picked person who is ruining Germany
8:53 AM – 9 Dec 2015

Time praised Angela Merkel as "Chancellor of the Free World".

"Rupert Murdoch Defends Trump: 'Complete Refugee Pause' Makes Sense' " https://t.co/HWOLO4RVAC
10:22 AM – 9 Dec 2015

A rapprochement with Murdoch, who strongly supported Trump's position on Muslim refugees, was reported in Breitbart and retweeted here by Trump.

Thank you, Piers, they don't know what they're getting into. https://t.co/UvKt1Go6nT
11:13 AM – 9 Dec 2015

Piers Morgan once again came to Trump's rescue, tweeting, "Have any of the 200k+ Brits who've signed the petition to ban Trump signed any petition to ban UK terror suspects returning from Iraq/Syria."

Thank you to respected columnist Katie Hopkins of Daily Mail https://t.co/LgtY0qdv9U for her powerful writing on the U.K.'s Muslim problems.
8:00 AM – 10 Dec 2015

Katie Hopkins appeared as a contestant on the British version of *The Apprentice* in 2007. She has since cultivated a reputation as an outspoken right-wing columnist, first with *The Sun* and then with *Mail Online*. Trump linked to her article headlined "Don't demonise Trump, he speaks for millions of Americans. And who can blame them for not wanting to end up like us?"

The politicians of the U.K. should watch Katie Hopkins of Daily https://t.co/LgtY0qdv9U on @FoxNews. Many people in the U.K. agree with me!
8:06 AM – 10 Dec 2015

Hopkins told Fox News "the truth is, a quarter of the population here in the UK are right behind Donald Trump".

In Britain, more Muslims join ISIS than join the British army. https://t.co/LQVNz7b2Eb
8:21 PM – 10 Dec 2015

The *Guardian* fact-checked this claim, concluding "At no point over the past three years has the number of active British Isis fighters eclipsed the number of serving Muslims in the British armed forces."

Looks like @tedcruz is getting ready to attack. I am leading by so much he must. I hope so, he will fall like all others. Will be easy!
7:49 AM – 11 Dec 2015

Dopey Prince @Alwaleed_Talal wants to control our U.S. politicians with daddy's money. Can't do it when I get elected. #Trump2016
10:53 PM – 11 Dec 2015

Prince Alwaleed, a Saudi billionaire, bailed Trump out twice during his financial troubles in the 1990s. Incensed by Trump's threat to ban Muslims, Prince Alwaleed sent a message to Trump by tweeting to his own 4 million Twitter followers: "You are a disgrace not only to the GOP [the Republican Party] but to all America. Withdraw from the US presidential race as you will never win."

I was disappointed that Ted Cruz would speak behind my back, get caught, and then deny it. Well, welcome to the wonderful world of politics!

5:31 PM – 13 Dec 2015

> Trump had been friendly with his rival until this point but Cruz was now rising in the polls. On 10 December *The New York Times* revealed Cruz had told a private fundraising event that Trump was facing a "challenging question" about whether he had the "judgment" to be president and have his finger on the nuclear button.

"@piersmorgan: Donald Trump vs Hillary Clinton would be the greatest presidential battle in history."

2:00 AM – 15 Dec 2015

> Trump once again retweets his friend Piers Morgan.

It was really strange when Hillary was missing from the podium last night. Not very presidential!

6:44 PM – 20 Dec 2015

> Trump is hinting that Clinton's lack of "stamina" indicated a serious secret health problem. Trump would develop this theme.

.@MissUniverse final 3 on now. Great people, great new owner @IMG. WATCH.

9:49 PM – 20 Dec 2015

Very sad what happened last night at the Miss Universe Pageant. I sold it 6 months ago for a record price. This would never have happened!

6:41 AM – 21 Dec 2015

> Shortly after crowning Miss Columbia, the host returned to the stage to explain the winner was actually Miss Philippines.

When I said that Hillary Clinton got schlonged by Obama, it meant got beaten badly. The media knows this. Often used word in politics!

10:37 PM – 22 Dec 2015

> The *Washington Post* found only a single previous instance of use of "schlonged" from a respected political source.

We need a PRESIDENT with strength, stamina, heart and incredible deal making skill if our country is ever going to be able to prosper again!

1:02 AM – 23 Dec 2015

It is hard to believe I am winning by so much when I am treated so badly by the media. New @CNN Poll amazing in ALL categories. 21 pt. Lead

12:20 PM – 23 Dec 2015

Hillary, when you complain about "a penchant for sexism," who are you referring to. I have great respect for women. BE CAREFUL!

6:17 PM – 23 Dec 2015

Next year will be an interesting one. I look forward to running against Hillary Clinton, a totally flawed candidate, and beating her soundly

5:35 PM – 24 Dec 2015

If Hillary thinks she can unleash her husband, with his terrible record of women abuse, while playing the women's card on me, she's wrong!

7:12 AM – 28 Dec 2015

2016

★ ★ ★ ★ ★

All Aboard the Trump Train

I will be on @FoxNews live, with members of my family, at 11:50 P.M. We will ring in the New Year together! MAKE AMERICA GREAT AGAIN!
7:44 PM – 31 Dec 2015

> In a live link from Mar a Lago, Trump broadcast his campaign message for ten minutes before delivering the final New Year countdown. Melania stood immobile at his side in an evening dress.

Well, the year has officially begun. I have many stops planned and will be working very hard to win so that we can turn our country around!
6:00 PM – 1 Jan 2016

"@codyraymille: I have never been interested in politics but because of you I want to get my political science degree. #trump2016" Great!
6:25 PM – 1 Jan 2016

The person that Hillary Clinton least wants to run against is, by far, me. It will be the largest voter turnout ever - she will be swamped!
6:40 PM – 1 Jan 2016

> The 2016 election would see 55 per cent of the voting age population cast ballots, well below the 57 per cent turnout for Obama's first election victory in 2008.

Thank you so much to https://t.co/8OMryrUVET for naming me the 2015 Man of the Year. This is indeed a great honor for me!
10:26 PM – 1 Jan 2016

> World Net Daily is a far-right website notorious for promoting conspiracy theories.

Hillary Clinton doesn't have the strength or stamina to be president. Jeb Bush is a low energy individual, but Hillary is not much better!

3:00 PM – 2 Jan 2016

> Trump often returned to this subject in the course of the campaign, accusing Hillary Clinton of hiding illness and insisting that she was physically unfit to be President. He, on the other hand, claimed to be vigorous and energetic, and his doctor issued a statement that showed, according to Trump, that he would be "the healthiest individual ever elected to the Presidency". Trump is here echoing the claim made by other authoritarian leaders to be strong men in every sense. Vladimir Putin likes to show off his martial arts skills and his prowess as a hunter and daredevil; Mussolini famously enjoyed tiring out his colleagues and showing off his muscles in staged photographs. Trump has not stripped to his vest for the cameras; his strength is entirely virtual.

I hope Bill Clinton starts talking about women's issues so that voters can see what a hypocrite he is and how Hillary abused those women!

3:04 PM – 2 Jan 2016

When I look at all of the money the special interests and lobbyists are giving to candidates, beware - the candidates are mere puppets $$$$!

4:01 PM – 2 Jan 2016

Remember, I am self-funding my campaign, the only one in either party. I'm not controlled by lobbyists or special interests- only the U.S.A.!

4:07 PM – 2 Jan 2016

Hillary said that guns don't keep you safe. If she really believes that she should demand that her heavily armed bodyguards quickly disarm!

9:27 AM – 3 Jan 2016

Love seeing union & non-union members alike are defecting to Trump. I will create jobs like no one else. Their #Dem leaders can't compete!

5:09 PM – 8 Jan 2016

Remember, get TIME magazine! I am on the cover. Take it out in 4 years and read it again! Just watch…

3:15 PM – 10 Jan 2016

> The cover pictured Trump addressing a rally under the headline "How Trump won: now he just needs the votes". The accompanying article was headlined "Donald Trump's art of the steal: how the real estate magnate took the Republican Party from its old bosses".

.@megynkelly recently said that she can't be wooed by Trump. She is so average in every way, who the hell wants to woo her!

3:20 PM – 11 Jan 2016

> Six months after Fox News anchor Megyn Kelly had grilled him on his coarse language about women in the first Republican debate, Trump still can't forget.

Sadly, there is no way that Ted Cruz can continue running in the Republican Primary unless he can erase doubt on eligibility. Dems will sue!

9:26 AM – 13 Jan 2016

> Trump stokes another birther conspiracy theory, this time concerning his rival for the Republican nomination.

[Retweet] @DRUDGE_REPORT: REUTERS ROLLING: TRUMP 39%, CRUZ 14.5%, BUSH 10.6%, CARSON 9.6%, RUBIO 6.7%…
1:23 PM – 13 Jan 2016

More radical Islam attacks today - it never ends! Strengthen the borders, we must be vigilant and smart. No more being politically correct.
9:47 PM – 15 Jan 2016

> Gunmen had attacked a restaurant and hotel in the centre of Ouagadougou, Burkina Faso, killing twenty-nine. Al Qaeda in the Islamic Maghreb claimed responsibility.

Ted Cruz was born in Canada and was a Canadian citizen until 15 months ago. Lawsuits have just been filed with more to follow. I told you so
6:40 AM – 16 Jan 2016

> Trump omitted to mention that Cruz had dual citizenship.

Ted Cruz said he "didn't know" that he was a Canadian Citizen. He also FORGOT to file his Goldman Sachs Million $ loan papers.Not believable
6:49 AM – 16 Jan 2016

Was there another loan that Ted Cruz FORGOT to file. Goldman Sachs owns him, he will do anything they demand. Not much of a reformer!
6:52 AM – 16 Jan 2016

> As President, Trump would appoint numerous past and present Goldman Sachs executives to his cabinet. These include the bank's former president, Gary Cohn, as chair of the National Economic Council and Steven Mnuchin as Treasury Secretary. In mid-March 2017 Trump nominated another Goldman Sachs employee, James Donovan, as Deputy to the Treasury Secretary. Trump's chief strategist, Steve Bannon, also worked

as a Goldman Sachs banker. The Mother Jones website reports that Trump is a member of a real estate partnership that has a $950 million loan put together by Goldman Sachs and the state-owned Bank of China – an arrangement that some experts believe violates the Constitution's emoluments clause.

Ted Cruz is falling in the polls. He is nervous. People are worried about his place of birth and his failure to report his loans from banks!

8:50 PM – 18 Jan 2016

I am greatly honored to receive Sarah Palin's endorsement tonight.

11:05 PM – 19 Jan 2016

John McCain, in an attempt to woo the Tea Party, had chosen Sarah Palin, then Governor of Alaksa, as his running mate in 2008. Palin then electrified the Republican Convention with a speech in which she described herself as "just your average hockey mom". Trump linked to a video of a much more recent speech by Palin. With Trump standing uneasily by her side, she gave her endorsement at a rally in Iowa, "Heads are spinning, media heads are spinning. This is going to be so much fun. Are you ready to make America great again?"… "Right wingin', bitter clingin', proud clingers of our guns, our god, and our religions, and our Constitution… He is from the private sector, not a politician, can I get a 'Hallelujah!'"

So sad that @CNN and many others refused to show the massive crowd at the arena yesterday in Oklahoma. Dishonest reporting!

9:04 AM – 21 Jan 2016

The media pool camera at these rallies focused on the podium, something Trump omitted to acknowledge as he used this line again and again to stir up his supporters.

"@WhiteGenocideTM: @realDonaldTrump Poor Jeb. I could've sworn I saw him outside Trump Tower the other day!"
10:51 AM – 22 Jan 2016

> Trump's Retweet presents a doctored photograph of his rival Jeb Bush holding a card reading "Vote Trump". The real interest, however, concerns the user's account itself. Called "White Genocide TM" it lists its location as "Jewmerica". Instead of the usual background photograph, the viewer is presented with a lurid banner slogan stating "GET THE FUCK OUT OF MY COUNTRY". The account also shockingly linked to a film called *Adolf Hitler: The Greatest Story Never Told*.
>
> Although there is no evidence that Trump harbours Nazi sympathies, the fact that he links to such a website shows how he is naturally attracted to dangerously far-right movements.

Based on @MegynKelly's conflict of interest and bias she should not be allowed to be a moderator of the next debate.
11:52 AM – 23 Jan 2016

I refuse to call Megyn Kelly a bimbo, because that would not be politically correct. Instead I will only call her a lightweight reporter!
6:44 AM – 27 Jan 2016

I hear that @SenTedCruz's $$ man, Robert Mercer, a good man, is very angry because Cruz lied to him about liquidating his (Ted's) holdings.?
2:52 PM – 28 Jan 2016

> Robert Mercer, a hedge-fund billionaire, would soon drop Ted Cruz and become Trump's key backer on his journey to the White House. Mercer certainly put money into the Trump campaign, but his real importance lies elsewhere. Mercer is a mathematical genius, and is believed to be one of the biggest investors in Cambridge Analytica. The company has developed an extremely sophisticated model which uses data gained via

Facebook and other social media to build character profiles of American voters. According to the famous pollster Frank Luntz, "They figured out how to win. There are no longer any experts apart from Cambridge Analytica." Crucially, Mercer was also one of the biggest investors in Steve Bannon's news website Breitbart.

A *New Yorker* profile of Mercer, published in March 2017, highlighted the depth of the connection between Steve Bannon and the Mercer family:

"Years before [Mercer] started supporting Trump, he began funding several conservative activists, including Steve Bannon; as far back as 2012, Bannon was the Mercers' de-facto political adviser. Some people who have observed the Mercers' political evolution worry that Bannon has become a Svengali to the whole family, exploiting its political inexperience and tapping its fortune to further his own ambitions. It was Bannon who urged the Mercers to invest in a data-analytics firm. He also encouraged the investment in Breitbart News… In an interview, Bannon praised the Mercers' strategic approach: 'The Mercers laid the groundwork for the Trump revolution. Irrefutably, when you look at donors during the past four years, they have had the single biggest impact of anybody.'"

Both Mercer and his influential daughter Rebekah are climate change sceptics, funding groups that seek to deny the established science and undermine action to address the problem.

"@piersmorgan: Trump won that debate. People can huff & puff all they like but he was the best candidate on the night. #GOPDebate

5:51 AM – 7 Feb 2016

Trump retweeted his loyal friend's verdict after the eighth GOP debate.

Lying Cruz put out a statement, "Trump & Rubio are w/ Obama on gay marriage." Cruz is the worst liar, crazy or very dishonest. Perhaps all 3?

11:20 PM – 11 Feb 2016

> Trump would soon hone this successful line of abuse into the catchphrase "Lyin' Ted".

How can Ted Cruz be an Evangelical Christian when he lies so much and is so dishonest?

7:03 AM – 12 Feb 2016

> Cruz was now Trump's closest rival in the polls. Trump's ability to attract the evangelical vote, despite his rackety personal life and the heretical theological views he seems to have loosely held for most of his life, was a remarkable feature of his campaign. His pious denunciation of Cruz, who is a genuine and extreme Christian fundamentalist, seems to have been a way of signalling his readiness to concede most of the demands made by his rival's base.

I will be in South Carolina all week. Saturday is BIG, BIG, BIG! Get out and vote - MAKE AMERICA GREAT AGAIN

8:55 AM – 15 Feb 2016

Response to the Pope:

1:07 PM – 18 Feb 2016

> A crisis point for the Trump campaign as he comes under attack from the Pope with potentially devastating consequences for the Catholic vote. After a visit to Mexico, Pope Francis had declared: "A person who thinks only about building walls, wherever they may be, and not building bridges, is not Christian."
>
> In this Tweet Trump directs his followers to his formal response:
>
> "For a religious leader to question a person's faith is disgraceful. I am proud to be a Christian and as President I will not

allow Christianity to be consistently attacked and weakened, unlike what is happening now, with our current President."

What a great night. Thank you South Carolina, a special place with truly amazing people! LOVE
10:01 PM – 20 Feb 2016

> Trump won with 32.5 per cent of the vote. Rubio and Cruz more or less tied for second. Jeb Bush scored less than 8 per cent. Bush announced he was dropping out of the race.

The failing @WSJ Wall Street Journal should fire both its pollster and its Editorial Board. Seldom has a paper been so wrong.Totally biased!
6:52 AM – 21 Feb 2016

> Yet another "failing" newspaper that was less than enthusiastic about Trump. When Rupert Murdoch purchased the *Wall Street Journal* in 2007, he promised to protect the newspaper's independence. This attack on his flagship paper by his friend Donald Trump suggests that he was as good as his word. On 22 March 2017 the *Wall Street Journal* was still attacking Trump over his unsupported claims that President Obama had authorized wiretaps in Trump Tower during the campaign: "The President clings to his assertion like a drunk to an empty gin bottle, rolling out his press spokesman to make more dubious claims."

Many people are now saying I won South Carolina because of the last debate. I showed anger and the people of our country are very angry!
11:12 AM – 22 Feb 2016

Unlike the other Republican candidates, I will be in Nevada all day and night - I won't be fleeing, in and out. I love & invest in Nevada!
12:11 PM – 23 Feb 2016

PM Great. Just reported on @FoxNews that many people who supported @JebBush are now supporting me. I knew that would happen, pundits didn't!

1:12 PM – 23 Feb 2016

THANK YOU NEVADA! #Trump2016 #MakeAmericaGreatAgain

1:25 AM – 24 Feb 2016

> Trump secured nearly 46 per cent of the vote, with Rubio and Cruz achieving 24 per cent and 21 per cent respectively.

Mitt Romney, who was one of the dumbest and worst candidates in the history of Republican politics, is now pushing me on tax returns. Dope!

7:34 AM – 25 Feb 2016

> Mitt Romney had called on Donald Trump to release his tax returns. Trump refused to do so on the grounds that they were still being audited by the US tax authorities. Tax experts pointed out that this was a feeble excuse as there was nothing to stop Trump from releasing his submission even if it were under audit. Trump would later change his position once more and flatly refuse to release his returns whether they were under audit or not.

I'm going to do what @MittRomney was totally unable to do- WIN!

11:44 AM – 25 Feb 2016

Lying Ted Cruz and lightweight choker Marco Rubio teamed up last night in a last ditch effort to stop our great movement. They failed!

11:15 AM – 26 Feb 2016

Tax experts throughout the media agree that no sane person would give their tax returns during an audit. After the audit, no problem!

10:20 AM – 27 Feb 2016

As I stated at the press conference on Friday regarding David Duke- I disavow.

12:35 PM – 28 Feb 2016

> With Super Tuesday looming, Trump gained support from an embarrassing backer. David Duke, leader of the Ku Klux Klan, told radio listeners: "Voting against Donald Trump at this point is really treason to your heritage." When asked for his reaction at a press conference, Trump answered, "I didn't even know he endorsed me… David Duke endorsed me? OK. Alright. I disavow. OK?" Trump had delayed for two days before making this grudging disavowal.

Thank you @SenatorSessions! #MakeAmericaGreatAgain #Trump2016 https://t.co/Szs0QF88HR https://t.co/UL6t60TTjP

8:09 PM – 28 Feb 2016

> Shortly after Trump's endorsement by the leader of the Ku Klux Klan, Alabama Senator Jeff Sessions came out for Trump. In 1986 a Senate committee heard testimony that he had called a black assistant US attorney "boy" while ordering him to be careful how he spoke to "white folks". Even though Sessions disputed this account, he was deemed unfit to be a judge. There were also claims he had joked about the Ku Klux Klan, saying he thought they "were OK" until he heard they smoked marijuana. Sessions would call accusations he had once supported the KKK "damnably false". Sessions is now the Attorney General.

Senator Sessions will serve as the Chairman of my National Security Advisory Committee.

8:20 PM – 3 Mar 2016

> Sessions's conversations with the Russian Ambassador to Washington while acting in this sensitive role would be embarrassingly revealed in March 2017. As a result Sessions, by now Attorney General, was obliged to recuse himself from

all investigations into links between the Trump campaign and Russia.

MAKE AMERICA GREAT AGAIN!

2:52 PM – 1 Mar 2016

Trump greets his supporters following his triumph on Super Tuesday.

Because of me, the Republican Party has taken in millions of new voters, a record. If they are not careful, they will all leave. Sad!

10:05 PM – 2 Mar 2016

"As predicted, Trump reaching out to make peace with Republican "establishment". If he becomes inevitable party would be..."

9:17 AM – 3 Mar 2016

In the wake of Super Tuesday Rupert Murdoch started to come on side. Here Trump retweets Murdoch's call for Republicans to rally behind him.

For all of today's voters please remember that I am the only candidate that is self funding my campaign, I am not bought and paid for!

8:22 AM – 5 Mar 2016

How do you fight millions of dollars of fraudulent commercials pushing for crooked politicians? I will be using Facebook & Twitter. Watch!

9:58 PM – 6 Mar 2016

Thank you Idaho! I love your potatoes- nobody grows them better. As President, I will protect your market.

5:48 PM – 7 Mar 2016

Trump would be smashed by Cruz in Idaho.

Bernie Sanders is lying when he says his disruptors aren't told to go to my events. Be careful Bernie, or my supporters will go to yours!

6:48 AM – 13 Mar 2016

The failing @nytimes is truly one of the worst newspapers. They knowingly write lies and never even call to fact check. Really bad people!

1:53 PM – 13 Mar 2016

> Trump's attack on *The New York Times* came after the newspaper had published a long investigation concluding that his Presidential campaign should be regarded as an attempt to attract attention to himself rather than as a serious attempt to prosecute a political programme.

Word is that, despite a record amount spent on negative and phony ads, I had a massive victory in Florida. Numbers out soon!

6:06 PM – 15 Mar 2016

I only wish my wonderful daughter Tiffany could have been with us at Mar-a-Lago for our great election victory. She is a winner!

9:33 PM – 15 Mar 2016

> A rare mention of Trump's only child by his second wife, Marla Maples, who was not present in Florida to celebrate his win and Rubio's dropping out of the race.

Yesterday was amazing—5 victories. Lyin' Ted Cruz had zero. Things are going very well!

12:04 PM – 16 Mar 2016

> Trump had won in Florida, Illinois, North Carolina and Missouri but lost in Ohio. His fifth victory was in the Northern Mariana Islands, a US dependency in the Pacific Ocean.

Everybody should boycott the @megynkelly show. Never worth watching. Always a hit on Trump! She is sick, & the most overrated person on tv.

4:55 PM – 18 Mar 2016

> Trump still has time to pursue his vendetta with the Fox News presenter Megyn Kelly who had still not been forgiven for asking him tough questions about women in the first Republican debate. His inability to forget a grudge was paradoxical. It demonstrated an alarming thin skin and a robust determination to finish every fight. This may have been part of his appeal: the invention and derision of enemies in the media and the political Establishment gave his campaign the air of a struggle against powerful opponents. "Unfairness" was one of his rallying cries, and many of his supporters believed the entire system was unfair to them economically and culturally.

Why is it that the horrendous protesters, who scream, curse punch, shut down roads/doors during my RALLIES, are never blamed by media? SAD!

11:13 AM – 20 Mar 2016

> Trump encouraged violence at his rallies. He said of one Black Lives Matter protestor who was kicked and hit by his supporters, "Maybe he should have been roughed up." At a rally in Iowa, Trump said: "If you see somebody getting ready to throw a tomato, knock the crap out of them, would you? Seriously. Okay? Just knock the hell – I promise you, I will pay for the legal fees. I promise, I promise. It won't be so much 'cause the courts agree with us too."

Do you all remember how beautiful and safe a place Brussels was. Not anymore, it is from a different world! U.S. must be vigilant and smart!

7:04 AM – 22 Mar 2016

Islamic State-inspired terrorist attacks had killed thirty-five (including three terrorists) at Brussels' airport and on its Metro. One of the victims was a young Muslim woman married to a driver on the Metro, who was left to bring up their three sons. Mohamed el-Bachiri later wrote a moving series of reflections on compassion and tolerance, *A Jihad for Love,* that became a major bestseller in the Netherlands and Belgium.

I have proven to be far more correct about terrorism than anybody- and it's not even close. Hopefully AZ and UT will be voting for me today!

10:32 AM – 22 Mar 2016

My heart & prayers go out to all of the victims of the terrible #Brussels tragedy. This madness must be stopped, and I will stop it.

1:21 PM – 22 Mar 2016

Note how Donald Trump first uses the Brussels atrocities to make a political point before going on to issue a message of sympathy to the victims.

Lyin' Ted Cruz just used a picture of Melania from a G.Q. shoot in his ad. Be careful, Lyin' Ted, or I will spill the beans on your wife!

8:53 PM – 22 Mar 2016

Another low point in Trump's presidential campaign. A Cruz supporting outlet had circulated a picture of a naked Melania Trump, as previously published in a Trump-sanctioned profile piece for *GQ* magazine, in a bid to shock conservative-minded voters. Trump's threat to "spill the beans" on Heidi Cruz was especially unpleasant, given that she is understood to have suffered from depression.

I will be the best by far in fighting terror. I'm the only one that was right from the beginning, & now Lyin' Ted & others are copying me.
2:54 PM – 23 Mar 2016

N.A.T.O. is obsolete and must be changed to additionally focus on terrorism as well as some of the things it is currently focused on!
6:47 AM – 24 Mar 2016

We pay a disproportionate share of the cost of N.A.T.O. Why? It is time to renegotiate, and the time is now!
6:59 AM – 24 Mar 2016

> One of Trump's strongest campaigning points. Most NATO members fail to meet the NATO obligation to devote 2 per cent of GDP to defence spending. Several NATO countries pay less than 1 per cent. Once in the White House, Donald Trump presented German Chancellor Angela Merkel with an invoice for $300 billion.

It is amazing how often I am right, only to be criticized by the media. Illegal immigration, take the oil, build the wall, Muslims, NATO!
9:38 AM – 24 Mar 2016

Just announced that as many as 5000 ISIS fighters have infiltrated Europe. Also, many in U.S. I TOLD YOU SO! I alone can fix this problem!
10:52 AM – 24 Mar 2016

> Trump had picked up the wrong end of the stick. Europol had said that it was worried about "5,000 suspects that have been radicalised in Europe, that have travelled to Syria and Iraq for conflict experience, some of whom, not all, have since come back to Europe". Almost all those responsible for the atrocities in London, Madrid, Brussels and Paris were born in the countries they attacked.

Europe and the U.S. must immediately stop taking in people from Syria. This will be the destruction of civilization as we know it! So sad!

10:55 AM – 24 Mar 2016

Nobody will protect our Nation like Donald J. Trump. Our military will be greatly strengthened and our borders will be strong. Illegals out!

2:20 PM – 26 Mar 2016

For the 1st time in American history, America's 16,500 border patrol agents have issue a presidential primary endorsement— me! Thank you.

9:25 AM – 1 Apr 2016

We must build a great wall between Mexico and the United States!

4:49 PM – 1 Apr 2016

> Trump linked to a *Mail Online* report depicting what it claimed to be drug smugglers scaling a fence in Arizona.

Unbelievable evening. Just made a speech in front 17,000 amazing New Yorkers in Bethpage, Long Island--- great to be home!

7:31 PM – 6 Apr 2016

So great to be in New York. Catching up on many things (remember, I am still running a major business while I campaign) and loving it!

7:03 AM – 8 Apr 2016

"@redneckgp: All you haters out there, STOP trashing the only candidate @realDonaldTrump that will put ALL OF YOU & AMERICA FIRST #trump"

9:32 PM – 8 Apr 2016

Dennis Bryant (Twitter handle "RedneckGP") at this point had seventy-five Twitter followers. He suddenly found himself retweeted to Trump's then 8 million followers. Trump loved to lift his supporters from obscurity. This was one way he established an emotional bond with his supporters.

Bernie Sanders says that Hillary Clinton is unqualified to be president. Based on her decision making ability, I can go along with that!

6:22 AM – 9 Apr 2016

I will be interviewed on @foxandfriends at 9:00 A.M. I will be talking about the rigged and boss controlled Republican primaries!

7:00 AM – 16 Apr 2016

Lyin' Ted Cruz will never be able to beat Hillary. Despite a rigged delegate system, I am hundreds of delegates ahead of him.

8:34 AM – 17 Apr 2016

Shortly after announcing his Presidential run in June 2015, Trump sought advice from his friend and adviser Roger Stone, a New York-based Republican strategist. According to the *Washington Post*, "Stone urged him to state that 'the system is rigged against the citizens' and that he is the lone candidate 'who cannot be bought'." Trump clearly took this advice very seriously indeed. Trump made constant claims of "rigging" against both Democrats and his fellow Republicans during his run for the presidency.

Crooked Hillary Clinton is spending a fortune on ads against me. I am the one person she doesn't want to run against. Will be such fun!

8:41 AM – 17 Apr 2016

This was the first of more than 200 Tweets mentioning "crooked Hillary".

Thank you New York, I will never forget!
10:22 PM – 19 Apr 2016

Though Trump had won the state comfortably, he was not triumphant in his hometown. Republican Manhattan voted for Kasich.

Had a meeting with the terrific @GovPenceIN of Indiana.
So excited to campaign in his wonderful state!
8:58 PM – 20 Apr 2016

Trump would later pick Mike Pence as his Vice Presidential running mate. Pence is one of the surprisingly large number of Irish-American Catholics in the Trump administration. The Governor of Indiana had come to national attention in March 2015 after signing a "religious freedom" law that was designed to allow businesses to refuse serving gay, bisexual and transgender people. Given the questions surrounding the Trump Presidency, there is every possibility that he may one day serve as Commander in Chief.

Passing what was once a vibrant manufacturing area in Pennsylvania. So sad! #MakeAmericaGreatAgain
5:11 PM – 25 Apr 2016

I am in Indiana where we just had a great rally. Fantastic people! Staying at a Holiday Inn Express - new and clean, not bad!
10:17 PM – 27 Apr 2016

Thank you to all for the wonderful reviews of my foreign policy speech. I will soon be speaking in great detail on numerous other topics!
5:41 AM – 28 Apr 2016

Trump spelled out his vision of an isolationist foreign policy: "America first will be the overriding theme of my administration."

The term "America First" was earlier used by the famous aviator and Fascist sympathizer Charles Lindbergh, who campaigned vigorously against the country's entry into World War Two. He blamed America's Jews and the British for the Roosevelt administration's preparations for war.

In his agenda-setting speech, Trump set out an eye-catching new approach to Russia: "I believe an easing of tensions and improved relations with Russia – from a position of strength – is possible. Common sense says this cycle of hostility must end. Some say the Russians won't be reasonable. I intend to find out. If we can't make a good deal for America, then we will quickly walk from the table."

Among the select audience at the Mayflower Hotel in Washington, DC to hear these words was the Russian Ambassador, Sergey Kislyak, who was seated in the front row.

Crooked Hillary Clinton, perhaps the most dishonest person to have ever run for the presidency, is also one of the all time great enablers!

8:46 AM – 29 Apr 2016

Trump later explained why he termed Hillary an "enabler" of Bill's infidelity: "It's only retribution for what she said. She is playing the woman's card to the hilt."

The "protesters" in California were thugs and criminals. Many are professionals. They should be dealt with strongly by law enforcement!

8:31 AM – 30 Apr 2016

Supporters of Donald Trump love to claim that anti-Trump protestors are paid by the billionaire financier George Soros, a notable supporter of Hillary Clinton. The figure of $18 an hour has been bandied about. The Hungarian-born investor, a Jew who survived the Nazi occupation during World War Two, has spent an estimated $12 billion on human rights work. Observers detect an element of anti-Semitism in some of the right-wing attacks on his support for liberal causes.

I will defeat Crooked Hillary Clinton on 11/8/2016. #Trump2016 #MakeAmericaGreatAgain
11:16 AM – 2 May 2016

Wow, Lyin' Ted Cruz really went wacko today. Made all sorts of crazy charges. Can't function under pressure - not very presidential. Sad!
4:02 PM – 3 May 2016

The battle for the Republican nomination takes a surreal turn. Ted Cruz's father Rafael, a Cuban-American preacher, told followers that a Trump victory could mean "the destruction of America". Trump hit back with the remarkable claim that Rafael Cruz had been in contact with the assassin of JFK, a conspiracy theory promoted by the tabloid *National Enquirer*. Trump informed Fox News: "I mean what was he doing with Lee Harvey Oswald, shortly before the death? Before the shooting? It's horrible." There is no evidence that Ted Cruz's father ever met or even spoke to Oswald.

Cruz then hit back, telling CNN: "This man is a pathological liar, he doesn't know the difference between truth and lies… in a pattern that is straight out of a psychology text book, he accuses everyone of lying… Whatever lie he's telling, at that minute he believes it… the man is utterly amoral… Donald is a bully… bullies don't come from strength they come from weakness." Cruz further described Trump as being "a narcissist at a level I don't think this country's ever seen… He is proud of being a serial philanderer… he describes his own battles with venereal diseases as his own personal Vietnam."

Lyin' Ted Cruz consistently said that he will, and must, win Indiana. If he doesn't he should drop out of the race-stop wasting time & money

6:08 PM – 3 May 2016

Thank you Indiana, we were just projected to be the winner. We have won in every category. You are very special people- I will never forget!

6:38 PM – 3 May 2016

> After his defeat in Indiana Ted Cruz suspended his campaign leaving Trump free to focus his attacks on Clinton.

Happy #CincoDeMayo! The best taco bowls are made in Trump Tower Grill. I love Hispanics!

1:57 PM – 5 May 2016

> This Tweet presented a photo of Trump eating tacos at his desk with a silver knife and fork.

So many great endorsements yesterday, except for Paul Ryan! We must put America first and MAKE AMERICA GREAT AGAIN!

5:26 AM – 6 May 2016

Paul Ryan said that I inherited something very special, the Republican Party. Wrong, I didn't inherit it, I won it with millions of voters!

7:08 AM – 6 May 2016

> Paul Ryan was (and remains) the Republican House Speaker and had refused to endorse Trump at this point.

.@KellyannePolls Kellyanne, you were fantastic on @meetthepress today. Keep going - I will win for the people. MAKE AMERICA GREAT AGAIN!

10:30 AM – 8 May 2016

This is the first mention of Kellyanne Conway, a pollster and strategist, soon to become a dominant presence in Trump's inner circle. Conway headed the action committee formed to promote Ted Cruz as Republican nominee, in which role she had criticized Trump for "offending his way to the nomination". In July 2016, with Cruz out of the way, she would officially became leader of Trump's campaign, making her the first woman to lead a Republican Presidential campaign. This was the fulcrum moment for Trump. Conway came with the backing not just of the Mercer family (she is a close friend and ally of Rebekah Mercer), but also as a package with Breitbart's Steve Bannon. According to *The New Yorker*, Bannon told Trump "I've never run a campaign… I'd only do this if Kellyanne came in as my partner."

Crooked Hillary just can't close the deal with Bernie. It will be the same way with ISIS, and China on trade, and Mexico at the border. Bad!
3:15 PM – 8 May 2016

Big wins in West Virginia and Nebraska. Get ready for November - Crooked Hillary, who is looking very bad against Crazy Bernie, will lose!
5:22 AM – 11 May 2016

Thanks Piers.
12:09 PM – 11 May 2016

Morgan had tweeted helpfully: "Trump surging in national polls incl crucial swing states. He's coming for you Hillary… start panicking!"

The failing @nytimes wrote yet another hit piece on me. All are impressed with how nicely I have treated women, they found nothing. A joke!
5:55 AM – 15 May 2016

The New York Times had conducted interviews with a dozen women who revealed "unwelcome romantic advances, unending commentary on the female form, a shrewd reliance on ambitious women, and unsettling workplace conduct". Trump would be confronted with much more damaging evidence of his treatment of women as election day approached.

Why doesn't the failing @nytimes write the real story on the Clintons and women? The media is TOTALLY dishonest!
6:32 AM – 15 May 2016

The media is really on a witch-hunt against me. False reporting, and plenty of it - but we will prevail!
2:26 PM – 15 May 2016

Wow, 30,000 e-mails were deleted by Crooked Hillary Clinton. She said they had to do with a wedding reception. Liar! How can she run?
6:29 AM – 17 May 2016

Trump's Democratic opponent Hillary Clinton was facing an FBI investigation about the use of a private server to deal with her emails when she was Secretary of State. When she was asked to present this email traffic she replied that 30,000 had been deleted because they were private.

Amazing that Crooked Hillary can do a hit ad on me concerning women when her husband was the WORST abuser of woman in U.S. political history
6:58 AM – 17 May 2016

Five years earlier, Trump had told Piers Morgan that Bill Clinton was "a lovely guy… a great guy" who had been treated "very, very harshly" over "the whole Monica thing". This was a reference to Bill Clinton's brief affair with the young White House intern Monica Lewinsky, which led to his impeachment.

Some low-life journalist claims that I "made a pass" at her 29 years ago. Never happened! Like the @nytimes story which has become a joke!

8:54 PM – 18 May 2016

> Lisa Belkin, now Chief National Correspondent for Yahoo News, had written about Trump's behaviour at a launch event when she was a twenty-six-year-old reporter at *The New York Times*: "I had interviewed Trump once for an article and was somehow invited to this event, which I attended with my now husband. I introduced him to Trump, we all chatted briefly, and then Bruce went off to get some hot chocolate or somesuch. After he'd walked away, Trump said there would be an even better afterparty and I was welcome to join him, but only if I came alone."

Thanks @piersmorgan! "Trump is the most unpredictable, extraordinary, entertaining&massively popular candidate this country has ever seen."

11:09 AM – 20 May 2016

How can Crooked Hillary say she cares about women when she is silent on radical Islam, which horribly oppresses women?

2:37 PM – 22 May 2016

I just released my financial disclosure forms, the largest numbers in the history of the F.E.C. Even the dishonest media thinks great!

5:41 AM – 24 May 2016

> Trump told the Federal Election Commission (FEC) that he had earned $557 million the previous financial year and had a net worth in excess of $10 billion dollars. Many experts have disputed these figures. Crucially Trump still refuses to release his tax return which would give a far more reliable picture.

Today we, together, won the Republican Nomination for President!

5:57 PM – 26 May 2016

> Trump passes the required delegate count and avoids the prospect of a contested convention in July, a momentous event both for the Republican Party and for American democracy. An insurgent candidate had secured the GOP nomination despite the entrenched hostility of the entire political Establishment. The United States had entered unknown territory.

Don't believe the biased and phony media quoting people who work for my campaign. The only quote that matters is a quote from me!

4:33 PM – 28 May 2016

> Trump here appears to be disowning comments made by his then campaign manager Paul Manafort who had told the *Huffington Post* Trump would "soften" his approach to a Muslim ban. The political lobbyist has a colourful past advising politicians and dictators around the world. Manafort had particularly strong ties with the Ukraine and had helped the pro-Kremlin government there. He would step away from the Trump campaign in August when reports highlighting his international connections threatened to become a distraction. Questions regarding Manafort's links to Russia would nevertheless persist.

Crooked Hillary Clinton is a fraud who has put the public and country at risk by her illegal and very stupid use of e-mails. Many missing!

5:16 PM – 1 Jun 2016

So great to have the endorsement and support of Paul Ryan. We will both be working very hard to Make America Great Again!

4:12 PM – 2 Jun 2016

The Speaker of the House of Representatives at last comes out in support of Trump.

The Clinton News Network, sometimes referred to as @CNN, is getting more and more biased. They act so indignant-hear them behind closed doors
4:36 PM – 5 Jun 2016

I am watching @CNN very little lately because they are so biased against me. Shows are predictable garbage! CNN and MSM is one big lie!
4:56 PM – 5 Jun 2016

Obama just endorsed Crooked Hillary. He wants four more years of Obama—but nobody else does!
1:22 PM – 9 Jun 2016

In reply, Hillary Clinton issued her most successful Tweet of the campaign, gaining over half a million Retweets. It simply called on Donald Trump to "Delete your account."

How long did it take your staff of 823 people to think that up-- and where are your 33,000 emails that you deleted?
3:40 PM – 9 Jun 2016

Trump duly fired back with a Tweet mocking Clinton as a machine candidate with 823 staff and reminding voters of her alleged criminal offence in deleting emails from her time as Secretary of State. It is worth noting the clever exploitation of numbers, which has echoes of the technique of Senator Joe McCarthy. The figure of 823 has a spurious precision, suggesting firstly that Trump has counted them personally and secondly that collectively the staffers and Hillary have achieved almost nothing (823 divided by 140 implies that it takes about seven staffers to compose each character of a Clinton Tweet). Most important of all it sets up an implied contrast between the two candidates, with Trump as a lone voice, an authentic outsider, his own man. Moreover, although the two numbers relate to completely different things, the jump from 823 to 33,000 adds to the shock value of the latter.

Mitt Romney had his chance to beat a failed president but he choked like a dog. Now he calls me racist-but I am least racist person there is

6:18 AM – 11 Jun 2016

Romney had accused Trump of promoting "trickle-down racism".

Horrific incident in FL. Praying for all the victims & their families. When will this stop? When will we get tough, smart & vigilant?

10:45 AM – 12 Jun 2016

Appreciate the congrats for being right on radical Islamic terrorism, I don't want congrats, I want toughness & vigilance. We must be smart!

11:43 AM – 12 Jun 2016

Omar Mateen, a twenty-nine-year-old security guard, had killed forty-nine people and wounded fifty-three others at a gay nightclub in Orlando. At this stage the motive was not clear though Islamic State was to claim responsibility. Six months later Mateen's widow was arrested and charged with aiding and abetting the attack.

AMERICA FIRST!

7:28 AM – 14 Jun 2016

This Tweet has been liked over 47,000 times.

Hillary took money and did favors for regimes that enslave women and murder gays.

12:16 PM – 21 Jun 2016

While attacking Clinton's ties with Saudi Arabia, Trump omits to mention his own business links with Middle Eastern states and other oppressive regimes.

Hillary says things can't change. I say they have to change. It's a choice between Americanism and her corrupt globalism. #Imwithyou
2:00 PM – 22 Jun 2016

Leaving now for a one night trip to Scotland in order to be at the Grand Opening of my great Turnberry Resort. Will be back on Sat. night!
7:52 PM – 23 Jun 2016

Just arrived in Scotland. Place is going wild over the vote. They took their country back, just like we will take America back. No games!
4:21 AM – 24 Jun 2016

Commercial and political opportunities merge seamlessly here: Trump the populist candidate hailing the Brexit result while plugging his Scottish golf club. A bit of media outreach was thrown into the mix with Trump fitting in a dinner at the resort with Rupert Murdoch and his new wife Jerry Hall.

Statement Regarding British Referendum on E.U. Membership https://t.co/GwWRxT3BVp
4:28 AM – 24 Jun 2016

Trump's statement read as follows:
"The people of the United Kingdom have exercised the sacred right of all free peoples. They have declared their independence from the European Union, and have voted to reassert control over their own politics, borders and economy. A Trump Administration pledges to strengthen our ties with a free and independent Britain, deepening our bonds in commerce,

culture and mutual defense. The whole world is more peaceful and stable when our two countries – and our two peoples – are united together, as they will be under a Trump Administration. Come November, the American people will have the chance to re-declare their independence. Americans will have a chance to vote for trade, immigration and foreign policies that put our citizens first. They will have the chance to reject today's rule by the global elite, and to embrace real change that delivers a government of, by and for the people. I hope America is watching, it will soon be time to believe in America again."

Self-determination is the sacred right of all free people's, and the people of the UK have exercised that right for all the world to see.
5:30 AM – 24 Jun 2016

America is proud to stand shoulder-to-shoulder w/a free & ind UK. We stand together as friends, as allies, & as a people w/a shared history.
5:32 AM – 24 Jun 2016

> Trump omitted to mention that a majority of Scots had voted to stay inside the European Union.

Many people are equating BREXIT, and what is going on in Great Britain, with what is happening in the U.S. People want their country back!
4:43 PM – 24 Jun 2016

> Trump here positions himself – alongside Nigel Farage, Marine Le Pen and Geert Wilders – as leader of a global movement of anti-system politicians.

Crooked Hillary Clinton, who called BREXIT 100% wrong (along with Obama), is now spending Wall Street money on an ad on my correct call.
6:33 AM – 26 Jun 2016

Hillary Clinton is not a change agent, just the same old status quo! She is spending a fortune, I am spending very little. Close in polls!

5:09 PM – 26 Jun 2016

In the second half of the twentieth century liberal Left politicians, of whom Hillary Clinton was one, captured the idea of radical change. By 2016 Clinton's progressive politics had become the symbol of a sclerotic Establishment. Trump took ruthless advantage.

Crooked Hillary -- Makes History! #ImWithYou #AmericaFirst

10:19 AM – 2 Jul 2016

The image that accompanied this Tweet depicted Hillary against a background of dollar bills, overlaid with a six-pointed star, similar to the Jewish Star of David, bearing the text "most corrupt candidate ever". Soon afterwards this original Tweet was deleted and replaced with an image presenting the text in an innocuous circle instead. But there was no apology.

It was just announced-by sources-that no charges will be brought against Crooked Hillary Clinton. Like I said, the system is totally rigged!

4:13 PM – 2 Jul 2016

Dishonest media is trying their absolute best to depict a star in a tweet as the Star of David rather than a Sheriff's Star, or plain star!

8:42 AM – 4 Jul 2016

The media had discovered that the image had originally appeared on far-right websites.

FBI director said Crooked Hillary compromised our national security. No charges. Wow! #RiggedSystem

10:39 AM – 5 Jul 2016

I don't think the voters will forget the rigged system that allowed Crooked Hillary to get away with "murder." Come November 8, she's out!
11:30 PM – 5 Jul 2016

> Extreme-Right websites (as well as Trump's close friend Rush Limbaugh) were disseminating the theory that Bill and Hillary Clinton had ordered rivals to be murdered. It looks as if Trump is giving a nod in their direction in this Tweet.

To all of my twitter followers, please contribute whatever you can to the campaign. We must beat Crooked Hillary.
4:58 PM – 6 Jul 2016

After today, Crooked Hillary can officially be called Lyin' Crooked Hillary.
8:52 PM – 7 Jul 2016

The media is so dishonest. If I make a statement, they twist it and turn it to make it sound bad or foolish.They think the public is stupid!
1:42 PM – 10 Jul 2016

Bernie Sanders, who has lost most of his leverage, has totally sold out to Crooked Hillary Clinton. He will endorse her today - fans angry!
8:36 AM – 12 Jul 2016

Bernie Sanders endorsing Crooked Hillary Clinton is like Occupy Wall Street endorsing Goldman Sachs.
12:01 PM – 12 Jul 2016

> An acute comment. Bernie Sanders was as much of an insurgent candidate as Trump himself. Sanders delivered his endorsement of Hillary Clinton as the "anyone but Trump" candidate through gritted teeth, and no wonder. Hillary Clinton's brand of Establishment politics failed to galvanize crucial sections of

the Democratic working-class base as well as leaving the left-wing movements who had been energized by Sanders feeling stranded. Some observers have speculated that Sanders might have beaten Trump to the White House had he secured the Democratic nomination.

To all the Bernie voters who want to stop bad trade deals & global special interests, we welcome you with open arms. People first.

12:04 PM – 12 Jul 2016

I am pleased to announce that I have chosen Governor Mike Pence as my Vice Presidential running mate. News conference tomorrow at 11:00 A.M.

9:50 AM – 15 Jul 2016

.@FoxNews is much better, and far more truthful, than @CNN, which is all negative. Guests are stacked for Crooked Hillary! I don't watch.

8:04 AM – 17 Jul 2016

Looking forward to being at the convention tonight to watch all of the wonderful speakers including my wife, Melania. Place looks beautiful!

12:28 PM – 18 Jul 2016

It was truly an honor to introduce my wife, Melania. Her speech and demeanor were absolutely incredible. Very proud! #GOPConvention

11:14 PM – 18 Jul 2016

Such a great honor to be the Republican Nominee for President of the United States. I will work hard and never let you down! AMERICA FIRST!

6:52 PM – 19 Jul 2016

The media is spending more time doing a forensic analysis of
Melania's speech than the FBI spent on Hillary's emails.
10:36 AM – 20 Jul 2016

> Masterful. After his nomination as Republican candidate,
> Trump's wife Melania was widely mocked for plagiarizing a
> speech by Michelle Obama. Trump cleverly managed to switch
> the agenda back to Hillary Clinton's alleged criminal behaviour
> while skewering the media and the FBI as co-conspirators
> against his candidacy.

I highly recommend the just out book - THE FIELD OF FIGHT -
by General Michael Flynn. How to defeat radical Islam.
10:49 PM – 22 Jul 2016

> Trump later appointed General Mike Flynn as his National
> Security Advisor. Flynn resigned just three weeks and three days
> into his role after it was revealed he had misled the Vice President
> Mike Pence about his dealings with the Russian Ambassador.

Leaked e-mails of DNC show plans to destroy Bernie Sanders.
Mock his heritage and much more. On-line from Wikileakes,
really vicious. RIGGED
5:55 AM – 23 Jul 2016

> This is the first mention of Wikileaks, the website set up by
> Julian Assange. It first came to public notice with the mass
> release of diplomatic cables, leaked by Bradley Manning, a
> serving US soldier. These caused acute embarrassment to the
> US government. Today Julian Assange is a fugitive from justice
> in London's Ecuadorian Embassy, from where he would come
> to exercise a profound influence over the Presidential election.
> He made no bones about the fact that he wanted to damage
> Hillary Clinton. Assange is a hero on the radical Left. Normally
> such a figure would be regarded as a traitor by any Republican
> Presidential candidate yet Donald Trump would form a tacit
> alliance with Assange and Wikileaks as the Presidential
> election approached.

The Wikileaks e-mail release today was so bad to Sanders that it will make it impossible for him to support her, unless he is a fraud!

4:20 PM – 23 Jul 2016

> The leaked emails showed that the Democratic party machine had tilted some of the primary contests against Sanders and in favour of Clinton. These revelations help to explain why Hillary Clinton, the classic Establishment triangulating candidate, failed to generate popular enthusiasm.

Wow, President Obama's brother, Malik, just announced that he is voting for me. Was probably treated badly by president- like everybody else!

6:56 AM – 24 Jul 2016

> Obama's estranged half brother is a darling of the alt-right for his contrarian agitation. He tweets to his 186,000 followers under the handle @ObamaMalik and his profile photograph shows him sporting a Make America Great Again red baseball cap.

The new joke in town is that Russia leaked the disastrous DNC e-mails, which should never have been written (stupid), because Putin likes me

6:31 AM – 25 Jul 2016

> In December 2015, six months before Trump secured the Republican nomination, Putin described him as "a colourful person, talented, without any doubt… It is not our business to decide his merits, that is for US voters, but he is absolutely the leader in the presidential race." Russian state media had followed Putin's lead in giving Trump favourable coverage. Four days before this Tweet by Trump, the head of the Duma's foreign affairs committee, Aleksey Pushkov, had added his support: "Clinton's credo is to strengthen US alliances against Russia; Trump's credo is only to respond to real threats. Aggressive banality versus common sense." In early

2017 the head of the FBI would confirm that Russian hackers had obtained emails relating to both the Republican and Democratic parties but that only those relating to the latter had been leaked.

The invention of email has proven to be a very bad thing for Crooked Hillary in that it has proven her to be both incompetent and a liar!

2:27 PM – 26 Jul 2016

In 2007, in a sworn deposition, Trump stated "I don't do the email thing".

In order to try and deflect the horror and stupidity of the Wikileakes disaster, the Dems said maybe it is Russia dealing with Trump. Crazy!

5:47 PM – 26 Jul 2016

For the record, I have ZERO investments in Russia.

5:50 PM – 26 Jul 2016

Questions surrounding Russian involvement in Trump's election campaign would continue to be asked.

Funny how the failing @nytimes is pushing Dems narrative that Russia is working for me because Putin said "Trump is a genius." America 1st!

4:43 AM – 27 Jul 2016

If Russia or any other country or person has Hillary Clinton's 33,000 illegally deleted emails, perhaps they should share them with the FBI!

11:16 AM – 27 Jul 2016

Eye-catching in the light of later claims that Russia helped Trump to win the Presidency by selectively releasing information it had hacked from the campaigns. Trump here appears to be asking

Russia to intervene in the election by releasing what it may have found on Hillary Clinton's private server.

Our country does not feel 'great already' to the millions of wonderful people living in poverty, violence and despair.

9:42 PM – 27 Jul 2016

Trump responds to Obama's speech to the Democratic National Convention: "America is already great. America is already strong. And I promise you, our strength, our greatness, does not depend on Donald Trump." The following day Clinton accepted the Democratic nomination and delivered her speech to the convention. Donald Trump sought to muscle in on the event by live-tweeting his own commentary which follows below.

Hillary will never reform Wall Street. She is owned by Wall Street!

10:52 PM – 28 Jul 2016

Hillary's vision is a borderless world where working people have no power, no jobs, no safety.

10:54 PM – 28 Jul 2016

Hillary's wars in the Middle East have unleashed destruction, terrorism and ISIS across the world.

10:57 PM – 28 Jul 2016

No one has worse judgement than Hillary Clinton - corruption and devastation follows her wherever she goes.

10:59 PM – 28 Jul 2016

The "Rust Belt" was created by politicians like the Clintons who allowed our jobs to be stolen from us by other countries like Mexico. END!

5:12 PM – 30 Jul 2016

Wow, NATO's top commander just announced that he agrees with me that alliance members must PAY THEIR BILLS. This is a general I will like!

5:18 PM – 30 Jul 2016

Nielson Media Research final numbers on ACCEPTANCE SPEECH: TRUMP 32.2 MILLION. CLINTON 27.8 MILLION. Thank you!

10:32 PM – 30 Jul 2016

I was viciously attacked by Mr. Khan at the Democratic Convention. Am I not allowed to respond? Hillary voted for the Iraq war, not me!

8:32 AM – 31 Jul 2016

Khizr Khan was the father of American military Captain Humayun Khan, killed in a suicide attack in Iraq in 2004 and posthumously awarded a Purple Heart and Bronze Star. Mr Khan and his wife Ghazala made a moving and dignified joint appearance on stage at the Democratic National Convention. With his wife at his side, Mr Khan declared that they were "patriotic American Muslims – with undivided loyalty to our country… If it was up to Donald Trump, [our son] never would have been in America. Donald Trump consistently smears the character of Muslims. He disrespects other minorities; women; judges; even his own party leadership."

Holding up his well-worn copy of the Constitution, Khan offered to lend it to Trump: "In this document, look for the words 'liberty' and 'equal protection of law'. Have you ever been to Arlington Cemetery? Go look at the graves of brave patriots who died defending the United States of America. You will see all faiths, genders and ethnicities. You have sacrificed nothing and no one."

Trump counter attacked, implying that Mrs Khan "wasn't allowed" to speak due to her Muslim faith. "If you look at his wife, she was standing there. She had nothing to say. She probably, maybe she wasn't allowed to have anything to say. You tell me."

As to sacrifices? Trump insisted he had "made lots of sacrifices": "I work very, very hard. I've created thousands and thousands of jobs, tens of thousands of jobs, built great structures. I've had tremendous success. I think I've done a lot." Trump did not mention that he had avoided serving in Vietnam.

I am not just running against Crooked Hillary Clinton, I am running against the very dishonest and totally biased media - but I will win!
8:53 PM – 6 Aug 2016

I love watching these poor, pathetic people (pundits) on television working so hard and so seriously to try and figure me out. They can't!
6:43 AM – 12 Aug 2016

Trump issued this Tweet in the wake of a row over his assertion that President Obama was "the founder of ISIS", the Islamic State. Under pressure, Trump claimed his remarks were sarcastic. Later still, Trump changed his tune again: "obviously I'm being sarcastic, but not that sarcastic, to be honest with you".

The failing @nytimes has become a newspaper of fiction. Their stories about me always quote non-existent unnamed sources. Very dishonest!
1:29 PM – 13 Aug 2016

I am truly enjoying myself while running for president. The people of our country are amazing - great numbers on November 8th!
1:39 PM – 13 Aug 2016

If the disgusting and corrupt media covered me honestly and didn't put false meaning into the words I say, I would be beating Hillary by 20%
7:37 AM – 14 Aug 2016

My rallies are not covered properly by the media. They never discuss the real message and never show crowd size or enthusiasm.
7:46 AM – 14 Aug 2016

I am not only fighting Crooked Hillary, I am fighting the dishonest and corrupt media and her government protection process. People get it!
11:55 AM – 14 Aug 2016

It is not "freedom of the press" when newspapers and others are allowed to say and write whatever they want even if it is completely false!
12:06 PM – 14 Aug 2016

I have always been the same person-remain true to self. The media wants me to change but it would be very dishonest to supporters to do so!
6:57 PM – 14 Aug 2016

> Trump yet again portrays himself as a victim of the so-called mainstream media. This is not entirely true. Trump enjoyed the consistent support of Fox, the largest cable news network.

'It's just a 2-point race, Clinton 38%, Trump 36%'
2:22 PM – 16 Aug 2016

They will soon be calling me MR. BREXIT!
7:11 AM – 18 Aug 2016

> A week later, Nigel Farage, cheerleader of the Leave.EU campaign, will join Trump on stage at a rally in Jackson, Mississippi.

Thank you to everyone for all of the nice comments, by Twitter, pundits and otherwise for my speech last night.
8:27 AM – 19 Aug 2016

#WheresHillary? Sleeping!!!!!
7:17 PM – 19 Aug 2016

> He uses "Where's Hillary?" as a hashtag in a clever attempt to spur a Twitter conversation.

.@AnnCoulter's new book, 'In Trump We Trust, comes out tomorrow. People are saying it's terrific - knowing Ann I am sure it is!
7:56 PM – 22 Aug 2016

> Coulter had tilted towards alt-right and white nationalist positions, and pivoted towards Russia. She had told Breitbart News in March: "The Left's hysteria about Russia isn't just an attempt to delegitimize Trump. It's the usual Christophobic fifth column rooting for the Islamization of the West."

The @WashingtonPost quickly put together a hit job book on me- comprised of copies of some of their inaccurate stories. Don't buy, boring!
8:02 PM – 22 Aug 2016

What do African-Americans and Hispanics have to lose by going with me. Look at the poverty, crime and educational statistics. I will fix it!
9:20 AM – 26 Aug 2016

I think that both candidates, Crooked Hillary and myself, should release detailed medical records. I have no problem in doing so! Hillary?
6:24 PM – 28 Aug 2016

> Once again, Trump is trying to tie Hillary's health into a campaign issue.

Great trip to Mexico today - wonderful leadership and high quality people! Look forward to our next meeting.
7:43 PM – 31 Aug 2016

> Mexican President Enrique Peña Nieto tweeted after his meeting with Trump, "I made it clear that Mexico will not pay for the wall." Even Trump had to admit that the two leaders "didn't discuss payment of the wall". However, Nieto was widely derided in Mexico for having the meeting at all.

Mexico will pay for the wall - 100%! #MakeAmericaGreatAgain #ImWithYou
11:58 PM – 31 Aug 2016

Wow, the failing @nytimes has not reported properly on Crooked's FBI release. They are at the back of the pack - no longer a credible source
7:55 AM – 4 Sep 2016

The polls are close so Crooked Hillary is getting out of bed and will campaign tomorrow. Why did she hammer 13 devices and acid-wash e-mails?
6:17 PM – 4 Sep 2016

Mainstream media never covered Hillary's massive "hacking" or coughing attack, yet it is #1 trending. What's up?
10:31 AM – 6 Sep 2016

.@CNN is unwatchable. Their news on me is fiction. They are a disgrace to the broadcasting industry and an arm of the Clinton campaign.
9:37 AM – 9 Sep 2016

Dummy writer @tonyschwartz, who wanted to do a second book with me for years (I said no), is now a hostile basket case who feels jilted!
12:47 AM – 10 Sep 2016

I havn't seen @tonyschwartz in many years, he hardly knows me. Never liked his style. Super lib, Crooked H supporter. Irrelevant dope!

12:57 AM – 10 Sep 2016

Tony Schwartz was the ghostwriter of Trump's bestselling book *The Art of the Deal*. In a blistering interview, Schwartz told *The New Yorker* that he had found it impossible to keep Trump "focused on any topic, other than his own self-aggrandizement, for more than a few minutes". Schwartz also said that Trump has "a stunning level of superficial knowledge and plain ignorance. That's why he so prefers TV as his first news source – information comes in easily digestible sound bites. I seriously doubt that Trump has ever read a book straight through in his adult life."

Wow, Hillary Clinton was SO INSULTING to my supporters, millions of amazing, hard working people. I think it will cost her at the Polls!

7:47 AM – 10 Sep 2016

Trump responds to Hilary Clinton's ill-judged phrase, "basket of deplorables". Deplorable would be embraced by Trump's more fervent supporters as a badge of honour. It is instructive to note the full context in which Clinton delivered the phrase while speaking to an audience of her supporters from the LGBT communities:

"We are living in a volatile political environment. You know, to just be grossly generalistic, you could put half of Trump's supporters into what I call the basket of deplorables. Right? The racist, sexist, homophobic, xenophobic, Islamaphobic – you name it. And unfortunately there are people like that. And he has lifted them up. He has given voice to their websites that used to only have 11,000 people – now 11 million. He tweets and retweets their offensive hateful mean-spirited rhetoric. Now, some of those folks – they are irredeemable, but thankfully they are not America."

"@brimyers813: Saw ur speech on Twitter. U give me
hope and optimism. I feel as though I am in the room with u.
I pray 4 ur/our success."
7:49 PM – 12 Sep 2016

I am now going to the brand new Trump International, Hotel
D.C. for a major statement.
8:23 AM – 16 Sep 2016

> A humiliating moment for Donald Trump. Under pressure
> from the Republican Establishment he was forced to admit
> President Obama was born in the United States. However, by
> an extraordinary sleight of hand, Trump turned this event to
> his advantage by using it to promote his new Washington, DC
> Hotel.

"Donald Trump's birther event is the greatest trick he's
ever pulled"
12:15 AM – 17 Sep 2016

Do people notice Hillary is copying my airplane rallies - she puts
the plane behind her like I have been doing from the beginning.
9:20 AM – 20 Sep 2016

Hillary Clinton is taking the day off again, she needs the rest.
Sleep well Hillary - see you at the debate!
9:23 AM – 20 Sep 2016

It is a MOVEMENT - not a campaign. Leaving the past behind,
changing our future. Together, we will MAKE AMERICA SAFE
AND GREAT AGAIN!
6:17 AM – 21 Sep 2016

My team of deplorables will be managing my Twitter account for
this evenings debate. Tune in! #DebateNight #TrumpPence16
5:31 PM – 26 Sep 2016

[Retweet] @DanScavino: Join @realDonaldTrump on his official social media platforms during tonight's debate ~ as @ TeamTrump manages rapid response…

6:30 PM – 26 Sep 2016

> Trump here retweets his social media director, Dan Scavino. Scavino is one of the more unlikely members of the Trump campaign team. He met the future President in 1990 when he caddied for Trump. He would go on to become general manager of Trump National Golf Club and travel the world with Trump visiting courses. He was appointed social media director of the campaign in February 2015. Scavino is said to sit next to Trump as he dictates his Twitter posts.
>
> The Tweets issued from the Trump account during the debate were all generated by Scavino.

This is the simple fact about @HillaryClinton: she is a typical politician - all talk, no action. #Debates2016

8:36 PM – 26 Sep 2016

.@HillaryClinton's 2008 Campaign And Supporters Trafficked In Rumors About Obama's Heritage #DebateNight

9:19 PM – 26 Sep 2016

> Here Trump blames Clinton for the birther controversy that he himself prosecuted so vigorously for half a decade.

Hillary Clinton is the only candidate on stage who voted for the Iraq War. #Debates2016 #MAGA

9:21 PM – 26 Sep 2016

Hillary Clinton failed all over the world. X LIBYA X SYRIA X IRAN X IRAQ X ASIA PIVOT X RUSSIAN RESET X BENGHAZI #DebateNight

9:26 PM – 26 Sep 2016

Nothing on emails. Nothing on the corrupt Clinton Foundation. And nothing on #Benghazi. #Debates2016 #debatenight

9:40 PM – 26 Sep 2016

Wow, did great in the debate polls (except for @CNN - which I don't watch). Thank you!

11:34 PM – 26 Sep 2016

Great debate poll numbers - I will be on @foxandfriends at 7:00 to discuss. Enjoy!

5:44 AM – 27 Sep 2016

> All mainstream polls and focus groups asserted that Donald Trump had lost resoundingly. But Trump sought consolation in the unofficial online polls.

The #1 trend on Twitter right now is #TrumpWon - thank you!

8:17 AM – 27 Sep 2016

'True blue-collar billionaire Donald Trump shows Hillary Clinton is out of touch'

8:49 AM – 27 Sep 2016

> Linking to a piece in the *Boston Herald*.

Did Crooked Hillary help disgusting (check out sex tape and past) Alicia M become a U.S. citizen so she could use her in the debate?

4:30 AM – 30 Sep 2016

> This notorious Tweet was one of the lowest points of Trump's Presidential campaign. The Alicia M referred to here is Alicia Machado who as Miss Venezuela won Trump's Miss Universe competition in 1996. Hillary Clinton had used her as a weapon against Trump during the first Presidential debate in order to illustrate Trump's long record of derogatory remarks towards women, as well as his casual racism. Clinton repeated Trump's description of Machado as "Miss Piggy", a reference to her

supposed weight gain after winning the beauty contest, and "Miss Housekeeping", a slur on her Hispanic background. Clinton summed up her attack as follows: "Her name is Alicia Machado and she has become a US citizen, and you can bet she's going to vote this November." Trump was unable to find an effective response during the debate but used Twitter in the early hours of the morning two days later to fight back.

For those few people knocking me for tweeting at three o'clock in the morning, at least you know I will be there, awake, to answer the call!

1:37 PM – 30 Sep 2016

This Tweet is a supreme example of Trump's ability to turn the tables on his opponents. Hillary Clinton had famously failed to wake in the night to respond to the attack on the American Embassy in Benghazi.

I know our complex tax laws better than anyone who has ever run for president and am the only one who can fix them. #failing@nytimes

6:22 AM – 2 Oct 2016

The New York Times had just revealed details of Trump's 1995 tax return which revealed he paid no tax after declaring a $916 million loss. With the artistry of a Judo black belt, Trump turned the story to his advantage.

I have created tens of thousands of jobs and will bring back great American prosperity. Hillary has only created jobs at the FBI and DOJ!

6:35 AM – 2 Oct 2016

Trump neatly contrasts himself the job creator versus "Crooked Hillary" who creates jobs only through her (presumed) criminal offences.

I will be watching the great Governor @Mike_Pence and live tweeting the VP debate tonight starting at 8:30pm est! Enjoy!

2:40 PM – 4 Oct 2016

Unable to resist upstaging his Vice Presidential running mate.

CLINTON'S CLOSE TIES TO PUTIN DESERVE SCRUTINY: https://t.co/wPYm5vQoyt #VPDebate

9:16 PM – 4 Oct 2016

This Tweet links to a long statement issued by the Trump campaign: *"Four Times When Hillary Clinton and Her Allies Sold Out American Interests to Putin in Exchange for Political and Financial Favor"*.

Mike Pence won big. We should all be proud of Mike!

9:36 PM – 4 Oct 2016

Volunteer to be a Trump Election Observer. Sign up today! #MakeAmericaGreatAgain

3:45 PM – 6 Oct 2016

Stoking voter fraud and election-rigging fears.

Here is my statement.

11:19 PM – 7 Oct 2016

This was the most dangerous moment of Trump's Presidential campaign. Even Trump's closest supporters believed he was finished after the release of an old tape in which he used outrageous and obscene language about women.

There were calls for Trump to quit the campaign and senior Republicans refused to support him. The crisis was so grave that Trump did not respond with a Tweet. Instead, after twenty-four hours of silence Trump released the following carefully prepared statement:

"I've never said I'm a perfect person, nor pretended to be

someone that I'm not. I've said and done things I regret, and the words released today on this more than a decade-old video are one of them. Anyone who knows me, know these words don't reflect who I am.

"I said it, it was wrong, and I apologize.

"I've travelled the country talking about change for America. But my travels have also changed me. I've spent time with grieving mothers who've lost their children, laid-off workers whose jobs have gone to other countries, and people from all walks of life who just want a better future. I have gotten to know the great people of our country, and I've been humbled by the faith they've placed in me. I pledge to be a better man tomorrow, and will never, ever let you down. Let's be honest. We're living in the real world. This is nothing more than a distraction from the important issues we are facing today. We are losing our jobs, we are less safe than we were eight years ago and Washington is broken. Hillary Clinton, and her kind, have run our country into the ground.

"I've said some foolish things, but there is a big difference between words and actions. Bill Clinton has actually abused women and Hillary has bullied, attacked, shamed and intimidated his victims. We will discuss this more in the coming days.

"See you at the debate on Sunday."

Certainly has been an interesting 24 hours!
9:48 AM – 8 Oct 2016

The following morning Trump returned to Twitter.

The media and establishment want me out of the race so badly - I WILL NEVER DROP OUT OF THE RACE, WILL NEVER LET MY SUPPORTERS DOWN! #MAGA
2:40 PM – 8 Oct 2016

The most impressive example of Trump turning defence into attack. In a remarkably short time Trump presented himself as a real human being who had never pretended to be something he was not, as champion of the people forgotten by a broken Washington Establishment and by "Hillary Clinton and her kind". He tried to make voters believe that Bill Clinton had actually behaved worse towards women, with Hillary's collusion, than Trump himself. A day later on Twitter, aware that this defence had been successful at least with his own supporters, Trump renewed his defiance of the "Establishment" who were trying to force him out of the race.

Tremendous support (except for some Republican "leadership"). Thank you.

8:00 AM – 9 Oct 2016

So many self-righteous hypocrites. Watch their poll numbers - and elections - go down!

9:12 AM – 9 Oct 2016

I'm not proud of my locker room talk. But this world has serious problems. We need serious leaders. #debate #BigLeagueTruth

8:13 PM – 9 Oct 2016

There's never been anyone more abusive to women in politics than Bill Clinton.My words were unfortunate-the Clintons' actions were far worse

8:23 PM – 9 Oct 2016

If I win-I am going to instruct my AG to get a special prosecutor to look into your situation bc there's never been anything like your lies.

8:27 PM – 9 Oct 2016

Chants of "LOCK HER UP!" were now common to Trump's rallies. At his debate with Clinton on 9 October, Trump assured her that she would be in jail after his election.

Basically nothing Hillary has said about her secret server has been true. #CrookedHillary

8:28 PM – 9 Oct 2016

History lesson: There's a big difference between Hillary Clinton and Abraham Lincoln. For one, his nickname is Honest Abe. #RattledHillary

9:00 PM – 9 Oct 2016

The world is most peaceful, and most prosperous when America is strongest.

9:07 PM – 9 Oct 2016

Despite winning the second debate in a landslide (every poll), it is hard to do well when Paul Ryan and others give zero support!

7:16 AM – 11 Oct 2016

Our very weak and ineffective leader, Paul Ryan, had a bad conference call where his members went wild at his disloyalty.

8:05 AM – 11 Oct 2016

> The Speaker of House, Paul Ryan, and the most senior ranking Republican, told his party that he would not be campaigning for Trump.

It is so nice that the shackles have been taken off me and I can now fight for America the way I want to.

9:00 AM – 11 Oct 2016

With the exception of cheating Bernie out of the nom the Dems have always proven to be far more loyal to each other than the Republicans!

9:15 AM – 11 Oct 2016

Disloyal R's are far more difficult than Crooked Hillary.
They come at you from all sides. They don't know how to win -
I will teach them!
9:48 AM – 11 Oct 2016

Wow. Unbelievable.
10:25 AM – 11 Oct 2016

> Trump linked to a report of a further tranche of emails hacked
> from the account of John Podesta, chairman of the Clinton
> campaign.

I hope people are looking at the disgraceful behavior of Hillary
Clinton as exposed by WikiLeaks. She is unfit to run.
12:43 PM – 11 Oct 2016

> The Democrats hit back, accusing Wikileaks, now spelt
> correctly by Trump in this Tweet, as being a "propaganda arm
> of the Russian government" seeking to help elect him.

Very little pick-up by the dishonest media of incredible information
provided by WikiLeaks. So dishonest! Rigged system!
8:46 AM – 12 Oct 2016

Why didn't the writer of the twelve year old article in People
Magazine mention the "incident" in her story. Because it did
not happen!
8:09 AM – 13 Oct 2016

> Natasha Stoynoff had claimed that Trump had made sexual
> advances during an interview at Mar a Lago. *People* editor-in-
> chief Jess Cagle stood by the reporter, calling her "a remarkable,
> ethical, honest and patriotic woman".

"This is a crossroads in the history of our civilization that will determine whether or not We The People reclaim control over our gov't!"
5:50 PM – 13 Oct 2016

100% fabricated and made-up charges, pushed strongly by the media and the Clinton Campaign, may poison the minds of the American Voter. FIX!
5:51 AM – 15 Oct 2016

> More and more women were going public with claims that Trump had abused them.

This election is being rigged by the media pushing false and unsubstantiated charges, and outright lies, in order to elect Crooked Hillary!
6:45 AM – 15 Oct 2016

Hillary Clinton should have been prosecuted and should be in jail. Instead she is running for president in what looks like a rigged election
7:23 AM – 15 Oct 2016

Nothing ever happened with any of these women. Totally made up nonsense to steal the election. Nobody has more respect for women than me!
1:29 PM – 15 Oct 2016

The failing @nytimes reporters don't even call us anymore, they just write whatever they want to write, making up sources along the way!
5:49 PM – 15 Oct 2016

Watched Saturday Night Live hit job on me.Time to retire the boring and unfunny show. Alec Baldwin portrayal stinks. Media rigging election!
6:14 AM – 16 Oct 2016

> Trump changes his mind about *Saturday Night Live*, the comedy
> sketch show he had hosted a year before.

Wow, interview released by Wikileakes shows "quid pro quo" in
Crooked Hillary e-mail probe.Such a dishonest person - & Paul
Ryan does zilch!
5:15 PM – 16 Oct 2016

"@THEREALMOGUL: 41% of American voters believe
the election could be "stolen" from DonaldTrump due to
widespread voter fraud. - Politico"
6:32 AM – 18 Oct 2016

> Trump's strategy of spreading disillusion in the electoral
> process has worked.

If we let Crooked run the govt, history will remember 2017 as
the year America lost its independence. #DrainTheSwamp
https://t.co/VpYiO8CnXQ
6:32 AM – 18 Oct 2016

It is time to #DrainTheSwamp in Washington, D.C! Vote Nov.
8th to take down the #RIGGED system!
1:25 PM – 18 Oct 2016

The media refuses to talk about the three new national polls
that have me in first place. Biggest crowds ever - watch what
happens!
10:33 PM – 21 Oct 2016

Former Prosecutor: The Clintons Are So Corrupt, Everything
'They Touch Turns To Molten Lead'
11:30 AM – 23 Oct 2016

"@piersmorgan: BOMBSHELL: FBI reopening its investigation into HillaryClinton's email server after new discovery!
8:30 PM – 28 Oct 2016

> The turning point in the presidential campaign. FBI Director James Comey writes to Congress stating that the FBI had reopened its investigation into Hillary Clinton's use of her private server after apparently "new" emails had been found on a laptop used by Anthony Weiner, the husband of Clinton's close aide Huma Abedin. Trump alerts his followers by retweeting Piers Morgan.

Wow, Twitter, Google and Facebook are burying the FBI criminal investigation of Clinton. Very dishonest media!
9:26 AM – 30 Oct 2016

> Trump uses no evidence to support this unlikely claim. In fact the use of Twitter hashtags, #ClintonEmails, #Comey, and #FBI had surged.

Thank you Orlando, Florida! We are just six days away from delivering justice for every forgotten man, woman and and child in this country!
4:30 PM – 2 Nov 2016

> Trump used "forgotten" to define his constituency and the basis of victory. The term has deep roots in modern US history. It is an echo both of Roosevelt's use of the "forgotten man" in a famous 1932 speech about those left at the bottom of American society without any government support, and of Sinclair Lewis's 1935 novel *It Can't Happen Here*. The anti-hero, Senator Buzz Windrip, exploits an existing political organization, the League of Forgotten Men, to win the 1936 election. One of the most popular films of the 1930s, *Gold Diggers of 1933*, had a spectacular musical number called "Remember My Forgotten Man" that featured returning soldiers from the First World War abandoned to poverty. The "forgotten" trope would be repeated on 9 November and thereafter.

225

[Retweet] @PaulaReidCBS: .@CBSNews confirms FBI found emails on #AnthonyWeiner computer, related to Hillary Clinton server, that are "new" & not previously reviewed.

6:30 PM – 3 Nov 2016

On 6 November, just two days before the election, James Comey wrote a further letter to Congress stating that the FBI had completed its review of the emails on Weiner's laptop. Comey said that he had found nothing to alter his earlier conclusion of July that, though she had been "extremely careless", Hillary Clinton had not committed a crime. Trump nevertheless used the FBI's volte face as further evidence that the whole system was "rigged". Clinton believes that the FBI's late intervention cost her victory. The Princeton Election Consortium point out that following Comey's first letter Trump gained a 4 per cent swing, half of which remained in place: "This was larger than the victory margin in Michigan, Pennsylvania, Florida, and Wisconsin. Many factors went into this year's Presidential race, but on the home stretch, Comey's letter appears to have been a critical factor." *The New York Times* later reported that Comey had been under pressure from within the FBI to tell Congress that emails had been found on Weiner's laptop before any assessment could be made as to their potential relevance. One surprise had been kept firmly under wraps. On 20 March 2017 Comey revealed the FBI had been actively investigating alleged links between the Russian government and the Trump team. The investigation began in July 2016. Congress and the American electorate had been kept entirely in the dark.

Starting tomorrow it's going to be #AmericaFirst! Thank you for a great morning Sarasota, Florida! Watch here: https://www. facebook.com/DonaldTrump/videos/10158077455590725/ ...

12:10 PM – 7 Nov 2016

TODAY WE MAKE AMERICA GREAT AGAIN!
6:43 AM – 8 Nov 2016

> This election day message has been retweeted over 340,000 times and liked by nearly 575,000 users.

I will be watching the election results from Trump Tower in Manhattan with my family and friends. Very exciting!
4:18 PM – 8 Nov 2016

Just out according to @CNN: "Utah officials report voting machine problems across entire country"
4:28 PM – 8 Nov 2016

> Trump prepares his excuse if he loses.

Don't let up, keep getting out to vote - this election is FAR FROM OVER! We are doing well but there is much time left. GO FLORIDA!
4:31 PM – 8 Nov 2016

[Retweet] @IvankaTrump: Such a surreal moment to vote for my father for President of the United States! Make your voice heard and vote! #Election2016 #MAGA #Voted
8:35 PM – 8 Nov 2016

Watching the returns at 9:45pm. #ElectionNight #MAGA
9:48 PM – 8 Nov 2016

Such a beautiful and important evening! The forgotten man and woman will never be forgotten again. We will all come together as never before
6:36 AM – 9 Nov 2016

> The only Tweet on the day Trump could rest in the knowledge that he was now President Elect.

227

After the Election

★ ★ ★ ★ ★

FAKE NEWS

A fantastic day in D.C. Met with President Obama for first time. Really good meeting, great chemistry. Melania liked Mrs. O a lot!
9:10 PM – 10 Nov 2016

> The honeymoon with the Obamas was short-lived. Some expected Trump to cut a more conventionally Presidential figure once he was elected, to "pivot" towards a more states-manlike style, but he would frustrate expectations.

Just had a very open and successful presidential election. Now professional protesters, incited by the media, are protesting. Very unfair!
9:19 PM – 10 Nov 2016

> The protests that erupted in the days after the election, mainly in the larger cities, provided a stark illustration of the division between Trump's electorate and the young, educated, liberal urban population on both coasts who were horrified by his racism, climate change denial and threats to clamp down on immigration. They were not, however, "professional" protesters.

Mitt Romney called to congratulate me on the win. Very nice!
9:45 AM – 13 Nov 2016

The Electoral College is actually genius in that it brings all states, including the smaller ones, into play. Campaigning is much different!
8:40 AM – 15 Nov 2016

> Trump made only one previous reference to the Electoral College. In the wake of Mitt Romney's loss on 6 November he tweeted that "The electoral college is a disaster for a democracy."

Very organized process taking place as I decide on Cabinet and many other positions. I am the only one who knows who the finalists are!

9:55 PM – 15 Nov 2016

> The host of *The Apprentice* as President Elect.

I have recieved and taken calls from many foreign leaders despite what the failing @nytimes said. Russia, U.K., China, Saudi Arabia, Japan, Australia, New Zealand, and more. I am always available to them. @nytimes is just upset that they looked like fools in their coverage of me.

7:17 AM – 16 Nov 2016

I am not trying to get "top level security clearance" for my children. This was a typically false news story.

6:28 AM – 16 Nov 2016

> In March it was revealed that Ivanka Trump was in the process of seeking security clearance, an office having been put aside for her in the West Wing of the White House.

I settled the Trump University lawsuit for a small fraction of the potential award because as President I have to focus on our country.

8:34 AM – 19 Nov 2016

The ONLY bad thing about winning the Presidency is that I did not have the time to go through a long but winning trial on Trump U. Too bad!

8:39 AM – 19 Nov 2016

> Trump had settled out of court for $25 million with students who complained that the courses in real estate offered by his "university" were inadequate, poorly resourced and badly taught. Trump's problems on this front are far from over. On 20 March, Trump's foe, the New York Attorney General Eric

Schneiderman, announced he had hired new prosecutors to pursue further claims of fraud against him.

Our wonderful future V.P. Mike Pence was harassed last night at the theater by the cast of Hamilton, cameras blazing.This should not happen!
8:48 AM – 19 Nov 2016

The Theater must always be a safe and special place.The cast of Hamilton was very rude last night to a very good man, Mike Pence. Apologize!
8:56 AM – 19 Nov 2016

The cast and producers of Hamilton, which I hear is highly overrated, should immediately apologize to Mike Pence for their terrible behaviour
6:22 AM – 20 Nov 2016

The musical based on Ron Chernow's bestselling biography of Alexander Hamilton – an unlikely marriage of hip hop and serious scholarship – became the most sensational theatrical phenomenon of recent times. The New York production has been sold out since August 2015, and the show has won eleven Tony Awards, a Grammy Award and the Pulitzer Prize for Drama. A US tour began in March 2017. It has been praised by both Barack Obama and Dick Cheney, and by almost all the critics who have seen it. Trump does not indicate who has told him the piece is "highly overrated", one of his signature dismissals.

Hamilton was the antithesis of Trump: a brilliant thinker and writer, and close ally of Washington, he co-authored the Federalist Papers with James Madison; he had an astonishing command of detail; he was the architect of a coherent and powerful national government, with an army and a central bank; and he was an ardent abolitionist at a time when most of his fellow founding fathers were slaveowners or supporters of slavery. He was also highly suspicious of populism and unchained political passion. Hamilton was one of the key shapers of a vigorous, outward-looking American capitalism. And he was an immigrant, an illegitimate orphan from the Caribbean.

The cast members' dignified statement in favour of tolerance and diversity, addressed to Mike Pence when he took his family to see the show, was widely reported. Pence himself defended the actors' right to speak out.

Many people would like to see @Nigel_Farage represent Great Britain as their Ambassador to the United States. He would do a great job!

9:22 PM – 21 Nov 2016

This idea was killed stone dead by British Prime Minister Theresa May.

Great meetings will take place today at Trump Tower concerning the formation of the people who will run our government for the next 8 years.

6:46 AM – 22 Nov 2016

Trump signalling that he expects to be a two-term President. Some of those selected, including National Security Advisor General Mike Flynn, would serve less than eight weeks.

Fidel Castro is dead!

8:08 AM – 26 Nov 2016

The tone of this Tweet contrasted sharply with the statement issued by President Obama: "History will record and judge the enormous impact of this singular figure on the people and world around him."

In addition to winning the Electoral College in a landslide,
I won the popular vote if you deduct the millions of people
who voted illegally
3:30 PM – 27 Nov 2016

> Far from a landslide, Trump won by one of the narrower
> Electoral College margins in history.

Serious voter fraud in Virginia, New Hampshire and California
- so why isn't the media reporting on this? Serious bias -
big problem!
7:31 PM – 27 Nov 2016

> Trump, irked by his failure to win the popular vote, continues
> to bang on about voter fraud. It cannot be repeated too
> often that Trump's thesis that there is widespread voter
> fraud in the US, particularly among minority communities
> in certain states, lacks any foundation in legal or scholarly
> research.

Just met with General Petraeus--was very impressed!
4:01 PM – 28 Nov 2016

> Petraeus would be passed over for any cabinet role.

.@CNN is so embarrassed by their total (100%) support of
Hillary Clinton, and yet her loss in a landslide, that they don't
know what to do.
10:03 PM – 28 Nov 2016

I thought that @CNN would get better after they failed so badly
in their support of Hillary Clinton however, since election, they
are worse!
6:34 AM – 29 Nov 2016

Nobody should be allowed to burn the American flag - if they do, there must be consequences - perhaps loss of citizenship or year in jail!

6:55 AM – 29 Nov 2016

> In 1989 the Supreme Court had ruled that flag burning constitutes symbolic speech that is protected by the First Amendment.

I will be holding a major news conference in New York City with my children on December 15 to discuss the fact that I will be leaving my … great business in total in order to fully focus on running the country in order to MAKE AMERICA GREAT AGAIN! While I am not mandated to …. do this under the law, I feel it is visually important, as President, to in no way have a conflict of interest with my various businesses..

Hence, legal documents are being crafted which take me completely out of business operations. The Presidency is a far more important task!

6:59 AM – 30 Nov 2016

> This conference would be postponed. Trump finally revealed on 11 January 2017 that he planned to hand control of his business empire to his adult sons as trustees. It quickly emerged that Trump had developed his plans without consulting the executive branch's ethics regulator, Walter Shaub, who gave his opinion: "This is not a blind trust – it's not even close. The only thing it has in common with a blind trust is the label 'trust'." Shaub's office had attempted to contact Trump's transition team but had been rebuffed.

"@TigerWoods: Can't wait to get back out there and mix it up with the boys. –TW #heroworldchallenge" Great to have you back Tiger - Special!

11:37 AM – 3 Dec 2016

> Golf would remain a priority.

Just tried watching Saturday Night Live - unwatchable! Totally biased, not funny and the Baldwin impersonation just can't get any worse. Sad

12:13 AM – 4 Dec 2016

Saturday Night Live has enjoyed record viewing figures since Trump's election.

If the press would cover me accurately & honorably, I would have far less reason to "tweet." Sadly, I don't know if that will ever happen!

11:00 AM – 5 Dec 2016

At the mid-point of the Presidential campaign, Donald Trump had told a rally of his supporters: "You know, I tweeted today. I tweeted, @RealDonaldTrump. Don't worry, I'll give it up once I'm president. I won't tweet anymore, I don't think. Not presidential."

In just the first 75 days following his inauguration, President Donald Trump issued nearly 400 Tweets from his personal account, an average of five a day.

Boeing is building a brand new 747 Air Force One for future presidents, but costs are out of control, more than $4 billion. Cancel order!

8:52 AM – 6 Dec 2016

I have NOTHING to do with The Apprentice except for fact that I conceived it with Mark B & have a big stake in it. Will devote ZERO TIME!

6:27 AM – 10 Dec 2016

Reports by @CNN that I will be working on The Apprentice during my Presidency, even part time, are ridiculous & untrue - FAKE NEWS!

9:11 AM – 10 Dec 2016

Trump Tweets the term "Fake News" for the first time.

Will be interviewed on @FoxNews at 10:00 P.M. Enjoy!
7:32 PM – 11 Dec 2016

Just watched @NBCNightlyNews - So biased, inaccurate and bad, point after point. Just can't get much worse, although @CNN is right up there!
8:02 PM – 11 Dec 2016

> In two successive Tweets the President Elect sets the boundaries of approved versus disapproved television networks.

Can you imagine if the election results were the opposite and WE tried to play the Russia/CIA card. It would be called conspiracy theory!
8:17 AM – 12 Dec 2016

Unless you catch "hackers" in the act, it is very hard to determine who was doing the hacking. Why wasn't this brought up before election?
8:21 AM – 12 Dec 2016

> Trump here appears to forget the numerous times Clinton had raised the issue during their nationally televised debates.

I have chosen one of the truly great business leaders of the world, Rex Tillerson, Chairman and CEO of ExxonMobil, to be Secretary of State.
6:43 AM – 13 Dec 2016

> Tillerson's credentials as a business executive were second to none. However his appointment raised fresh questions about Trump's Russian connections. Tillerson had enjoyed close business dealings with Putin's Russia since 1999. In 2013 Putin personally awarded Tillerson Russia's Order of Friendship.
>
> As Exxon chief executive, Tillerson was responsible for a series of deals with Russian state-owned oil giant Rosneft which were thwarted when President Obama imposed sanctions on

Russia in 2014 following Putin's annexation of Crimea. Tillerson argued for the sanctions to be lifted.

Has anyone looked at the really poor numbers of @VanityFair Magazine. Way down, big trouble, dead! Graydon Carter, no talent, will be out!

5:05 AM – 15 Dec 2016

Another feud, this time with a glamorous literary institution. *Vanity Fair*'s circulation figures stood at 1.2 million in the middle of 2016, a considerable result for a print magazine in the digital age. Its website, meanwhile, attracted 14.3 million visitors in October 2016, a quarter more than it received the previous year. Trump's anger seemed to have been provoked a couple of days before his Tweet by a review in *Vanity Fair* of Trump Grill, the steakhouse in the lobby of Trump Tower. The restaurant reviewer described it as perhaps the "worst restaurant in America" with pretentious, overpriced menus and incompetently cooked ingredients. Trump's eagerness to defend the most obscure niches of his brand from any and all critics, even after his election to the most powerful office in the free world, suggests that during his tenure as President he will find it difficult to step away from his business interests.

As for Graydon Carter, he has written contemptuously about Trump since 1983 when, as editor of the satirical magazine *Spy*, he coined the term "Short-fingered vulgarian" for Trump, who has never forgiven him. Trump has regularly tweeted that Carter is "talentless", "a disaster", "on the way out" and "a total loser".

If Russia, or some other entity, was hacking, why did the White House wait so long to act? Why did they only complain after Hillary lost?

9:24 AM – 15 Dec 2016

Last night in Orlando, Florida, was incredible - massive crowd - THANK YOU FLORIDA! Today at 3:00 P.M. I will be in Alabama for last rally!

5:05 AM – 17 Dec 2016

"China steals United States Navy research drone in international waters – rips it out of water and takes it to China in unpresidented act,"

4:30 AM – 17 Dec 2016

> This early-morning Tweet with its notable spelling error was deleted and a new version issued.

If my many supporters acted and threatened people like those who lost the election are doing, they would be scorned & called terrible names!

4:54 PM – 18 Dec 2016

> Trump was irked by protests across the nation as the Electoral College prepared to declare the formal result of its vote.

We did it! Thank you to all of my great supporters, we just officially won the election (despite all of the distorted and inaccurate media).

6:51 PM – 19 Dec 2016

Bill Clinton stated that I called him after the election. Wrong, he called me (with a very nice congratulations). He "doesn't know much" …

8:03 AM – 20 Dec 2016

I would have done even better in the election, if that is possible, if the winner was based on popular vote - but would campaign differently

8:24 AM – 21 Dec 2016

> Trump's crushing loss in the popular vote tally remained a sore point.

Someone incorrectly stated that the phrase "DRAIN THE SWAMP" was no longer being used by me. Actually, we will always be trying to DTS.

11:41 AM – 22 Dec 2016

> The phrase Drain the Swamp, a favourite at rallies, was shorthand for Trump's desire to clean out what he regarded, not without justification, as the corrupt Washington Establishment.

The United States must greatly strengthen and expand its nuclear capability until such time as the world comes to its senses regarding nukes

11:50 AM – 22 Dec 2016

The so-called "A" list celebrities are all wanting tixs to the inauguration, but look what they did for Hillary, NOTHING. I want the PEOPLE!

8:59 PM – 22 Dec 2016

> The inauguration celebration committee was having great difficulty finding performers.

Vladimir Putin said today about Hillary and Dems: "In my opinion, it is humiliating. One must be able to lose with dignity." So true!

4:13 PM – 23 Dec 2016

> Trump, in late December, was still quoting Putin as a source of statesmanlike wisdom.

.@NBCNews purposely left out this part of my nuclear qoute: "until such time as the world comes to its senses regarding nukes." Dishonest!

3:59 PM – 24 Dec 2016

Merry Christmas and a very, very, very , very Happy New Year to everyone!

12:48 PM – 25 Dec 2016

An important moment. The alt-right felt it had regained the freedom to say "Merry Christmas" rather than "Happy Holidays".

The world was gloomy before I won - there was no hope. Now the market is up nearly 10% and Christmas spending is over a trillion dollars!

3:32 PM – 26 Dec 2016

By the end of March 2017, however, the Dow Jones index would be experiencing its longest slide since 2011, losing value for over eight consecutive days.

I gave millions of dollars to DJT Foundation, raised or recieved millions more, ALL of which is given to charity, and media won't report!

6:53 PM – 26 Dec 2016

Misleading. As the *Washington Post*'s dogged reporter David Fahrenthold had revealed after an extensive investigation, much of the money received by the Trump Foundation had been used for dubious purposes such as the purchase of a 6ft portrait of Trump, albeit at a charity auction, and to settle a legal bill of $260,000 in relation to one of his private businesses. In 2013, despite a prohibition on political donations, $25,000 was given to Florida Attorney General Pam Bondi's re-election campaign.

The U.S. Consumer Confidence Index for December surged nearly four points to 113.7, THE HIGHEST LEVEL IN MORE THAN 15 YEARS! Thanks Donald!

10:10 PM – 27 Dec 2016

Doing my best to disregard the many inflammatory President O statements and roadblocks.Thought it was going to be a smooth transition - NOT!

9:07 AM – 28 Dec 2016

My Administration will follow two simple rules: BUY AMERICAN and HIRE AMERICAN! #USA

9:54 AM – 29 Dec 2016

Great move on delay (by V. Putin) - I always knew he was very smart!

2:41 PM – 30 Dec 2016

Russians are playing @CNN and @NBCNews for such fools - funny to watch, they don't have a clue! @FoxNews totally gets it!

5:18 PM – 30 Dec 2016

> Obama had launched a new round of sanctions and ejected thirty-five diplomats from the Russian Embassy in Washington following confirmation by the intelligence services that Russia had hacked the Democratic Party. Putin surprised everybody by not responding with the usual tit-for-tat. It later emerged that General Mike Flynn had privately suggested to the Russian Ambassador that Obama's moves might be rolled back after Trump became President.

Happy New Year to all, including to my many enemies and those who have fought me and lost so badly they just don't know what to do. Love!

8:17 AM – 31 Dec 2016

@CNN just released a book called "Unprecedented" which explores the 2016 race & victory. Hope it does well but used worst cover photo of me!

1:32 PM – 2 Jan 2017

North Korea just stated that it is in the final stages of developing a nuclear weapon capable of reaching parts of the U.S. It won't happen!

6:05 PM – 2 Jan 2017

The "Intelligence" briefing on so-called "Russian hacking" was delayed until Friday, perhaps more time needed to build a case. Very strange!
7:22 AM – 4 Jan 2017

Julian Assange said "a 14 year old could have hacked Podesta" - why was DNC so careless? Also said Russians did not give him the info!
7:22 AM – 4 Jan 2017

A fascinating moment. The President Elect preferring the word of a fugitive from justice, and an enemy of the Establishment, rather than the sober conclusions of the American intelligence agencies.

"@FoxNews: Julian Assange on U.S. media coverage: "It's very dishonest." #Hannity " More dishonest than anyone knows
5:10 AM – 4 Jan 2017

With two weeks to go before he enters the White House, Donald Trump continues to view Julian Assange as an authority.

Intelligence stated very strongly there was absolutely no evidence that hacking affected the election results. Voting machines not touched!
3:56 AM – 7 Jan 2017

This Tweet, issued in the early hours of the morning, misses the key point. On 6 January, a US intelligence report concluded that "Russian President Vladimir Putin ordered an influence campaign in 2016 aimed at the US presidential election." It also concluded with "high confidence" that the Russians had passed material to Wikileaks. Voting machines were not the issue.

Having a good relationship with Russia is a good thing, not a bad thing. Only "stupid" people, or fools, would think that it is bad! We..... have enough problems around the world without yet another one. When I am President, Russia will respect us far more than they do now and.... both countries will, perhaps, work together to solve some of the many great and pressing problems and issues of the WORLD!

7:21 AM – 7 Jan 2017

Trump defends his Russia policy, and makes a sensible point.

Meryl Streep, one of the most over-rated actresses in Hollywood, doesn't know me but attacked last night at the Golden Globes. She is a..... Hillary flunky who lost big. For the 100th time, I never "mocked" a disabled reporter (would never do that) but simply showed him....... groveling" when he totally changed a 16 year old story that he had written in order to make me look bad. Just more very dishonest media!

3:43 AM – 9 Jan 2017

Yet another celebrity enemy appears in Trump's crosshairs. Streep, who has won innumerable awards for her acting, made a speech attacking the President Elect while collecting another: "There was one performance this year that stunned me. It sank its hooks in my heart. Not because it was good. It was – there was nothing good about it. But it was effective, and it did its job. It made its intended audience laugh and show their teeth. It was that moment when the person asking to sit in the most respected seat in our country imitated a disabled reporter, someone he outranked in privilege, power, and the capacity to fight back. It – it kind of broke my heart when I saw it. And I still can't get it out of my head because it wasn't in a movie. It was real life. And this instinct to humiliate, when it's modeled by someone in the public platform, by someone powerful, it filters down into everybody's life, because it kind of gives permission for other people to do the same thing. Disrespect invites disrespect. Violence incites violence. When the powerful use their position to bully others, we all lose."

Russia just said the unverified report paid for by political opponents is "A COMPLETE AND TOTAL FABRICATION, UTTER NONSENSE." Very unfair!

4:13 AM – 11 Jan 2017

> This is the pivotal moment when relations between the President Elect and the US intelligence agencies descend into a vicious life-or-death struggle. News website Buzz Feed published an intelligence dossier which detailed links between Donald Trump, his campaign team and Putin's Russia. The dossier, which included lurid, unproven allegations about Trump and Russian prostitutes, was prepared by Christopher Steele, a former British intelligence officer. Members of the Trump campaign team believe that the publication of this report was a deliberate attempt by US intelligence agencies, helped by Britain's MI6, to destabilize his Presidency even before he had reached the White House.

I win an election easily, a great "movement" is verified, and crooked opponents try to belittle our victory with FAKE NEWS. A sorry state!

4:44 AM – 11 Jan 2017

Intelligence agencies should never have allowed this fake news to "leak" into the public. One last shot at me. Are we living in Nazi Germany?

4:48 AM – 11 Jan 2017

Russia has never tried to use leverage over me.
I HAVE NOTHING TO DO WITH RUSSIA - NO DEALS,
NO LOANS, NO NOTHING!

7:31 AM – 11 Jan 2017

Totally made up facts by sleazebag political operatives, both Democrats and Republicans - FAKE NEWS! Russia says nothing exists. Probably…

3:11 AM – 13 Jan 2017

released by "Intelligence" even knowing there is no proof, and never will be. My people will have a full report on hacking within 90 days!

3:16 AM – 13 Jan 2017

Thank you to General Motors and Walmart for starting the big jobs push back into the U.S.!

9:55 AM – 17 Jan 2017

> These announcements related mostly to plans set in place long before Trump's victory.

The forgotten men and women of our country will be forgotten no longer. From this moment on, it's going to be #AmericaFirst

9:54 AM – 20 Jan 2017

A fantastic day and evening in Washington D.C. Thank you to @FoxNews and so many other news outlets for the GREAT reviews of the speech!

3:53 AM – 21 Jan 2017

> Trump wakes up very early on his first day as President.

Had a great meeting at CIA Headquarters yesterday, packed house, paid great respect to Wall, long standing ovations, amazing people. WIN!

4:35 AM – 22 Jan 2017

> One of the first tasks of Presidents is to address the serving members of the CIA in front of the memorial wall recording their colleagues who have fallen in the line of duty. Until Trump, this task had been performed respectfully. The new US President devoted a large portion of his speech to making inaccurate claims about the size of his inauguration crowd and counting the number of times he had appeared on the cover of *Time* magazine. Outgoing CIA director John Brennan condemned what he called Trump's "despicable display of self-aggrandizement".

247

I will be asking for a major investigation into VOTER FRAUD, including those registered to vote in two states, those who are illegal and.... even, those registered to vote who are dead (and many for a long time). Depending on results, we will strengthen up voting procedures!
4:13 AM – 25 Jan 2017

Interview with David Muir of @ABC News in 10 minutes. Enjoy!
6:48 PM – 25 Jan 2017

> This interview took place in the White House. During the tour of the residence that the President gave David Muir, Trump showed him a panoramic photograph of the crowd at his inauguration, the size of which had become the subject of a furious dispute with the media. Aerial photographic evidence and police estimates had shown that Trump's audience was much smaller than Obama's. Trump and his spokespeople insisted that it was the largest crowd in the modern history of inaugural events. "Look at this tremendous sea of love," Trump said to Muir. It was a moment when Trump's need to be adored, to feel himself the subject of uncritical devotion, was on unguarded display.

Statement on International Holocaust Remembrance Day: https://www.whitehouse.gov/the-press-office/2017/01/27/statement-president-international-holocaust-remembrance-day ...
12:20 PM – 27 Jan 2017

> This prepared statement, tweeted out by Donald Trump on International Holocaust Remembrance Day, failed to mention the 6 million Jewish victims. There was no subsequent amplification, correction or apology.

The failing @nytimes has been wrong about me from the very beginning. Said I would lose the primaries, then the general election. FAKE NEWS!
5:04 PM – 28 Jan 2017

The coverage about me in the @nytimes and the @washingtonpost gas [sic] been so false and angry that the times actually apologised to its dwindling subscribers and readers. They got me wrong right from the beginning and still have not changed course, and never will. DISHONEST.
8:16 AM – 28 Jan 2017

> Not particularly dishonest, compared with the man who invented a fictitious apology by *The New York Times* to its subscribers, whose number passed 3 million at the beginning of February.

Our country needs strong borders and extreme vetting, NOW. Look what is happening all over Europe and, indeed, the world - a horrible mess!
5:08 AM – 29 Jan 2017

There is nothing nice about searching for terrorists before they can enter our country. This was a big part of my campaign. Study the world!
4:27 AM – 30 Jan 2017

If the ban were announced with a one week notice, the "bad" would rush into our country during that week. A lot of bad "dudes" out there!
5:31 AM – 30 Jan 2017

> These early-morning Tweets attempted to defend Trump's announcement that citizens from seven Muslim-majority countries were barred with immediate effect from entering the United States.

Everybody is arguing whether or not it is a BAN. Call it what you want, it is about keeping bad people (with bad intentions) out of country!
4:50 AM – 1 Feb 2017

Do you believe it? The Obama Administration agreed to take thousands of illegal immigrants from Australia. Why? I will study this dumb deal!

7:55 PM – 1 Feb 2017

Thank you to Prime Minister of Australia for telling the truth about our very civil conversation that FAKE NEWS media lied about. Very nice!

6:34 AM – 3 Feb 2017

> The *Washington Post* had reported that Donald Trump had slammed down the phone on Australian Prime Minister Malcolm Turnbull, after he tried to get the President to confirm that the US would honour the pledge given by Obama to take 1,250 refugees from an Australian detention centre. "This is the worst deal ever," Trump is said to have replied, accusing Australia of seeking to export "the next Boston bombers." (The Boston bombers were American citizens.)
>
> Australian officials confirmed that the account given by the *Washington Post* was "substantially accurate", stating that the conversation was "robust" and "shorter than expected". Malcolm Turnbull later said: "These conversations are conducted candidly, frankly, privately. If you see reports of them, I'm not going to add to them." In a press release enumerating the calls between Trump and world leaders, the White House did not name the Australian Prime Minister, referring to him as the "Australian President".

The opinion of this so-called judge, which essentially takes law-enforcement away from our country, is ridiculous and will be overturned!

5:12 AM – 4 Feb 2017

What is our country coming to when a judge can halt a Homeland Security travel ban and anyone, even with bad intentions, can come into U.S.?

12:44 AM – 4 Feb 2017

The judge opens up our country to potential terrorists
and others that do not have our best interests at heart.
Bad people are very happy!
4:48 PM – 4 Feb 2017

Just cannot believe a judge would put our country in such
peril. If something happens blame him and court system.
People pouring in. Bad!
12:39 PM – 5 Feb 2017

In Seattle, WA, US District Court Senior Judge James L. Robarts had made an interim order suspending the President's travel ban on certain Muslim nations, pending a full hearing of a case brought on the grounds that the ban was unconstitutional. He had the power to do this under the terms of the US Constitution, which in its first three articles created the basis of the government of the United States.

Article 1 created the Legislature – the House of Representatives and the Senate; Article 2 created the Executive – the President, the Vice President and the Departments; Article 3 created the Judiciary – the Federal Courts and the Supreme Court.

Each branch of the Administration is constrained by limits enforced by the other branches. The Judicial branch, for example, has the power to declare any law or executive act unconstitutional. These are the essential elements of the US Constitution: the separation of powers and the system of checks and balances.

It follows that the President, whose office is created by the Constitution, is subject to it and to any amendments which may have been passed (there have been twenty-seven ratified so far).

It further follows that everything in the above Tweets is nonsense, born of an ignorance which is either genuine (which would be worrying) or perverse (which would be sinister). Trump has offered no evidence offered to support the assertion that people, bad or otherwise, are "pouring in".

The Attorney General of Washington State, Bob Ferguson,

summed up the situation: "We are a nation of law. Not even the President can violate the Constitution."

My daughter Ivanka has been treated so unfairly by @Nordstrom. She is a great person -- always pushing me to do the right thing! Terrible!

7:51 AM – 8 Feb 2017

> The American department store Nordstrom dropped Ivanka Trump's line of products after a grassroots campaign had successfully encouraged women not to buy them.

Melania and I are hosting Japanese Prime Minister Shinzo Abe and Mrs. Abe at Mar-a-Lago in Palm Beach, Fla. They are a wonderful couple!

5:33 AM – 11 Feb 2017

A working dinner tonight with Prime Minister Abe of Japan, and his representatives, at the Winter White House (Mar-a-Lago). Very good talks!

3:24 PM – 11 Feb 2017

Just leaving Florida. Big crowds of enthusiastic supporters lining the road that the FAKE NEWS media refuses to mention. Very dishonest!

2:19 PM – 12 Feb 2017

The real story here is why are there so many illegal leaks coming out of Washington? Will these leaks be happening as I deal on N.Korea etc?

6:28 AM – 14 Feb 2017

Information is being illegally given to the failing @nytimes & @washingtonpost by the intelligence community (NSA and FBI?).Just like Russia

4:19 AM – 15 Feb 2017

The war between the Trump White House and the intelligence services gets even worse. Here Trump accuses the National Security Agency and the Federal Bureau of Investigation of leaking information to the press in order to damage him.

The real scandal here is that classified information is illegally given out by "intelligence" like candy. Very un-American!
5:13 AM – 15 Feb 2017

> Trump is perhaps attempting to switch attention from the accusations that he has colluded with Russia on to the leaks from intelligence agencies which suggest that he has done so.

The Democrats had to come up with a story as to why they lost the election, and so badly (306), so they made up a story - RUSSIA. Fake news!
6:39 AM – 16 Feb 2017

> The '306' is his Electoral College total.

Thank you for all of the nice statements on the Press Conference yesterday. Rush Limbaugh said one of greatest ever. Fake media not happy!
3:43 AM – 17 Feb 2017

"One of the most effective press conferences I've ever seen!" says Rush Limbaugh. Yet FAKE MEDIA calls it differently. Dishonest.
6:15 PM – 17 Feb 2017

> This press conference was almost universally described as a disaster. Who exactly is Rush Limbaugh, who so strongly bucks the trend? He is a far-right-wing Republican broadcaster and talk-show host who has expressed some strong opinions, among them that African-Americans have been systematically trained from an early age to hate the

United States; that consent is irrelevant in sexual relations, and that feminism "was established so as to allow unattractive women easier access to the mainstream of society". Limbaugh has a reputation for inaccuracy and has always been a strong supporter of Donald Trump.

The FAKE NEWS media (failing @nytimes, @NBCNews, @ABC, @CBS, @CNN) is not my enemy, it is the enemy of the American People!

1:48 PM – 17 Feb 2017

Trump draws a new dividing line.

I will not be attending the White House Correspondents' Association Dinner this year. Please wish everyone well and have a great evening!

11:21 PM – 25 Feb 2017

Trump was the first President to miss the White House Correspondents' dinner since Ronald Reagan in 1981. Reagan was recovering after an assassination attempt.

Since November 8th, Election Day, the Stock Market has posted $3.2 trillion in GAINS and consumer confidence is at a 15 year high. Jobs!

11:00 AM – 2 Mar 2017

True. However the stock market surge was very little use to Donald Trump's "forgotten men and women", very few of whom own stocks and shares.

Terrible! Just found out that Obama had my "wires tapped" in Trump Tower just before the victory. Nothing found. This is McCarthyism!

3:35 AM – 4 Mar 2017

Trump provided no evidence to support this claim.

Just out: The same Russian Ambassador that met Jeff Sessions visited the Obama White House 22 times, and 4 times last year alone.

3:42 AM – 4 Mar 2017

Is it legal for a sitting President to be "wire tapping" a race for president prior to an election? Turned down by court earlier. A NEW LOW!

3:49 AM – 4 Mar 2017

I'd bet a good lawyer could make a great case out of the fact that President Obama was tapping my phones in October, just prior to Election!

3:52 AM – 4 Mar 2017

How low has President Obama gone to tapp my phones during the very sacred election process. This is Nixon/Watergate. Bad (or sick) guy!

4:02 AM – 4 Mar 2017

Arnold Schwarzenegger isn't voluntarily leaving the Apprentice, he was fired by his bad (pathetic) ratings, not by me. Sad end to great show

5:19 AM – 4 Mar 2017

In this extraordinary sequence of Tweets, despatched in less than two hours before dawn on 4 March, Donald Trump accused his predecessor of illegally tapping his phone and of being malevolent or mentally ill; attempted to conflate Obama's routine meetings with the Russian Ambassador at the White House with Trump's Attorney General Jeff Sessions's undeclared discussions during the election with the representative of a foreign power; and poured scorn on Arnold Schwarzenegger for his failure to sustain Trump's TV franchise.

The accusations of surveillance seem to have been based on a Fox News programme broadcast late the previous night. James Comey, Director of the FBI, stonily denied that any such surveillance had taken place in his testimony to Congress on 20 March.

Here, in the early hours of the morning, was Trump at his most undisciplined and wildly expressive, giving vent to his fears and insecurities. He believes he is a victim of mysterious operations by intelligence agencies controlled by his enemies; he attempts to deflect attention from conversations (which may have been entirely innocent) between his Attorney General Jeff Sessions, then a Senator and an active member of Trump's election team, and the representative of Putin's government. Finally he rages against yet another celebrity enemy who failed to support him, while reminding his followers that he dominated the ratings with a TV show of which he remains executive producer. Show business, paranoia and politics come together in a remarkable cocktail. Twitter is the medium which allows Trump to expose these thoughts to the world in real time.

Whether his administration turns out to be long or short, Trump intends to use his Twitter account to keep the world hooked on his version of events. As the 45th President of the United States rails against 'FAKE NEWS', he remains @realDonaldTrump.

Endnotes

1. Julia Pace, "Inside the origins of Trump's high-octane Twitter account", 31 May 2016, AP The Big Story, http://bigstory.ap.org/article/1695fc61ab2544459f2c41515b982ccf/inside-origins-trumps-high-octane-twitter-account

2. By September of 2009, after six months of tweeting, Trump had managed to gain only 12,000 followers.

3. The data gathered by Twitter records the type of device Tweets are written on. It is commonly accepted that Trump prefers to use a mobile phone with an Android operating system while his employees use iPhones. "Two people write Trump's tweets: He writes the angrier ones", *Washington Post*, 12 August 2016.

4. Paul Johnson, *A History of the American People* (Weidenfeld and Nicolson, 1997), pp. 272–81.

5. See Richard Hofstadter, "The paranoid style in American politics" in *Harper's Magazine*, November 1964. Maria died in poverty while her ghost-writers fought over her book earnings.

6. See Lorraine Boissoneault, "How the 19th century Know-Nothing Party reshaped American politics" in the *Smithsonian* magazine, 26 January 2017.

7. B. S. Viault, *American History Since 1865* (McGraw-Hill, 1989) has a succinct summary of the Populist programme, and that of its predecessor, the National Greenback party, at pp. 114–16.

8. For Bryan as a precursor of Trump see Tim Reuter, "Before Donald Trump there was William Jennings Bryan", in *Forbes* magazine, 20 June 2016.

9. See Benjamin Hufbauer, "How Trump's favourite movie explains him" in www.politico.com, 6 June 2016.

10. See comparisons by Bill Kauffman, "Why they love Trump" in *The American Conservative*, 12 January 2106. For Hearst's politics, see Ben H. Procter, *William Randolph Hearst: The Early Years* (OUP, 1998, especially Chs 8–11), and David Nasaw, *The Chief* (Houghton Miflin, 2000). Hearst is portrayed vividly and accurately as a major figure in Gore Vidal's novel *Empire*.

11. See Jeet Heer, "Donald Trump, gutter journalist" in *New Republic*, 11 August 2016.

12. See Doris Goodwin, *No Ordinary Time* (Simon & Schuster, 1995) pp. 57–8; "FDR's first Fireside Chat" in *Radio Digest*, February 1939; "The Fireside Chats" in www.history.com.

13. M. Sheldon, *Father Coughlin: The Tumultuous Life of the Priest of the Little Flower* (Little Brown, 1973), p. 4.

14. A. Brinkley, *Voices of Protest: Huey Long, Father Coughlin and the Great Depression* (Knopf, 1982).

15. Sinclair Lewis, *It Can't Happen Here* (Doubleday, 1935), Ch. 19.

16. Quoted in Ronald Bailey's *Reason Magazine*, July 1997.

17. In fairness one should say that the Kennedy dynasty were active supporters of McCarthy. Bobby, later a liberal hero, actually worked for him.

18. Thomas C. Reeves, *The Life And Times of Joe McCarthy* (Stein and Day, 1982), p. 674. Reeves's assessment is striking because his biography generally tries to restore McCarthy's reputation.

19. Ibid., p. 224.

20. For McCarthy's shifting numbers see ibid., pp. 226–42. Male homosexual acts were then criminal throughout the United States. McCarthy was frequently accused of being homosexual himself. This was almost certainly wrong, but his most prominent supporter Cardinal Spellman was himself gay and McCarthy's chief counsel, Roy Cohn, preyed upon young blond men. See Jeffrey Toobin, "The Dirty Trickster", in *The New Yorker*, 2 June 2008.

21. Richard Rovere, *Senator Joe McCarthy* (University of California Press, 1996), p. 134.

22. Reeves, op. cit. p. 672.

23. After leaving McCarthy Cohn built up a lucrative legal practice representing gangsters. See Michelle Dean, "A mentor in shamelessness", *Guardian*, 20 April 2016. Cohn is now dead.

24. See Sidney Blumenthal, "A short history of the Trump family", in the *London Review of Books*, 16 February 2017. Although Blumenthal is a longtime Clinton supporter, his account of Cohn and Trump is wholly reliable.

25. See Buchanan's colourful interview for the Hudson Union Society, published 7 August 2014 on m.youtube.com/watch?v=SC5BmBYs63E

26. See Rick Perlstein, *Nixonland* (Scribner, 2008), p. 444.

27. *Time*, 5 January 1970.

28. See "Donald Trump rallies a new 'Silent Majority' in a visit to Arizona", *New York Times*, 11 July 2015.

29. See for example Monica Crowley in the *Washington Times*, 1 June 2016, and Earl Ofari Hutchinson in the *Huffington Post*, 18 June 2016.

30. See "Two Clintons, 41 years. $3 billion", in the *Washington Post*, 19 November 2015. During the 2016 campaign Hillary Clinton raised a further $623 million herself and was supported by a further $804 million through her party and political action committees (*Washington Post*, 1 February 2017, graphic).

31. Interview, Isaac Chotiner, slate.com.

32. "The reclusive hedge fund tycoon behind the Trump Presidency", Jane Mayer, *New Yorker*, 27 March 2017.

33. Ibid.

34. We are indebted to Alastair Crooke, Conflicts Forum Weekly Comment 3–10 March 2017, "The Trump–Bannon paradox 'History is seasonal and winter is coming'".

Trump Bibliography

When Trump writes more than 140 characters... his books and their blurbs.

The Art of the Deal, 1987 co-written with Tony Schwartz
"Here is Trump in action – how he runs his organization and how he runs his life – as he meets the people he needs to meet, chats with family and friends, clashes with enemies, and challenges conventional thinking. But even a maverick plays by rules, and Trump has formulated time-tested guidelines for success. He isolates the common elements in his greatest accomplishments; he shatters myths; he names names, spells out the zeros, and fully reveals the dealmaker's art. And throughout, Trump talks – really talks – about how he does it. *Trump: The Art of the Deal* is an unguarded look at the mind of a brilliant entrepreneur and an unprecedented education in the practice of deal-making. It's the most streetwise business book there is – and the ultimate read for anyone interested in achieving money and success, and knowing the man behind the spotlight."

Surviving at the Top, 1990, co-written with Charles Leerhsen,
republished in 1991 as *The Art of Survival*
"Trump is back in a book with a distinctly personal edge, taking the reader behind the scenes on the business deals that have kept his name continually in the headlines. Here too for the first time is Trump's account of the decline and fall of his celebrated marriage to Ivana."

The Art of the Comeback, 1997, co-written with Kate Bohner
"Trump's story begins when many real estate moguls went belly-up in what he calls the Great Depression of 1990. Trump reveals how he renegotiated millions of dollars in bank loans and survived the recession, paving the way for a resurgence... Blunt, outrageous, smart as hell, and full of hilarious stories – check out his chapter "The Art of the Prenuptial Agreement" – Trump tells it like it is: the women in his life; the wild and woolly deals; negotiating tactics; his investment philosophy; and his strategy for success or coming back from adversity."

The America We Deserve, 2000, co-written with Dave Shiflett
"Any political leader who won't face the future head-on is putting the American Dream at risk. That dream has made this the best country in history. It's the dream my father and mother dreamed, the one they made true for our family. It's the one that took me to the top. When you mess with the American Dream, you're on the fighting side of Trump. I'm not worried about whether or not the intellectual / journalistic / political establishment thinks I've got the stuff to talk about saving the American Dream... My business experience shows me that it works and I want to do everything possible to see that regular Americans can enjoy the same opportunity for success and security that I have had."

How to Get Rich, 2004, co-written with Meredith McIver
"First he made five billion dollars. Then he made 'The Apprentice'. Now The Donald shows you how to make a fortune, Trump style.

Real estate titan, bestselling author, and TV impresario Donald J. Trump reveals the secrets of his success in this candid and unprecedented book of business wisdom and advice... Trump tells all – about the lessons learned from 'The Apprentice', his real estate empire, his position as head of the 20,000-member Trump Organization, and his most important role, as a father who has successfully taught his children the value of money and hard work."

The Way to the Top: The Best Business Advice I Ever Received, 2004
"The host of the hit reality show 'The Apprentice' presents an invaluable collection of grounded, hard-hitting advice on business success, from people who have made it to the boss's chair at some of America's most thriving companies... A telling to-do list for the aspiring professional, *The Way to the Top* belongs on every business bookshelf."

Think Like a Billionaire: Everything You Need to Know About Success, Real Estate, and Life, 2004
"It's not good enough to want it. You've got to know how to get it. Real estate titan, bestselling author, and TV star Donald J. Trump is the man to teach you the billionaire mind-set – how to think about money, career skills, and life... And once you've earned your money, you've got to learn to spend it well. Trump presents his consumer guide to the best things in life, from wine to golf clubs to engagement rings... As Donald Trump proves, getting rich is easy. *Staying* rich is harder. Your chances are better, and you'll have more fun, if you think like a billionaire. This is the book that will help you make a real difference in your life."

The Best Golf Advice I Ever Received, 2005

"The host and co-producer of the megahit reality show *The Apprentice* presents a unique collection of golf advice… Everyone who plays golf has that little nugget of information they turn to on the course. But never before has such an array of golfing advice been pulled together in one place. Donald Trump, himself an avid – and very good – golfer, asked his friends, colleagues, and playing companions to offer thoughts on everything from the mental game to the swing to putting to playing golf the right way."

How to Build a Fortune: Your Plan for Success from the World's Most Famous Businessman, 2006

"Do you sweat the bills every month? Do you work too hard and receive too little? Do you want more? What if you could make Donald Trump your personal wealth creation coach? What if you could learn the secrets of a self-made billionaire? Now you can. Introducing 'How to Build a Fortune,' a new home study product from Trump University (trumpuniversity.com). Learn directly from Donald Trump! Get your personal plan for success from the world's most famous businessman, Donald Trump. You know Donald Trump has the know how. Now, he shows how. And you are going to benefit!"

Why We Want You to be Rich: Two Men – One Message, 2006, Donald Trump and Robert Kiyosaki, co-written with Meredith McIver and Sharon Lechter

"*Rich Dad, Poor Dad* author and motivational speaker Robert T. Kiyosaki and celebrity rich man Donald J. Trump join forces to come to the aid of America's shrinking middle class… The entitlement mentality is epidemic, creating people who expect their countries, employers, or families to take care of them… [Trump and Kiyosaki] believe you cannot solve money problems with money. You can only solve money problems with financial education. Trump and Kiyosaki want to teach you to be rich."

Think BIG and Kick Ass in Business and Life, 2007,
co-written with Bill Zanker

"For the first time ever, you too can learn Trump's secrets to thinking BIG and kicking ass! Learn: Momentum: the Big Mo. How to get it and how to get it back. Revenge: how and when to get it (and why it's so sweet) 'I love you, now sign this!' Why contracts in business and personal life are so important.

"…These strategies are proven and attested to by those who've learned to think BIG from Donald Trump and found success in their own lives even when the world seems to be against them."

The Best Real Estate Advice I Ever Received: 100 Top Experts Share Their Strategies, 2007

"Donald Trump has gathered in one book the best advice on real estate from the brightest and most experienced people… 'Mom said, "If you don't have big breasts, put ribbons in your pigtails." Good salesmanship is nothing more than maximizing the positive and minimizing the negative…' – Barbara Corcoran, Founder of the Corcoran Group, New York City's leading real estate company."

Trump 101: The Way to Success, 2007, co-written with
Meredith McIver

"In *Trump 101*, Trump himself becomes your personal mentor and coach as he shares tips, tactics, and strategies, all designed to help you make the most of yourself, your career, and your life. Each chapter covers a basic rule or belief, and shows you how to make it work for you. Learn the vital qualities and skills that every successful businessperson needs."

Never Give Up: How I Turned My Biggest Challenges into Success, 2008

"In *Never Give Up*, Donald Trump tells the dramatic stories of his biggest challenges, lowest moments, and worst mistakes – and how he uses tenacity and creativity to turn defeat into victory. Each chapter includes an inspiring story from Trump's career and concludes with expert commentary and coaching from adversity researcher and author Paul Stoltz. Inspirational and intelligent, *Never Give Up* will help you deal with your own personal challenges, failures, and weaknesses."

Think Like a Champion: An Informal Education in Business and Life, 2009, with Meredith McIver

"Over the years, Donald Trump has written many bestselling books, and he has also written short pieces that summarize his singularly successful tenets on how to live the good life, both personally and professionally. These have been personally selected by Donald Trump for this book, giving his special perspective in what amounts to an 'informal education' on how to succeed in business and life. The pieces are engaging, informative, and educational, presenting the clearest picture yet into the mind and heart of an extraordinary individual."

Midas Touch: Why Some Entrepreneurs Get Rich – and Why Most Don't, 2011, co-written with Robert T. Kiyosaki

"In a world of high unemployment and an economy that needs new jobs to recover, who isn't hungry for a solution, something that will speed economic recovery? Many look to the government, but it's becoming more and more obvious that governments can't create real jobs. Trump and Kiyosaki believe that only one group can bring our world back to prosperity: Entrepreneurs. And, especially, entrepreneurs with the Midas Touch."

Time to Get Tough: Making America No. 1 Again, 2011,
co-writer uncredited

"Trump has the answers America has been looking for, an agenda for making America number one again, including:

- How to put OPEC out of business
- How to create American jobs by forcing Communist China into truly fair trade
- How to retire our debt without endangering long-established programs – like Social Security, Medicare, and Medicaid – that millions of Americans depend on
- How to undo the fraud of Obamanomics and the disaster of Obamacare

Blunt, straightforward, and honest, it's all trademark Trump, setting out a common sense agenda to restore American prosperity and make our nation respected once again."

Crippled America: How to Make America Great Again, 2015,
co-writer uncredited, republished and updated as *Great Again: How to Fix Our Crippled America*, 2016

"Look at the state of the world right now. It's a terrible mess, and that's putting it mildly. There has never been a more dangerous time. The politicians and special interests in Washington, DC, are directly responsible for the mess we are in. So why should we continue listening to them? It's time to bring America back to its rightful owners – the American people. I'm not going to play the same game politicians have been playing for decades – all talk, no action, while special interests and lobbyists dictate our laws. I am shaking up the establishment on both sides of the political aisle because I can't be bought. I want to bring America back, to make it great and prosperous again, and to be sure we are respected by our allies and feared by our adversaries... This book is my blueprint for how to Make America Great Again. It's not hard. We just need someone with the courage to say what needs to be said."

Fiction

Trump Tower, 2012, now credited solely to Jeffrey Robinson, the original cover for the novel stated Donald J. Trump with Jeffrey Robinson

"At Trump Tower – the iconic Manhattan building on the corner of 56th Street and Fifth Avenue – there exists a world of luxury, glamour, sex, lust, and naked power. But at Trump Tower, nothing is quite what it seems to be. Move in and meet your neighbors:

"The 'garbage' traders who are willing to do business with South American money brokers; the power couple, a TV anchor and her broker husband, for whom sex is sometimes an elaborate game; the Hollywood agent who is plotting to own the world; the British rock star under house arrest who sends out for good times, sex, and rock n' roll; the model with one of the most famous faces in the world who just happens to be kept by two men who don't know of each other's existence; the Broadway star who is banned from the building; one of the richest men in the world who believes his innocent daughter is still innocent; the business owner who is being forced out by someone who wants her business; the mysterious and venomous woman who wants to build a tropical rainforest; the assistant to the Director of Operations who is willing to do anything to get the General Manager's job; and Pierre Belasco, the General Manager and ringmaster of Trump Tower whose job is 'ultimate discretion.'

"…Leave your modesty downstairs. 'Trump Tower' is the sexiest novel of the decade."

The sole cover quote is by Trump:

"Jeffrey Robinson's novel TRUMP TOWER *bares it all. Here is the drama of the Ultra Rich, the Ultra Powerful, and the Ultra Beautiful who call the most glamorous address in the country their home. I can't wait to see it on television!",* DONALD J. TRUMP

A Trump Twitter Lexicon

"inverted commas" – cynicism
????? – incredulity
!!!!!!! – extreme incredulity
BLOCK CAPITALS – anger

	Tweets to April 2017
	(figures are rounded)

Grabbing attention and signing off

Enjoy!	400
Wow!	300
Sad!	250
Stay tuned…	45

Binary divisions

The best – the worst	585
Smart – stupid	550
Success – failure	525
Strong – weak	445
Stamina – low energy	30

Put downs

Bad	590
Crooked	280
Failing, failure	240
Losers, haters	150
Worst	130
Dishonest	120
Lightweight	100
Fraud	70
Lying	60
Rigged	50
Fake News	35
Overrated, highly overrated	35
Irrelevant	30
Vicious, viciously	20
Out of control	16

Praise (usually self-reflexive)

Great, greatest	4400
Big	1100
Amazing	535
Nice	500
The Best!	485
Success	455
Winner, winning	335
Ratings	235
Tremendous	100
Terrific	95
Huge	95

"I…", "…me", the power of authoritarian assurance

"Everyone is / Many people are saying / asking / wanting me…"
"Nobody has more respect for […fill in blank…] than me"
"I alone can fix…"

Significant and not so significant others

The Obamas (Michelle and Barack)	2495
The Clintons (Hillary, Bill and Chelsea)	970
Mitt Romney	430
Fox & Friends	380
Ted Cruz	300
Ivanka Trump	250
Megyn Kelly	170
Sean Hannity	160
Melania Trump	120
Piers Morgan	100
Anthony Weiner	80
Vladimir Putin	65
Lawrence O'Donnell	20
Mike Pence	14
Tiffany Trump	7
Barron Trump	2

Written regrets

"I regret…"	0
"I am sorry…"	0
"I apologize…"	0

Hashtags

#Trump2016	960
#MakeAmericaGreatAgain	580
#CelebApprentice/#CelebrityApprentice	445
#MAGA	245
#AmericaFirst	90
#BigLeagueTruth	60
#TrumpTrain	50
#CrookedHillary	40+
#MissUniverse	21
#MissUSA	11

Twitter Glossary

In part drawn from the (official) Twitter glossary

@username
A username is how you're identified on Twitter, and is always preceded immediately by the @ symbol.

For instance, Donald Trump is @realDonaldTrump

.@username
Starting a tweet with an @ followed by someone's Twitter handle is considered by Twitter to be a reply. This means it will only show up to the followers of both these accounts.

If a dot is inserted before the mention (e.g. .@realDonaldTrump), the Tweet will be broadcast to everyone.

#
See "hashtag".

bio
Your bio is a short (up to 160 characters) personal description that appears in your profile that serves to characterize your persona on Twitter.

As of April 2017, the bio for @realDonaldTrump reads: "45th President of the United States of America".

follow
Subscribing to a Twitter account is called "following". Anyone on Twitter can follow or unfollow anyone else at any time.

@realDonaldTrump follows forty-three Twitter accounts, a mix of his preferred journalists, family members and the promotional accounts of his golf resorts and hotels.

follow(s), follower
A follow is the result of someone following your Twitter account. You can see how many follows (or followers) you have from your Twitter profile.

As of April 2017, @realDonaldTrump had 27.2 million followers.

hacking
Gaining unauthorized access to an account via phishing, password guessing, or session stealing. Usually this is followed by unauthorized posts from the account. Hacked accounts are sometimes referred to as "compromised".

hashtag
A hashtag is any word or phrase immediately preceded by the # symbol. When you click or tap on a hashtag, you'll see other Tweets containing the same keyword or topic.

header photo
Your personal image that you upload, which appears at the top of your profile.

Home
Your Home timeline displays a stream of Tweets from accounts you have chosen to follow on Twitter.

like (n. and v.)

Liking a Tweet indicates that you appreciate it. Tap the heart icon to like a Tweet and the author will see that you appreciate it.

@realDonaldTrump has written over 34k Tweets. As of April 2017 he has only "liked" forty-seven Tweets written by other users.

live tweeting

When watching an event or broadcast some users chose to tweet their opinions and reactions. Users often include a hashtag related to the event in their Tweets.

mention

Mentioning other accounts in your Tweet by including the @ sign followed directly by their username is called a "mention". Also refers to Tweets in which your @username was included.

parody

You can create parody accounts on Twitter to spoof or make fun of something in jest, as well as commentary and fan accounts.

@realDonaldTrump was chosen as Trump's handle to distinguish it from the parody accounts that already existed when he joined Twitter. The number continues to rocket, and includes @RealDonalDrumpf and @Donaldshair. @MatureTrumpTwts (bio "Alternative parody account of how a mature, more presidential Trump should tweet"), has 123k followers.

phishing

Tricking a user to give up their username and password. This can happen by sending the user to fake sign-in page, a page promising to get you more followers, or just simply asking for the username and password via a DM or email.

profile

Your profile displays information you choose to share publicly, as well as all of the Tweets you've posted. Your profile along with your @username identify you on Twitter.

@realDonaldTrump states his location as Washington, DC.

profile photo
Your personal image found under the Me icon. It's also the picture that appears next to each of your Tweets.

@PiersMorgan presents a shot of himself seated with Trump leaning on his shoulder as his profile photo.

Retweet (n.)
A Tweet that you forward to your followers is known as a Retweet. Often used to pass along news or other valuable discoveries on Twitter, Retweets always retain original attribution.

retweet (v.)
The act of sharing another account's Tweet to all of your followers by clicking or tapping on the Retweet button.

For much of his Twitter career, @realDonaldTrump copied and pasted users' messages into new Tweets that he would then issue instead of simply using the Retweet function.

timestamp
The date and time a Tweet was posted to Twitter. A Tweet's timestamp can be found in grey text in the detail view of any Tweet.

The original timing of some of Trump's Tweets have proved hard to retrieve, but the authors have attempted to present them as accurately as possible.

trends
A trend is a topic or hashtag determined algorithmically to be one of the most popular on Twitter at that moment.

Tweet (n.)

A Tweet may contain photos, videos, links and up to 140 characters of text.

@realDonaldTrump has used Tweet length-extending tools at points during his Twitter career.

tweet (v.)

The act of sending a Tweet. Tweets get shown in Twitter timelines or are embedded in websites and blogs.

Twitter

An information network made up of 140-character messages (including photos, videos and links) from all over the world.

Twitter Polls

Twitter Polls allow you to weigh in on questions posed by other people on Twitter. You can also easily create your own poll and see the results instantly.

unfollow

See "follow".

URL, URLs

A URL (Uniform Resource Locator) is a web address that points to a unique page on the internet.

@realDonaldTrump often points his users to sources of information this way.

viral

Information such as a Tweet or image that is circulated rapidly and widely on the Internet and takes on a life of its own, "going viral".

Acronyms

ABC	American Broadcasting Company
ACA	Affordable Care Act ("Obamacare")
BLM	Black Lives Matter protest
CBS	Columbia Broadcasting System network
CIA	Central Intelligence Agency
CNBC	Consumer News and Business Channel
CNN	Cable News Network (or the "Clinton News Network")
CPAC	Conservative Political Action Conference
DNC	Democratic National Convention
DOJ	Department of Justice
EPA	Environmental Protection Agency
FBI	Federal Bureau of Investigation
FEC	Federal Election Commission
FLOTUS	First Lady of the United States
GCHQ	Government Communications Headquarters
GDP	Gross Domestic Product
GMA	*Good Morning America*, ABC network's morning news show
GOP	Grand Old Party (the Republican Party)
IN	Indiana

MAGA	Make America Great Again!
MSM	Mainstream Media
NATO	North Atlantic Treaty Organization
NBC	National Broadcasting Company network
NH	New Hampshire
NJ	New Jersey
NRA	National Rifle Association
NSA	National Security Agency
NYT	*New York Times*
OPEC	Organization of Petroleum Exporting Countries
OWS	Occupy Wall Street protest
PAC	Political Action Committee
PEOTUS	Presidential Elect of the United States
POTUS	President of the United States
QVC	Quality Value Convenience, home shopping network
RNC	Republican National Convention
RT	*Russia Today* news channel
SCOTUS	Supreme Court of the United States
SNL	*Saturday Night Live*, NBC comedy sketch show
UN	United Nations
VP	Vice President
WH	White House
WSJ	*Wall Street Journal*

Acknowledgements

Brendan Brown's Trump Twitter Archive – www.trumptwitterarchive. com – has been an invaluable resource. Mr Brown has created a comprehensive database of Trump's Twitter output. Its fully searchable content, which is free to access, includes Tweets that Trump sought to delete. Thanks to Mr Brown's archive, they have been preserved.

We are grateful to all those who have helped us with the writing and publication of this book. Richard Heller has generously shared insight and advice on the antecedents for Trump, and drafted much of the historical section of the introduction. Robin Bailey has given us his acerbic and brilliant observations on a number of Tweets. We would like to thank Professor Peter Swaab for his observations about Donald Trump's use of the English language. Lindsay Codsi read the manuscript with her renowned expert eye. Livvy Moore played a crucial role in helping the timely publication of this work. We thank Christian Duck for her calm production of the book in the face of pressing deadlines. Lastly we would like to thank Neil Belton, our publisher, for coming up with the idea. His enthusiasm for and dedication to the project has been utterly invaluable. He too has helped greatly with commentary on President Trump's Tweets.